Cornelsen English Grammar

English Edition

Cornelsen

Cornelsen English Grammar
English Edition

(inhaltlich identisch mit der *Großen Ausgabe*, Bestellnummer 53342)

Erarbeitet von
StD Erich Fleischhack, Ebern; Prof. Hellmut Schwarz, Mannheim

Übersetzt von
John Eastwood, Somerset

Verlagsredaktion
Filiz Bahşi (verantwortliche Redakteurin), Michael Ferguson (Projektleitung), Dr. Marion Kiffe, Hartmut Tschepe *sowie* Cornelia Giesen, Antje Stahn (Assistenz)

Beratende Mitwirkung
John Eastwood, Somerset; Jennifer Seidl, München

Grafik
Katharina Wieker, Berlin (S. 57, 62, 81, 91, 117, 126, 140, 166, 167, 183)

Umschlaggestaltung
Knut Waisznor

Technische Umsetzung
Peter Richter, Eva Schmidt

Ergänzend zu dieser Grammatik gibt es zwei Übungsbücher mit beigelegtem Lösungsschlüssel:
Cornelsen English Grammar · Practice Book 1, Bestellnummer 63119;
Cornelsen English Grammar · Practice Book 2, Bestellnummer 63127.

Bild- und Textquellen
s. Verzeichnis auf S. 248

 http://www.cornelsen.de

1. Auflage   €   Druck 4 3 2 1   Jahr 04 03 02 01

Alle Drucke dieser Auflage sind inhaltlich unverändert und können im Unterricht nebeneinander verwendet werden.

© 2001 Cornelsen Verlag, Berlin
Das Werk und seine Teile sind urheberrechtlich geschützt.
Jede Verwertung in anderen als den gesetzlich zugelassenen Fällen bedarf deshalb der vorherigen schriftlichen Einwilligung des Verlages.

Druck CS-Druck Cornelsen Stürtz, Berlin

ISBN 3-464-06310-0

Bestellnummer 63100

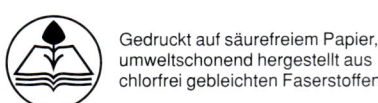 Gedruckt auf säurefreiem Papier, umweltschonend hergestellt aus chlorfrei gebleichten Faserstoffen.

Contents

	page	section
Using this book	6	

The sentence

	page	section
Sentence types	7	1
Statements	8	2-3
Questions	10	4-8
Summary: word order in statements and questions	14	9
Inversion	15	10
Question tags	16	11-12
Imperatives/Commands	17	13
Exclamations	18	14
Main clauses and subordinate clauses	19	15-16
Clause elements	20	17-20

The verb

	page	section
Summary	23	21
Modal auxiliaries	23	22-48
Be, have and *do*	36	49-57
The short forms of the auxiliaries	40	58-60
Full verbs	42	61-71
Summary: the tenses of the full verbs	50	72-73
The tenses of the full verbs	54	74-94
Simple present	54	74-75
Present progressive	56	76-77
Simple present and present progressive in contrast	57	78
Present perfect (simple form)	58	79-80
Present perfect progressive	60	81-82
Present perfect (simple form) and present perfect progressive in contrast	61	83
Since and *for* with the present perfect	62	84
Simple past	63	85-86
Present perfect and simple past in contrast	65	87
Past progressive	66	88-89
Simple past and past progressive in contrast	67	90
Past perfect	67	91-92
Past perfect progressive	69	93-94
Ways of expressing future time	70	95-106
Will-future	70	95-96
Going to-future	71	97-98
Present progressive	72	99
Simple present	72	100
Future progressive	73	101-102
Future perfect	74	103-104
Other ways of expressing future time	75	106
The passive	76	107-117
Non-finite forms of the verb	83	118
The infinitive	84	119-134
The *-ing* form	93	135
The gerund	94	136-150
The participle	104	151-163
Phrasal and prepositional verbs	113	164-167

Contents

	page	section

The noun

	page	section
Kinds of nouns	**116**	168
The gender of nouns	**117**	169
Countable nouns	**119**	170-174
Plural nouns	**122**	175
Collective nouns	**123**	176
Uncountable nouns	**124**	177
Common determiners with countable and uncountable nouns	**125**	178
The possessive form and the *of*-phrase	**126**	179-180

The article

	page	section
Forms and pronunciation	**129**	181
The definite article	**130**	182-188
The indefinite article	**134**	189-195

The adjective

	page	section
Use	**136**	196
Comparison	**137**	197-200
One/Ones after adjectives	**140**	201
The adjective used as a noun	**141**	202

The adverb

	page	section
Adjectives and adverbs in contrast	**142**	203
Kinds of adverbs	**143**	204
Forms	**143**	205-208
Adverbs or adjectives after certain verbs	**146**	209
Comparison	**146**	210-213
Position	**148**	214-215
English verbal expressions for German adverbs	**150**	216

Quantifiers

	page	section
Introduction	**151**	217
Some and *any*	**152**	218
A lot of/Lots of, much, many, (a) little and *(a) few*	**153**	219
Every, each and *any*	**155**	220
All	**156**	221
Both, either and *neither*	**157**	222
No and *none*	**158**	223
Compounds with *some, any, every* and *no*	**159**	224

	page	section

Pronouns

	page	section
Introduction	**160**	226
The personal pronoun	**160**	227-229
The possessive determiner and the possessive pronoun	**162**	230-231
The reflexive pronoun	**164**	232-234
The emphasizing pronoun	**166**	235-236
The demonstrative determiner and the demonstrative pronoun	**167**	237-238
The prop-word *one*	**168**	239

Question words

	page	section
Introduction	**169**	240
Summary	**169**	241
Who	**170**	242
Who and *which*	**170**	243
What and *which*	**171**	244
Fixed phrases with question words	**172**	245

Prepositions

	page	section
Forms and functions	**173**	246
Meanings	**174**	247
Frequent prepositions of place and direction	**183**	248
Phrases of time with *at*, *in* and *on*	**184**	249
Fixed phrases with prepositions	**185**	250

Complex sentences

	page	section
Conditional sentences	**186**	251-257
Relative clauses	**194**	258-266
Adverbial clauses	**199**	267-272
Indirect speech	**201**	273-280

Appendix

	page	section
Common mistakes	**209**	281
Word formation	**215**	282-289
American English	**218**	290-298
Emphasis	**220**	299-301
Punctuation	**222**	302-304
Numbers	**224**	305-309
Irregular verbs	**227**	310
Grammatical terms	**230**	311
Index	**235**	

Using this book

What's in the *Cornelsen English Grammar*?

- The *Cornelsen English Grammar* presents the basic facts of English grammar as clearly and simply as possible. Its main concern is to explain how to form sentences in correct, standard English and how to use them in context.

- Each grammar topic has as its starting-point a good number of examples (always on the left-hand side of the page). Form, meaning and use are made clear by explanations and rules on the right-hand side of the page. In most cases there are also translations to facilitate understanding. Most of the examples are of present-day spoken or written English.

- In some cases there is information about stylistic variation. Structures which occur mainly in American English are labelled *AE*, while *BE* stands for *British English*. A distinction is also made between formal and informal English: By formal English we mean the language used in speeches, business correspondence, reports and the like. Informal English is the type of English spoken or written in everyday life, e.g. in personal letters, and in most modern novels.

What's the meaning of the colours, symbols, etc.?

They are used to show the relative importance of grammatical structures:

I think Emily will like it here. *Ich glaube, Emily wird es hier gefallen.*	The most frequently used structures are highlighted in yellow.
Queen to visit Russia in June *Queen besucht Russland im Juni*	Less frequent structures are not highlighted.
Note You're being very aggressive today. *Du bist heute aber sehr aggressiv.*	Structures which you do not need to use actively come under the heading *Note*. Some additional information is also included in the notes.
Ich habe meine Uhr gestern verloren. **not:** I have lost my watch yesterday. **but:** I lost my watch yesterday.	The warning triangle indicates structures where it is especially easy to make mistakes. (A summary of common mistakes and how to avoid them can be found in the appendix on pages 209-214.)
'any' = jeder beliebige*...	The handwriting in red at the end of many of the sections gives a brief summary of the most important points.

How do I find what I'm looking for?

- If you are looking for a particular grammar point, you may find it in the list of contents (pages 3-5).

- The alphabetical index at the back of the book contains all the grammatical terms used and the topics covered, together with a reference to the relevant section. The index also contains many individual words with grammatical information on their use. For example, the index entry *United States* has the information *singular*: In English the name of this country is followed by a singular verb (page 245).

- Cross-references at the end of many sections (e.g. ▶ Modal auxiliaries: 22-48) lead to other parts of the *Cornelsen English Grammar* where further information can be found.

---

* In order to make the grammatical rules as clear and easy to understand as possible, only the masculine form, e.g. of adjectives and pronouns, has been given.

1-20 The sentence

1 Sentence types
2-3 Statements
4-8 Questions
9 Summary: word order in statements and questions
10 Inversion
11-12 Question tags
13 Imperatives/Commands
14 Exclamations
15-16 Main clauses and subordinate clauses
17-20 Clause elements

1 Sentence types

There are four **sentence types**, each with a different use: statements, questions, imperatives and exclamations. They can be positive or negative.

a I speak English.
I don't speak Spanish.

A **statement** gives information.

Do you like skateboarding?
Why didn't you come yesterday?

A **question** asks for information.

Wait a moment, please.
Don't forget your rucksack.

An **imperative** (or **command**) is used to get someone to do something.

How fantastic the view is!
What a terrible accident!

An **exclamation** expresses feelings.

b 1 Could you open the window, please?
2 Have I ever criticized you?
3 I want that to be done quickly.

Besides its **main use**, a sentence can sometimes have **other uses**. A question form can express a command (example 1) or give information (example 2). A command can also be expressed in the form of a statement (example 3).

▶ Statements: 2-3
▶ Questions: 4-8
▶ Imperatives: 13
▶ Exclamations: 14

Statements

2 Positive statements

subject	verb*	
Our parrot	can talk.	
The pupils	are doing	a test.
John	gave	me a nice present.
Mrs Wood	is	a tourist guide.
The house	looked	mysterious in the moonlight.
My sister	works	in a travel agency.
We	lived	in York from 1990 to 1995.
Sarah	had taken	me for a ride on her motorbike.

The word order in a positive statement is **subject – verb***. The verb can be followed by an object, a subject complement or an adverb or adverb phrase.

'A virus ate my homework.'

Perhaps Claire will phone.
Vielleicht ruft Claire an.

'Go away,' she shouted.
„Geh weg", rief sie.

If you come, I'll make spaghetti.
Wenn du kommst, mache ich Spaghetti.

She teaches jazz dance every morning.
Sie unterrichtet jeden Morgen Jazzdance.

In contrast to German, the word order **subject – verb** stays the same

- when there is an **adverb or adverbial phrase at the beginning of the sentence**
- **after direct speech**, when the subject is a pronoun
- in a **main clause** which comes **after another clause**.

In English a **verb** *(teaches)* and an **object** *(jazzdance)* are **closely linked** together. In contrast to German, they are not normally separated.

▶ Word order in subordinate clauses: 16 ⚠ 2
▶ Position of the direct and indirect object: 20
▶ Position of the object with phrasal verbs: 166 a-c
▶ Position of adverbs: 214, 215
▶ Inversion: 10

Word order in positive statements:
subject – verb

---

* The word *verb* in English has two different meanings: the **part of speech** and the **clause element**.

The sentence 9 Statements

3 Negative statements

a

	verb			
	auxiliary + *not*	main verb*		
Mrs Ashton	is not	using	the computer.	
Lisa and I	have not	finished	our project.	
We	should not	be	here.	

We form a negative statement with an **auxiliary + *not***.

▶ Negative short forms: 59

b

	verb			
	auxiliary + *not*	main verb		
You	have not been	listening	for quite a time.	
I	will not have	finished	that by Friday.	
Mum	should not have been	told	that story.	

If there are two or more auxiliaries, ***not*** comes **after the first auxiliary**.

c

	verb			
	form of *do* + *not*	main verb		
(My parents		like	my nose ring.)	
My parents	do not	like	my nose ring.	
That music	does not	sound	very exciting.	
The girls	did not	tidy	their room.	

If there is no auxiliary verb in the positive statement, the negative statement is formed with a form of the **auxiliary *do* + *not***. After *do/does/did* the main verb is in the infinitive form (*like, sound, tidy*).

▶ *Be, have* and *do* used as full verbs: 51-52, 54-55, 57

⚠ Steve **does** the housework regularly.
Steve **does not do** the housework regularly.

Steve **did** the housework yesterday.
Steve **did not do** the housework yesterday.

We form a negative statement with the **full verb *do*** in the same way. We use *do/does* + *not* in the simple present and *did* + *not* in the simple past.

Notes

1 (We **do not** watch TV in the morning.)
We **never** watch TV in the morning.

Nobody left the room.
They heard **nothing** unusual.

Besides *not*, there are other negative words such as *no, nobody, nothing, never*, etc. We use them without *do/does/did*.

2 I **don't think** you have read Sally's letter.
(I think you haven't read Sally's letter.)

When verbs like *think, believe, suppose* and *imagine* introduce a negative sentence, the word *not* usually goes with the first verb (*think*), not with the second verb (*read*).

*In negative statements:
auxiliary + 'not' + main verb*

---

* We use *main verb* to speak about the function a full verb has in a sentence. (*Full verb* however refers to a verb class.)

Questions

4 Yes/No questions and questions with a question word

Did your friends enjoy the party?
Would you like to come to my next party?

What's your favourite film?
How many times have you seen it?

Can't you come on Saturday?
Why didn't Nick phone?

Have you ever been to Las Vegas?
When were you there?

There are two kinds of questions:

- **yes/no questions,** which can be answered with *yes* or *no*,
- **questions with a question word**.

Questions, like statements, can be **negative**.

As a general rule, yes/no questions are spoken with a rising **intonation** and questions with a question word with a falling intonation.

▶ Question words: 240-245
▶ Indirect questions: 279

'What did you take that I didn't?'

The sentence 11 Questions

5 Word order (except in subject questions)

a

question word	auxiliary	subject	main verb	
	Is	Scott	cooking	pasta?
	Can	the girls	drive	a moped?
What	has	Julie	bought?	
When	will	the parcel	arrive?	

We form a question from a statement by putting the **auxiliary before the subject** (subject-auxiliary inversion).
Scott is cooking pasta. (statement)
Is   Scott cooking pasta? (question)

▶ Inversion: 10 a

b

question word	auxiliary do/does/did	subject	main verb	
		(The Bells	live	in Chelsea.)
	Do	the Bells	live	in Chelsea?
		(Jenny	likes	horses.)
	Does	Jenny	like	horses?
		(Fran	went	to L.A. in May.)
When	did	Fran	go	to L.A.?
		(She	visited	her pen pal.)
Who	did	she	visit?	

If there is no auxiliary in the statement, then in the question we use a **form of the auxiliary do before the subject**. The main verb is in the infinitive form (live, like, go, visit).

c (John has been waiting for an hour now.)
How long has John been waiting now?

(The files might have been destroyed by a virus.)
Might the files have been destroyed by a virus?

If there are two or more auxiliaries, we put the **first auxiliary before the subject**.

(Jenny does the shopping every Friday.)
What does Jenny do every Friday?

(Anne went for a job interview yesterday.)
What did Anne do yesterday?

In order to form a **question with the full verb do** we use **do/does** in the simple present and **did** in the simple past.

d

question word	auxiliary + n't	subject	main verb	
	Isn't	Kathy	working	today?
Why	doesn't	Brian	buy	a car?

Who did the Windsors not invite to the wedding?

In **negative questions** we use the negative form of the auxiliary.

In formal English the **long form not** comes after the subject.

e (The children are laughing at a cartoon film.)
What are the children laughing at?
Worüber lachen die Kinder?

(The findings are based on extensive research.)
On what are the findings based?
Worauf basieren die Forschungsergebnisse?

In English a **preposition** which is closely linked to a question word usually comes **at the end** of the question.

In formal English the **preposition** comes **before** the question word.

The sentence | **12** | **Questions**

> **Note**
> Where did you say you were yesterday?
> *Wo, sagtest du, wart ihr gestern?*
>
> What do you think John told Sarah?
> *Was, glaubst du, hat John Sarah erzählt?*

In complex questions, the word order in the subordinate clause is the same as in a statement: subject – verb (*you were*, *John told*).

Word order in questions where we don't ask about the subject:
(question word) – auxiliary – subject – main verb

6 Word order in subject questions

subject (question word)	verb	
(Simon	is singing.)	
Who	is singing?	
(Tina's brother	can't find	a job.)
Whose brother	can't find	a job?
(The film	made	Kate nervous.)
What	made	Kate nervous?
(Tram number 14	goes	to the town centre.)
Which tram	goes	to the town centre?

When we **ask about the subject** of a statement, the question word (e.g. *who*, *what*) becomes the subject. The word order is the same as in a statement: subject – verb.

subject question	object question
(Liz likes Marc.)	(Liz likes Marc.)
Who likes Marc?	Who does Liz like?
Wer mag Marc?	*Wen mag Liz?*
(Noise causes headaches.)	(Noise causes headaches.)
What causes headaches?	What does noise cause?
Was verursacht Kopfschmerzen?	*Was verursacht Lärm?*

We can use *who*, *whose*, *what*, *which* and *how much/many* to **ask about the subject or the object**. In subject questions we do not use *do/does/did*.

Subject questions without 'do/does/did'!

The sentence 13 Questions

7 Answering questions: yes/no questions

a Is it still snowing? – Yes.
   Did you see that red car? – No.
   Are you hungry? – Yes.

We can answer **yes/no questions** with a simple *yes* or *no*. However, this is not very usual because it is a little impolite.

b Can you use the Internet? – Yes, I can.
   Does Mel know Tony? – No, she doesn't.
   Have you got your videos? – Yes, we have.
   Is Mike going with us? – Yes, he is.

Short answers are usually more polite. A short answer has the form *yes/no* + personal pronoun + auxiliary (+ *n't*).
In short answers with *yes* we always use the long form of the auxiliary. The short form of the auxiliary cannot be used here.

▶ Short forms of the auxiliaries: 58-60

c Would you like a cup of tea?
   – Yes, please. Thank you. /
   Yes, I'd love one. Thank you. /
   No, thanks. Not just now.

We do not usually answer requests, offers and suggestions with just a short answer. We use a **more polite expression**.

d Is Nicole Jeff's girlfriend?
   – I'm not sure. / I don't think so. She may (be).
   Has Daniel left school?
   – Yes, of course. / No, of course not.

Instead of a short answer we can often use expressions such as **I'm not sure, I don't know, of course (not), I (don't) think so, … may (be), certainly** or **perhaps**.

e Does the restaurant open on Sundays?
   – I suppose so. / I suppose it does.
   I don't think so. / I don't think it does.

If we answer a yes/no question with **believe, imagine, suppose** or **think**, we can use **so** instead of a subordinate clause.

   Can you come on Saturday?
   – I hope so. / I'm afraid not.

After *hope, be afraid* and *guess*, we use *so* in a positive sentence and *not* in a negative sentence.

f Are the Smiths from Bristol?
   – No, they aren't. They're from Dover.
   Do you like Indian food?
   – Not very much. I prefer Chinese.

We often need to add **more information** after a short answer in order to keep the conversation going.

'Are you sure your tie* didn't flop over the bar-code* scanner?'

How might the man answer?

I'm not sure. / I don't think so.

tie Krawatte
bar-code Strichkode

The sentence | **14** | **Summary: word order**

8 Answering questions: questions with a question word

a What's the time? – Five.
   When does the concert start? – At eight.
   Where are the tickets? – In my pocket.
   Why couldn't you come last Friday?
   – (Because) I was ill. I'm sorry.

We answer **questions with a question word** by giving only the information that is asked for. Answering in a complete sentence can sound very formal (e.g. *I couldn't come last Friday because I was ill.*).

b Who told you the answer?
   – Emma. / Emma did.

When answering a subject question, we often use an **auxiliary**.

c Who wants to go for a hamburger?
   – Me. / I do.

We often use **me** and not **I**. But when there is a verb, we have to use *I*: *I do/did/am/have/can*.

▶ Use of subject and object form of the personal pronoun: 227 b/c

d Who are you talking about?
   – You. / Patrick.
   – Über dich. / Über Patrick.

In contrast to German, when there is a **preposition** at the end of a question, it is not repeated in a short answer.

9 Summary: word order in statements and questions

		subject	verb		
		The music	stopped.		**Statements**
		My mother	doesn't like	video clips.	
		I	can't babysit	tomorrow.	

question word	auxiliary	subject	main verb		
	Are	the children	playing?		**Questions** where we **don't ask about the subject**
	Do	your friends	like	fast food?	
How long	have	they	known	each other?	
Why	didn't	you	phone	yesterday?	

		question word	verb		
		Who	is coming	to your party?	**Subject questions**
		Which of you	can send	e-mails?	
		What	caused	the accident?	

'My screen is hard to read. Can I have a bigger monitor?'

10 Inversion

a

	verb	subject	
	Is	he	from Bangor?

(He is from Bangor.)

The word order in questions is **verb – subject**. We call this word order **inversion**: subject and verb change their position in the sentence.

Inversion can also occur in statements. The following types of word order are possible:

	verb	subject	
Outside	was	a huge dog.	

- **verb – subject** (subject-verb inversion)

	auxiliary	subject	main verb	
Seldom	have	I	seen	such brutality.
(Have		you	seen	such brutality?)

(Lee rarely pays his debts.)
Rarely	does	Lee	pay	his debts.
(Does		Lee	pay	his debts?)

- **auxiliary – subject – main verb** (subject-auxiliary inversion).

If there is no auxiliary verb in the sentence, then we use *do/does/did*.

b We were at the Blur concert last night. – So was I.
　　　　　　　　　　　　… – Ich auch.

Liz can do karate. – So can her brother.
　　　　　　… – Ihr Bruder auch.

My parents love camping. – So do we.
　　　　　　　… – Wir auch.

My sister doesn't like boygroups. – Neither/Nor does mine.
　　　　　　　　　… – Meine auch nicht.

We use inversion after **so** (auch) and after **neither/nor** (auch nicht).

We saw the royal wedding on TV. – So did we.
　　　　　　　　　… – We did too.
I can't speak Russian. – Neither/Nor can I.
　　　　　　… – I can't either.

Instead of using *so* with inversion, we can add **too**, and instead of *neither/nor* + inversion, we can use **not either**. With *too* and *either* the word order is the same as in statements (subject – verb).

c On the table sat two cats.
Auf dem Tisch saßen zwei Katzen.

Some **adverbial phrases of place** can come at the beginning of a sentence when they need special emphasis. Then we have to use inversion.

d At no time was the general aware of the danger.
Zu keiner Zeit war sich der General der Gefahr bewusst.

Never in my life have I felt so embarrassed.
Niemals in meinem Leben war ich so verlegen.

Only later did we realize who the man was.
Erst später wurde uns klar, wer der Mann war.

There are some **adverbials** which have a **restrictive** or **negative meaning**. We can use them at the beginning of a sentence with inversion. This structure is mostly used in formal written English. The adverbials with a restrictive or negative meaning include:

seldom, rarely	selten
never	niemals
at no time	zu keiner Zeit
in no way, on no account	auf keinen Fall
in/under no circumstances	unter keinen Umständen
not until (tomorrow/…)	erst (morgen/…)
only (later/then/…)	erst (später/dann/…)
hardly ever	kaum jemals

e 'I don't like Brian,' said John.
'Have you seen him lately?' asked Sue.

'I don't like Brian,' he said.
'Have you seen him lately?' she asked.

We often use inversion after **direct speech**.

But we use the normal word order (subject – verb) when the subject is a pronoun.

Notes

1 Here comes the bus.
Da ist der Bus.
There go my last five dollars.
Da verschwinden meine letzten fünf Dollar.

Here and *there* can come at the beginning of a sentence when they are linked to the verbs *be*, *come* or *go*. We use inversion after *here/there*.

2 Here it comes.
There they go.

We use the normal word order (subject – verb) when the subject is a pronoun.

Question tags

11 Forms

Marc is playing squash, isn't he?
The thief has been caught, hasn't he?
Mike can repair cars, can't he?
Your girlfriend lives in Glasgow, doesn't she?
You saw Vicky last week, didn't you?

We form a **question tag** with the (first) auxiliary of the statement + personal pronoun. If there is no auxiliary we use *do/does/did*.

- If the **statement** is **positive**, then the **question tag** is **negative**.

Craig isn't coming, is he?
You haven't seen Kate, have you?
Sandra can't play the guitar, can she?
We don't have to leave now, do we?
Steve and Amy didn't pay for their tickets, did they?

- If the **statement** is **negative**, then the **question tag** is **positive**.

▶ Negative statements: 3
▶ Questions: 5

⚠ I'm wrong, aren't I?

The question tag after **I am** is **aren't I**.

12 Use

a It's too cold in here, isn't it?
           …, nicht wahr?
– Yes, it is. I'll turn on the heating.
That didn't take long, did it?
           …, nicht wahr?
– No, it was easier than I expected.

Question tags (in German: *nicht wahr?, gell?, oder?, ja?*) are often used in conversation when we **expect someone to agree** with what we have said. In this case the **voice goes down** at the end of the sentence (falling intonation).

The sentence | 17 | **Imperatives/Commands**

b The film starts at 8.15, <u>doesn't it?</u>
..., *oder?*
– No, it doesn't. It starts earlier.

You can't ride a motorbike, <u>can you?</u>
..., *oder?*
– Yes, I can. I used to have one.

We can also use question tags when we are unsure about something and want to **ask if it is true**. In this case the **voice goes up** at the end of the sentence (rising intonation).

> **Notes**
>
> **1** Shut the windows, will you/would you/can you/could you?
> *Schließ bitte die Fenster!*
> Don't forget to phone me, will you?
> *Vergiss bitte nicht, mich anzurufen!*
> Be quiet now, won't you/can't you?
> *Seid jetzt endlich ruhig!*
>
> Let's go for a pizza, shall we?
> *Wollen wir nicht eine Pizza essen gehen?*
>
> **2** I'll see you tomorrow, OK?
> Your wife speaks Japanese, right?

After an imperative we can add the question tags *will you?*, *would you?*, *can you?*, *could you?*, *won't you?* or *can't you?* We can do this to make a request, an offer, a suggestion, etc., or to give the imperative more emphasis.

After a suggestion with *let's* + infinitive (without *to*) we can add the question tag *shall we?*

In American English the question tags *OK?* and *right?* are often used.

▶ American English: 290-298

Positive statement (+) → negative question tag (–)
Negative statement (–) → positive question tag (+)

13 Imperatives/Commands

a Listen.
Hör/Hört/Hören Sie zu!

Just sign here.
Unterschreiben Sie bitte hier!

Please take a seat.
Turn the music down, please.

⚠ Stop that terrible noise!

The **imperative** has the same form as the infinitive (without *to*). There is one form for both singular and plural.

As in German, we use the imperative to get someone to do something.

In a request we can use the imperative with *please*.

In contrast to German, in English we use an **exclamation mark** only when the sentence is really an exclamation.

▶ Punctuation: 302-304

b Don't listen.
Hör/Hört/Hören Sie nicht zu!

c Let's go to a disco.
Gehen wir (doch) in eine Disko.
Let's not argue. / Don't let's argue.
Lasst uns nicht streiten.

We form the **negative imperative** with *do not* (short form: *don't*).

The imperative form ***let's*** (= *let us*) **+ infinitive** (without *to*) is used for suggestions and requests which include the speaker.

> **Notes**

1 **Do have** another cup of coffee.
Trinken Sie doch noch eine Tasse Kaffee!
Do help me with the homework, please.
Hilf mir doch bitte bei den Hausaufgaben!

If we want to add emphasis, we can use *do* + imperative.

2 **You get** the coats, I'll get a taxi.
Sie holen die Mäntel, …
Don't you phone me again tonight.
Rufen Sie mich heute Abend bloß nicht wieder an!

In English, as in German, we can put *you* before the imperative. The negative form is *don't you* + verb.

3 **Could** you please help me with this exercise, Mr Smith?
Könnten Sie mir bitte bei dieser Aufgabe helfen, Mr Smith?
Can you be quiet, please?
Kannst du bitte ruhig sein?

Requests and commands can also be expressed by means of modal auxiliaries, usually in questions. This is more polite than an imperative.

▶ Emphasis: 299-301
▶ Requests and commands with *can, could, will* anc *would*: 43
▶ Commands in indirect speech: 274a, 280a

14 Exclamations

a How nice to see you!
Wie schön, euch zu treffen!

What a silly mistake you made!
Was für einen dummen Fehler du gemacht hast!

Fantastic!
Fantastisch!

Oh dear!
Ach du liebe Zeit! / Ach du meine Güte!

Exclamations express the speaker's **feelings**, e.g. pleasure, annoyance, surprise.

'How romantic! Breakfast in bed!'

b **How kind** you are!
How badly the team played!
How we ran!

What a view we had!
What an awful sweatshirt she is wearing!
What silly questions you asked!

Exclamations often begin with **how** or **what**.

How can come before an adjective or an adverb, or it can be on its own.

What comes before a noun or an adjective + noun. A singular noun has the indefinite article (*a, an*).

The word order in the rest of the sentence is subject – verb.

 A private bathroom – **what luxury!**
Ein eigenes Bad – was für ein Luxus!

When the **noun** is **uncountable**, there is no article between *what* and the noun.

▶ Uncountable nouns: 177, 178

c **How kind!**
What an awful dress!

Exclamations can also be just a **simple phrase** with **how** or **what**.

The sentence | **19** | **Main clauses and subordinate clauses**

Main clauses and subordinate clauses

A **main clause** can **stand on its own** as a statement, question, command or exclamation. But it can also be combined **with another main clause** or with a **subordinate clause**.

▶ Complex sentences: 251-280

15 Compound sentence

main clause		main clause
I like windsurfing,	and	I enjoy sailing.
Shall we go out,	or	shall we stay at home?
Write the letter,	but	don't post it yet.

When **main clauses** are **combined**, they form a **compound sentence**. The main clauses are usually linked by a coordinating conjunction such as *and*, *or* or *but*.

16 Complex sentence

a

main clause	subordinate clause
I'll phone you	when we get home.
Adam can't come	because he's babysitting.
This isn't the man	who served me.
Where's the shop	that sells posters?
Do you know	where Samantha lives?
Can you tell me	what 'RAM' means?
I forgot the magazines	lying on the table.

When a **main clause** is **combined with** a **subordinate clause**, they form a **complex sentence**. The clauses can be linked by a **subordinating conjunction** (e.g. *when, because, after*), by a relative pronoun (e.g. *who, that*) or by a question word (e.g. *where, what, how*).

We can also use a participle construction instead of a subordinate clause.

▶ Participle: 151-163

b

subordinate clause	main clause
If it's hot,	we'll go for a swim.
Wenn es heiß ist,	*gehen wir schwimmen.*

As in German, a **subordinate clause** with *when, if, as,* etc. can also come **before the main clause**. When this happens, there is often a comma between the clauses in English.

                      subject verb
If it rains tomorrow, we   can go to the cinema.
Wenn es morgen regnet, können wir ja ins Kino gehen.

In contrast to German, the subject – verb **word order in the main clause** does not change when the sentence begins with a subordinate clause.

                      subject verb
Kim stopped talking when Peter joined us.
Kim hörte auf zu reden, als Peter zu uns kam.

The **word order in an adverbial clause** is the same as in the main clause: subject – verb.

Clause elements

17 Subject and verb*

clause			
subject	verb		
Becky	is laughing.		
subject	verb	complement	
Shopping	can be	fun.	
subject	verb	object	
Andrew	has bought	a new CD-player.	
subject	verb	object	complement
We	voted	Mike	team captain.
subject	verb	object	object
She	gave	her mother	the keys.
subject	verb	adverbial	
My pen pal	lives	in Montreal.	
subject	verb	adverbial	adverbial
Luke	was	in Rio	last year.

A clause is made up of **clause elements**.
The **subject** refers to a person or thing. It is the topic, what the sentence is about.
The **verb*** and its **complementation** (the elements that follow it) tell us something about the subject. The verb complementation depends on the kind of verb we use and can be:
- a **complement**
- an **object**
- an **adverbial**.

18 Complementation of the verb: subject complement and object complement

subject	verb	subject complement
Pedro	got	nervous.
He	became	chairman.

The **subject complement**, which can be an adjective or a noun, relates to the subject. It is linked to the subject by a linking verb.
Such verbs include: *appear, be, become, feel, get* (= werden), *grow* (= werden), *look, remain, seem, sound, turn* (= werden).

	verb	object	object complement
The waiting	made	Pedro	nervous.
They	made	him	chairman.

The **object complement**, which can be an adjective or a noun, relates to the object. It comes after a verb + object.
Verbs we can use in this structure include: *appoint, believe, call, consider, elect, find, make, name, think*.

---

* The word *verb* in English has two different meanings: the **part of speech** and the **clause element**.

The sentence **21** **Clause elements**

19 Complementation of the verb: objects

	indirect object	direct object
She sent	her husband	a fax.

As in German, English has verbs which can have **two objects**:
- an **indirect object** (in German often called *Personenobjekt*),
- a **direct object** (in German often called *Sachobjekt*).

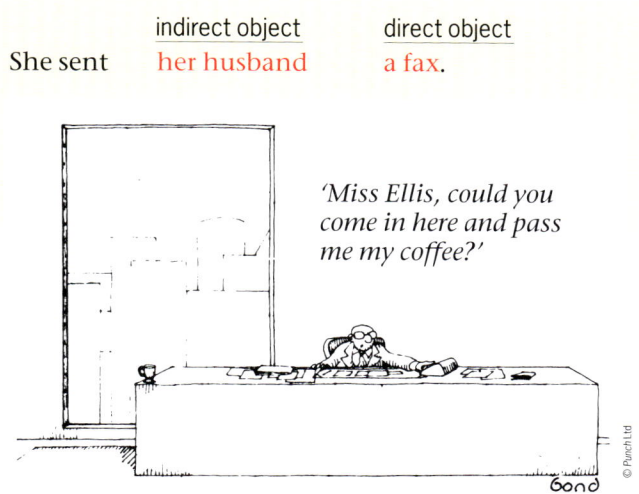

'Miss Ellis, could you come in here and pass me my coffee?'

> **Note**
>
> I saw that it was a mistake.
> We wanted to talk to you.
> Marc enjoys reading books about zoos.

We can also use a subordinate clause or an infinitive or gerund construction as complement of the verb.

20 The position of the indirect and the direct object

a

	indirect object	direct object
I lent	Katie	my camera.
I made	my friend	some sandwiches.

When a **verb** has **two objects**, the normal word order is **indirect object – direct object**. Such verbs include: *bring, buy, cook, fetch, get, give, leave, lend, make, offer, order, pass, promise, read, refuse, sell, send, show, take, teach, tell, throw, write.*

b

	direct object	to/for + indirect object
I lent	my camera	to Katie.
I made	some sandwiches	for my friend.

If the indirect object needs to be more prominent, the word order is **direct object – indirect object**.
When the indirect object comes at the end, we always use **to** or **for**. We use *for* with the verbs *buy, cook, fetch, get, make* and *order*.

 Who did you lend your camera to?
Wem…?
Who did you make the sandwiches for?
Für wen …?

In **questions** about the indirect object we always use **to** or **for** (at the end of the sentence).

c

	direct object	to/for + indirect object
I lent	it	to Katie.
I made	them	for my friend.
I lent	it	to her.
I made	them	for him/her.

When the direct object is a **pronoun**, the word order is **direct object – to/for + indirect object**.

When there are two pronouns after the verb, the word order is usually the same: direct object – to/for + indirect object.

'Press these flowers into a scanner & e-mail them to my wife, please, Monique.'

d

	direct object	to + indirect object
Could you explain	the problem?	
Could you explain	the problem	to the team?
I'll try to describe	the scene	to you.
We mentioned	the idea	to our teacher.

There are **some verbs** where we always use **to** with the indirect object. The word order is normally **direct object – to + indirect object**. Such verbs include: announce, deliver, describe, explain, introduce, mention, point out, report, say, suggest.

	direct object	to + indirect object
1 He suggested	a solution	to us.

	to + indirect object	direct object
2 He suggested	to us	a surprising solution.

If we want to draw attention to the direct object, the word order is **to + indirect object – direct object** (example 2).

Debbie erklärte ihrem Vater das Problem.
not: Debbie explained ~~her father the problem~~.
but: Debbie explained the problem to her father.

Kannst du mir das erklären?
not: Can you explain ~~me that~~?
but: Can you explain that to me?

The verb

21-167 The verb

21 Summary

can, could, will, would, must, may, might, shall, should, ought to, need not

be, have, do

play, read, work, think, like, hear, …

English verbs can be divided into three groups:

- **modal auxiliaries**, also called *modal auxiliary verbs*, *modal verbs* or *modals*,
- **primary verbs**, those that can be used either as auxiliaries or as full verbs,
- **full verbs**.

▶ Modal auxiliaries: 22-48
▶ *Be*, *have* and *do*: 49-57
▶ Full verbs: 61-71

22-48 Modal auxiliaries

- 22 Forms
- 23 Characteristics
- 24 Functions
- 25-35 Summary
- 36-37 Ability: *can* and *could* – substitute form: *be able to*
- 38-39 Permission: *can*, *may* and *could* – substitute form: *be allowed to*
  Prohibition: *can't*, *may not* and *mustn't* – substitute form: *be not allowed to*
- 40-41 Strong obligation or necessity: *must* – substitute form: *have to*
  Lack of obligation or necessity: *needn't* – substitute form: *not have to*
- 42 Obligation, instructions and advice: *should*, *ought to*, *had better*, *be to*, *be supposed to* and *must*
- 43 Requests: *Can/Could you …?* and *Will/Would you …?*
- 44 Offers and invitations: *Can/Could I …?*, *Will/Won't you …?*, *Would/ Wouldn't you …?* and *May I/we …?*
- 45 Suggestions: *Shall I/we …?*, *Can't/Couldn't …?*, *can* and *could*
- 46 Refusals and rejections: *won't* and *wouldn't*
- 47 Possibility and probability: *can*, *could*, *will*, *would*, *must*, *may*, *might*, *should* and *ought to*
- 48 Typical behaviour: *will* and *would*

22 Forms

positive		negative	
long forms	short forms	long forms	short forms
can	–	cannot	can't [kɑːnt]
could	–	could not	couldn't
will	'll	will not	won't [wəʊnt]
would	'd	would not	wouldn't
must	–	must not	mustn't ['mʌsnt]
may	–	may not	–
might	–	might not	mightn't
shall	'll	shall not	shan't [ʃɑːnt]
should	'd	should not	shouldn't
ought to	–	ought not to	oughtn't to
		need not	needn't

▶ Short forms of the auxiliaries: 58, 59a

The verb | **24** | **Modal auxiliaries**

23 Characteristics

a | I **can drive** a motorbike.
You **mustn't read** my e-mails.
Jason **ought to be** in London now.

> After a modal auxiliary we use an **infinitive without to**. Note that **ought** is always used with **to**.

b | I/You/He/She/It / We/You/They **can** speak Russian.

> There is **one form** for all persons. There is **no -s** in the 3rd person singular.

c | I **can't** understand this poem.
Can you sing?

> As with other auxiliaries, we form **negatives** and **questions without do/does/did**.

d | It's fun to **be able to** find friends on the net.
She hates **having to** get up early.
I haven't **been able to** contact Jenny.
We **had to** buy a new TV set.
I hope we**'ll be allowed to** use a dictionary in the test.

> Modal auxiliaries
> - have no infinitive form
> - have no -ing form
> - have no past participle
> - cannot form all the verb tenses.
>
> This is why some modals have **substitute forms** with a similar meaning. With these substitutes, we can form the infinitive, the -ing form and all the tenses.

e | She isn't answering the phone. She **must be taking** a shower.
I **may be playing** squash tomorrow.
Tim is very tired. He **must have been working** hard all day.

> Modal auxiliaries have no **-ing form**. But the verb after the modal can be in the -ing form: be + -ing form, have been + -ing form.

f | 1 **Can** you help me with these suitcases?
2 That **must** be Tom. I know his voice.
3 **Could** I have a glass of water, please?
4 **Can** you call back in the afternoon?
5 I **must** go to the bank tomorrow.
6 **Could** you babysit for us next weekend?

> Modal auxiliaries usually refer to the **present** (examples 1-3) or the **future** (examples 4-6).

g | Where **can** I **have left** my anorak?
Wo kann ich nur meinen Anorak liegen gelassen haben?

Paul **may have gone** to town.
Paul ist vielleicht in die Stadt gegangen.

You **could have asked** me before you took my bike.
Du hättest mich fragen können, …

> When used with the **perfect infinitive** (have + past participle), modal auxiliaries (except shall) can also refer to the **past**.

Modal auxiliaries:
– always with an infinitive without 'to'
– no '-s' in the third person singular
– negatives and questions without 'do/does/did'

24 Functions

A modal auxiliary adds **something extra to the meaning of a sentence**. It expresses the speaker's purpose or attitude (communicative function). There are two main functions of modal auxiliaries:

a   You can have my car. I'm not going out today.
    Du kannst mein Auto haben … (= Ich erlaube es dir.)

    Couldn't I bring a few friends home after school?
    Könnte ich nicht nach der Schule ein paar Freunde mit nach Hause bringen? (= Ich bitte dich, …)

    I think you should explain the problem to Ben. He'll understand.
    Ich glaube, du solltest Ben das Problem erklären. Er wird es verstehen. (= Ich rate dir, …)

    The speaker wants to **influence other people**.
    He gives permission, makes a request, advises, etc.

b   There's someone at the door.
    It will be the postman. (fairly certain)
    It could be the postman. (probable)
    It may be the postman. (possible)

    The speaker wants to express an **assumption** that something is certain, probable or possible.

Summary

This summary lists the **modal auxiliaries** and their various **functions**. In sections 36-48 you will find further details about the use of these modal auxiliaries.

25 Can/Can't

Vicky can play the piano very well.
I can't carry the box. It's too heavy.
You can get all kinds of things at the new shop.
That can't be Mike. He's much taller.
You can have my Walkman if you like.
Tim can't drive a car because he isn't old enough.
Can I have your pen, please?
Can/Can't we go to the coast tomorrow?
Can I show you my new video game?

- Ability and inability

- Possibility

- Permission and prohibition

- Requests and orders
- Suggestions
- Offers and invitations

26 Could/Couldn't

Jenny could swim when she was three.
John couldn't play tennis last week. He was ill.
Gemma could be at her aunt's.
I could watch TV after 9 pm when I was twelve.
The fans couldn't enter the concert hall.
Could you help me with the translation?
Could/Couldn't someone open a window?

- Ability and inability in the past

- Probability
- Permission and prohibition in the past

- Requests and orders
- Suggestions

The verb | **26** | **Modal auxiliaries**

27 Will/Won't

Will you sit down, please?
Will you have another cup of tea?
Won't you tell me about your problem?
That's the phone. It'll be Andrew.
I'm sure Tracy stole that money, but she won't admit it.
Ed will sit in a pub for hours and chat with the landlord.

- Requests and orders
- Offers and invitations

- Probability
- Refusal and rejection
- Typical behaviour

▶ Will-future: 96

pile up   sich stapeln
flip through   durchblättern
periodically   regelmäßig

28 Would/Wouldn't

Would you pass me the sugar, please?
Would you like some more coffee?
A short walk after lunch would do us good.
Judy knew all about our plan, but she wouldn't give any details.
When Sarah was a little girl, she would dance when she heard music.

- Requests and orders
- Offers and invitations
- Probability
- Refusal and rejection in the past

- Typical behaviour in the past

29 Must

I must go to the bank to get some money.
In Britain traffic must keep to the left.
You've been working all day. You must be tired.
The film is great. You simply must see it.

- Strong obligation and necessity

- Probability
- Firm advice

30 Mustn't

You mustn't smoke here.

- Prohibition

31 Needn't

You needn't go home yet. • Lack of obligation or necessity

32 May/May not

You may be wrong.
May I help you?
You may leave earlier today.
Students may not use the staff canteen.

• Possibility
• Offers
• Permission and prohibition

'Hold on – there may be a vacancy* in our finance department* …'

vacancy freie Stelle
department Abteilung

33 Might

There might be snow tomorrow. • Possibility

34 Shall

Shall I do the shopping for you?
Shall we have a break?

• Suggestions

35 Should/Ought to

We all should save/ought to save energy.
You should book/ought to book the hotel in good time.
The roads should be/ought to be less crowded today.

• Obligation
• Advice
• Probability

Ability: can and could – substitute form: be able to

36 Forms

	positive	negative
present tense:	can am/are/is able to	cannot (can't) am/are/is not able to
past tense:	could was/were able to	could not was/were not able to
present perfect:	have/has been able to	have/has not been able to
will-future:	will be able to	will not (won't) be able to

▶ Short forms of the auxiliaries: 58, 59

37 Use

a   Most teenagers can use a computer. /
   Most teenagers are able to use a computer.
   Die meisten Jugendlichen können mit einem Computer umgehen.

In the **present tense** we use *can* or *am/is/are able to*. *Can* is more usual.

b   I could ride a horse when I was ten. /
   I was able to ride a horse when I was ten.
   Ich konnte mit zehn Jahren reiten.

The **past tense forms** *could* and *was/were able to* both express a **general ability** which existed in the past. *Could* is more usual.

c   The road was icy, but Jane was able to stop/managed to stop the car.
   Die Straße war vereist, aber Jane konnte das Auto anhalten.

We do not normally use *could* in a positive statement when we mean that someone had a chance to do something in a **specific situation** in the past and actually did it. In this case we use **was/were able to** or **managed to**.

   The little girl fell in the river. Luckily, she could swim (= general ability), so she was able to reach the river bank and pull herself out (= ability in a specific situation).

Note the different use of **could** and **was/were able to**.

d   Could you speak French fluently after your year in Paris? – No, I'm afraid I couldn't speak really fluently.
   Konntest du nach deinem Jahr in Paris fließend Französisch sprechen? – Nein, ich konnte leider nicht wirklich fließend sprechen.

We can always use *could/couldn't* in **questions** and in **negative statements**.

e   I could hear you, but I couldn't see you.
   Ich konnte dich hören, aber ich konnte dich nicht sehen.

With **verbs of perception** (*see*, *hear*, etc.) we use *could*, not *was/were able to*.

The verb **29** **Modal auxiliaries**

f **Have** you **been able to** contact Jane since she moved?
Hast du Jane erreichen können, seitdem sie weggezogen ist?
I'**ll be able to** buy some CDs with this money.
Ich werde mir von diesem Geld ein paar CDs kaufen können.

In **compound tenses**, e.g. the present perfect or the *will*-future, we use *be able to*.

▶ Tenses of the full verbs: 79
▶ Ways of expressing future time: 95

g **Could** you turn the TV on, please?
Könntest du bitte den Fernseher anmachen?
I **could** come tomorrow.
Ich könnte morgen kommen.

When **could** means the same as the German **könnte**, it refers to the present or the future.

h You **could have told** me last week.
Du hättest es mir schon letzte Woche sagen können.
(*Aber du hast es nicht getan.*)

We use **could** + **perfect infinitive** to talk about possible actions in the **past**.

You **couldn't have done** anything.
Du hättest nichts tun können.
(*Auch wenn du es versucht hättest.*)

▶ Perfect infinitive: 120

Ability:
— in the present tense: 'can'
— in the past tense: 'could' and 'was/were able to'
— compound tenses with 'be able to'

Permission: can, may *and* could *– substitute form:* be allowed to
Prohibition: can't, may not *and* mustn't *– substitute form:* be not allowed to

38 Forms

	positive	negative
present tense:	can, may am/are/is allowed to	cannot (can't), may not, must not am/are/is not allowed to
past tense:	could was/were allowed to	could not was/were not allowed to
present perfect:	have/has been allowed to	have/has not been allowed to
will-future:	will be allowed to	will not (won't) be allowed to

▶ Short forms of the auxiliaries: 58, 59

39 Use

a You **can** use my camera.
Sie können/dürfen meine Kamera benutzen.

You **aren't allowed to** smoke on the plane, I'm afraid.
Sie können/dürfen im Flugzeug leider nicht rauchen.

In the **present tense** *can* and *can't* are used when the **speaker** is **giving or refusing permission**.
Be (not) allowed to is used when we mean that **someone else** is **giving or refusing permission**.

The verb | 30 | **Modal auxiliaries**

b   Can/Could I leave half an hour earlier today, please?
    – Yes, of course.
    Kann/Könnte ich heute bitte eine halbe Stunde früher gehen?

    May I leave half an hour earlier today, please?
    – Certainly.
    Darf/Dürfte ich heute bitte eine halbe Stunde früher gehen?

To **ask for permission**, we can use *Can I/we …?*, *Could I/we …?* or *May I/we …?*
May I/we …? is especially polite.

'Dad, can I borrow the gun tonight?'

c   You mustn't pull the cat's tail.
    Du darfst die Katze nicht am Schwanz ziehen.
    You must not talk during an exam.
    Man darf während einer Klausur nicht sprechen.

Mustn't is used either to **prohibit** something on the authority of the speaker, or for a general rule which prohibits something.

d   On Saturdays we could always stay up till midnight.
    An Samstagen durften wir immer bis Mitternacht aufbleiben.

    Yesterday Julie was allowed to stay up till midnight.
    Gestern durfte Julie bis Mitternacht aufbleiben.

The **past tense forms** *could* and *was/were allowed to* express a **general permission** in the past. For **permission in a specific situation** in the past we use only *was/were allowed to*.

e   I've always been allowed to go to parties.
    Ich habe schon immer auf Partys gehen dürfen.
    I'll be allowed to go to discos when I'm eighteen.
    Ich darf in die Disko gehen, wenn ich achtzehn bin.

Compound tenses, e.g. the present perfect or the *will*-future, are formed with *be allowed to*.

▶ Tenses of the full verbs: 79
▶ Ways of expressing future time: 95

f   You may smoke in this part of the restaurant.
    Sie dürfen in diesem Teil des Restaurants rauchen.
    Magazines may not be taken out of the waiting room.
    Zeitschriften dürfen nicht aus dem Wartezimmer mitgenommen werden.

In formal English *may* and *may not* can be used to **give and refuse permission**.

Permission/prohibition:
– *in the present tense: 'can, can't, may (not)' and 'am/is/are (not) allowed to'*
– *prohibition: 'mustn't'*
– *in the past tense: 'could, couldn't' and 'was/were (not) allowed to'*
– *compound tenses with 'be allowed to'*

The verb | **31** | **Modal auxiliaries**

Strong obligation or necessity: must – *substitute form:* have to
Lack of obligation or necessity: needn't – *substitute form:* not have to

40 Forms

	positive	negative
present tense:	must have to/has to have got to/has got to	need not (needn't) do not have to/does not have to have not got to/has not got to
past tense:	had to	did not have to
present perfect:	have had to/has had to	have not had to/has not had to
will-future:	will have to	will not (won't) have to

▶ Short forms of the auxiliaries: 58, 59

41 Use

a

I'm exhausted. I must sit down.
… Ich muss mich hinsetzen.

Dogs must be kept on leads.
Hunde müssen an der Leine geführt werden.

Sorry, I have to go now. The taxi is waiting.
Ich muss jetzt leider gehen. Das Taxi wartet.

I've got to go. I'm late. See you!
Ich muss gehen. …

In the **present tense** we use *must*, *have to* and *have got to*.

Must is used when the necessity or obligation is **felt by the speaker**.

Must is also used in official regulations.

Have to is used mostly to talk about necessity which is **imposed by someone else**. It often arises from the **situation**.

Have got to is found mainly in informal English. It is used like *have to*.

Doctor to Ally: You must take this medicine twice a day.
Arzt zu Ally: Sie müssen diese Medizin zweimal täglich nehmen.

Ally to mother: I have to take/I have got to take this medicine twice a day.
Ally zur Mutter: Ich muss diese Medizin zweimal täglich nehmen.

Note the different use of **must** and **have to/have got to**.

Wir müssen die Hausaufgaben morgen abgeben.
not: We ~~must~~ give in the homework tomorrow.
but: We have to give in the homework tomorrow.

Be careful not to use *must* too often. The English equivalent of German *müssen* is usually **have to**.

The verb | **32** | **Modal auxiliaries**

⚠️ You **needn't** tell Dan about the party. He knows.
*Du musst Dan nichts über die Party sagen. /
Du brauchst Dan nichts über die Party zu sagen. …*

You **mustn't** tell Dan about the party. It's a surprise.
Du darfst Dan nichts über die Party sagen. …

needn't = lack of necessity
(German: *nicht müssen/nicht brauchen*)

mustn't = prohibition (German: *nicht dürfen*)

b   You **needn't have seen** the doctor.
Du hättest nicht zum Arzt gehen müssen/brauchen.
but:
I'm glad you **didn't have to see** the doctor.
Ich bin froh, dass du nicht zum Arzt gehen musstest.

Needn't + perfect infinitive expresses the idea that something was done in the **past** which later turned out to be unnecessary.

▶ Perfect infinitive: 120

> **Note**
>
> | modal auxiliary | full verb |
> |---|---|
> | You **needn't** go now. | You **don't need to** go now. |
> | *Du brauchst jetzt nicht zu gehen.* | *Du brauchst jetzt nicht zu gehen.* |
> | **Need** we go now? | **Do** we **need to** go now? |
> | *Müssen wir jetzt gehen?* | *Müssen wir jetzt gehen?* |
> | | I think you **need to** go now. |
> | | *Ich glaube, du musst jetzt gehen.* |
> | | I **didn't need to** go then. |
> | | *Ich brauchte dann nicht zu gehen.* |

Need can be a modal auxiliary or a full verb. As a modal auxiliary, it is used only in the present tense, mainly in negative statements and less often in questions. The full verb *need* is used in the same way as other full verbs.

▶ Full verbs: 61

c   Yesterday we **had to** get up early.
Gestern mussten wir früh aufstehen.

When **did** you **have to** get up? – At 5.30.
Wann musstet ihr aufstehen? – …

The **past tense** of *must* and *have to/have got to* is *had to*.

Past tense **negatives** and **questions** are formed with *did*.

d   We**'ve** never **had to** play against such a good team.
Wir haben noch nie gegen so eine gute Mannschaft spielen müssen.

We**'ll have to** train hard next week.
Wir müssen nächste Woche hart trainieren.

Compound tenses, e.g. the present perfect or the *will*-future, are formed with *have to*.

▶ Tenses of the full verbs: 79
▶ Ways of expressing future time: 95

Strong obligation or necessity:
– in the present tense: 'must' and 'have to/have got to'
– in the past tense: 'had to'
– compound tenses with 'have to'

42 Obligation, instructions and advice: should, ought to, had better, be to, be supposed to *and* must

a If you make a promise, you should keep it.
Wenn Sie ein Versprechen machen, sollten Sie es halten.
You shouldn't sit at the computer for hours and hours.
Du solltest nicht stundenlang am Computer sitzen.
You ought to take a bus. It's too far to walk.
Sie sollten einen Bus nehmen. …

We use *should* and *ought to* to express an **obligation** or to give **advice**.

You shouldn't have drunk so much.
Du hättest nicht so viel trinken sollen.

We use **should/ought to + perfect infinitive** to talk about a **past** obligation which was not met.

▶ Perfect infinitive: 120

Besides *should* and *ought to*, there are **other ways** of expressing advice or obligation.

b It's raining. You had better take an umbrella.
… Es wäre besser, wenn du einen Schirm mitnehmen würdest. / Du solltest lieber einen Schirm mitnehmen.

We'd better not eat much before we go to the fitness studio.
Wir sollten lieber nicht so viel essen, bevor wir ins Fitnessstudio gehen.

Had better (short form: *'d better*) is used when we give **advice** and expect it to be taken. Note that after *had better* the infinitive is without *to*. The negative is *had better not*.

c Mum says you're to be back before ten.
Mama sagt, du sollst vor zehn zu Hause sein.
What am I to do first? What did you say?
Was soll ich als erstes tun? …

We use **be to** to report other people's **instructions**, or to ask about them.

d You're supposed to answer all the questions on the form.
Sie sollten alle Fragen auf dem Formular beantworten.
The boys were supposed to be here by ten.
Die Jungen sollten um zehn Uhr hier sein/hätten um zehn Uhr hier sein sollen.

We use **be supposed to** to say that someone should do something because they have an **obligation** to do it or have **agreed** to do it.

e You simply/really must see the exhibition.
Du musst die Ausstellung unbedingt sehen.

We use **must** to **strongly advise** or **recommend** something. We often use *simply* or *really* for emphasis.

Obligation or advice: 'should' and 'ought to'

43 Requests: Can/Could you …? *and* Will/Would you …?

Can/Could you turn the music down, please?
Kannst/Könntest du bitte die Musik leiser stellen?

Will/Would you help me to download these files?
Würden Sie mir helfen, diese Dateien herunterzuladen?

We use *Can/Could you …?* and *Will/Would you …?* to make a **request**. *Could you …?* and *Would you …?* are more polite than *Can you …?* and *Will you …?*

The verb | **34** | **Modal auxiliaries**

44 Offers and invitations: Can/Could I …?, Will/Won't you …?, Would/Wouldn't you …? *and* May I/we …?

Can/Could I get you a drink?
Kann ich Ihnen (vielleicht) etwas zu trinken holen?

Will/Won't you join us?
Willst/Möchtest Du (nicht) mitkommen?

Would/Wouldn't you like some more cake?
Möchten Sie (nicht) noch etwas Kuchen?

May we send you our catalogue?
Dürfen wir Ihnen unseren Katalog schicken?

When we want to **offer** somebody something or **invite** somebody to do something, we can use *Can/Could I …?*, *Will/Won't you …?*, *Would/Wouldn't you …?* and *May I/we …?* *Could I …?* is more polite than *Can I …?* *Won't you …?* and *Wouldn't you …?* are more insistent than *Will you …?* and *Would you …?*

We use *May I/we …?* for a very polite offer.

45 Suggestions: Shall I/we …?, Can't/Couldn't …?, can *and* could

Shall we buy a DVD player?
Sollen wir einen DVD-Spieler kaufen?

Can't we meet you at the cinema?
Können wir euch nicht am Kino treffen?

Couldn't we go to town tomorrow?
Könnten wir morgen nicht in die Stadt gehen?

You can/could watch TV while I'm away.
Du kannst/könntest fernsehen, während ich weg bin.

Shall I/we …?, *Can't/Couldn't …?*, *can* and *could* are used to make **suggestions**.

46 Refusals and rejections: won't *and* wouldn't

My mother knows I love dogs, but she won't let us have one.
Meine Mutter weiß, dass ich Hunde liebe, aber sie lässt uns keinen haben.

Paul knew the secret, but he wouldn't tell me.
Paul kannte das Geheimnis, aber er weigerte sich, es mir zu verraten.

Won't expresses a **refusal in the present**.

Wouldn't expresses a **refusal in the past**.

Requests: 'Can/Could you …?' and 'Will/Would you …?'
Offers and invitations: 'Can/Could I …?, Will/Won't you …?,
 Would/Wouldn't you …?' and 'May I/we …?'
Suggestions: 'Shall I/we …?, Can't/Couldn't …?, can' and 'could'
Refusals and rejections: 'won't' and 'wouldn't'

The verb 35 Modal auxiliaries

47 *Possibility and probability:* can, could, will, would, must, may, might, should *and* ought to

a The lights are on. Craig must be at home.
　　　　… *Craig muss zu Hause sein.*
There's a fax for you. – Oh, it will be from Jeff.
　　　　… *– Oh, es wird von Jeff sein.*
Too bad Leo is injured. With him in the team they would win.
… *Mit ihm in der Mannschaft würden sie gewinnen.*
Kathy should be/ought to be in the office by now.
Kathy müsste/dürfte jetzt eigentlich im Büro sein.
That parcel could be a birthday present.
Das Paket kann/könnte ein Geburtstagsgeschenk sein.
Steve hasn't phoned. He may still be in bed.
　　　　… *Vielleicht ist er noch im Bett.*
It's cold. It might even snow.
　　… *Es könnte sogar schneien.*
The weather can be quite nice in England.
Das Wetter kann in England ziemlich schön sein.

By using certain modal auxiliaries, the speaker can express an assumption about how **certain**, **probable** or **possible** he thinks something is.

'… and a little knot* here, and this rope should last one more jump …'

knot Knoten

b

positive	negative
must	cannot
will	will not
would	would not
ought to	ought not to
should	should not
could	could not
may	may not
might	might not
can	cannot

The modal auxiliaries express **different degrees** of certainty or probability:

• fairly certain

• probable

• possible.

▶ Short forms of the modal auxiliaries: 22

Das kann Peter sein.
not: That can be Peter.
but: That may/might/could be Peter.

c I posted the letter yesterday. It can't have arrived today.
　　　　… *Er kann heute noch nicht angekommen sein.*
Laura is late. – She may have met friends.
　　　　… *– Sie hat vielleicht Freunde getroffen.*

With a **modal auxiliary + perfect infinitive**, we can talk about things that certainly, probably or possibly happened or did not happen in the **past**.

▶ Perfect infinitive: 120

48 *Typical behaviour:* will *and* would

Granny will sit in the park and feed the birds all day.
Oma sitzt immer den ganzen Tag im Park und füttert Vögel.

Will can express **typical behaviour in the present**.

When I was a child, I would play in the fields every day.
… *habe ich immer den ganzen Tag auf den Feldern gespielt.*

Would can express **typical behaviour in the past**.

▶ *Used to:* 86 d

The verb | **36** | **Be, have and do**

49-57 Be, have *and* do

   49 *Be*, *have* and *do* used as auxiliaries
50-52 *Be* used as a full verb
53-55 *Have* used as a full verb
56-57 *Do* used as a full verb

49 Be, have *and* do *used as auxiliaries*

Be, have and *do* are special verbs. They can be auxiliaries or full verbs. As **auxiliaries**, they help to form certain verb tenses.

Mike is writing lyrics for his new song.
My snowboard was made in Austria, not Korea.

Tim has just phoned.
I was too late. The last bus had left.

Does Becky work in the supermarket? – I don't know.
Helen didn't forget your birthday, did she?
Don't be late.

Be used as an auxiliary:
- progressive form: a form of *be* + *-ing* form
- passive: a form of *be* + past participle

Have used as an auxiliary:
- present perfect: *have/has* + past participle
- past perfect: *had* + past participle

Do used as an auxiliary:
- questions and negatives in the simple present
- questions and negatives in the simple past
- the negative imperative

▶ *-ing* form: 65
▶ Forms of the past participle: 66
▶ Short forms of the auxiliaries: 58, 59
▶ Word order in questions: 5
▶ Negative statements: 3

'When did you last feed that goldfish?'

> **Note**
>
> She does look nervous.
> I did tell you. I'm sure.

We can use the auxiliary *do* to emphasize a full verb in the simple present or simple past.

▶ Emphasis: 299-301

Be *used as a full verb*

50 Forms

a

infinitive	present tense	past tense	past participle	-ing form
be	I am he/she/it is we/you/they are	I/he/she/it was we/you/they were	been	being

b Is Sarah in Mr Wilson's class?
I wasn't in Mr Wilson's class last year.
Was your brother in his class?

Don't be silly.

When we form **negative statements** and **questions** with *be* in the simple present or simple past, we do **not use *do/does/did***.

The negative imperative is *don't be* …

▶ Short forms of the auxiliaries: 58, 59

51 Be *used as a linking verb*

I'm a research scientist.
The new girl is nice.
We have often been here.

The full verb *be* **links** a **subject and** a **complement**.
The complement can be a noun (*a research scientist*) or an adjective (*nice*). *Be* can also link a subject and an **adverbial** (*here*).

> **Note**
>
> You're being very aggressive today.
> *Du bist heute aber sehr aggressiv.*

We can use *be* in the progressive form to describe temporary behaviour.

52 There + be

a There's someone on the phone for you.
Es ist jemand für dich am Telefon.

There are some good programmes on TV over Christmas.
Weihnachten gibt es einige gute Sendungen im Fernsehen.

Will there be anything to eat at the party?
Gibt es auf der Party etwas zu essen?

We use **there + a form of *be*** to say that something is present or exists.
The German equivalent of *there + be* is *es ist/sind* or *es gibt*, or the verbs *liegen* or *stehen* are used.
Be agrees in number with the following pronoun or noun (*There's someone* …, *There are some good programmes* …).

b There's only five days left.
Es sind nur noch fünf Tage.

In informal English, *there + is* is sometimes used with a noun in the plural.

Have *used as a full verb*

53 Forms

infinitive	present tense	past tense	past participle	-ing form
have	I/you/we/they have he/she/it has I/you/we/they don't have he/she/it doesn't have Do I/you/we/they have? Does he/she/it have?	I/you/he/… had I/you/he/… did not have Did I/you/he/… have?	had	having
	I/you/we/they have got he/she/it has got I/you/we/they haven't got he/she/it hasn't got Have I/you/we/they got? Has he/she/it got?			

54 Have *used as a state verb*

Our friends have (got) a new house.
My girlfriend has (got) brown eyes.
I have (got) a terrible stomach ache.

Mike's father has got two cars.
Mike's father has two cars.

Our neighbours haven't got pets.
Our neighbours don't have pets.

Have you got any brothers or sisters?
Do you have any brothers or sisters?

When it means the same as the German *haben* or *besitzen*, *have (got)* is a **state verb**, and so it is not used in the progressive form.

In British English **have** and **have got** are both possible. *Have got* is preferred in informal English and is used mainly in the simple present. In American English *have* is normally used.

▶ American English: 291
▶ State verbs and activity verbs: 69, 70

55 Have *used as an activity verb*

I have a shower every morning.
We don't often have lunch in town.
We're just having a drink.
Come on. Let's have some fun.
Did Sue have a good time in Spain?

In expressions like *have a shower, have breakfast*, etc., *have* is an **activity verb**. As an activity verb, *have* can be used in both the simple form and the progressive form.

Some common **expressions** with *have*:
have a shower — (sich) duschen
have breakfast — frühstücken
have lunch — (zu) Mittag essen
have dinner — zu Abend essen
have a drink — etwas trinken
have fun — sich vergnügen
have a go — es ausprobieren
have a good time — viel Spaß haben
have a party — eine Party geben/machen
have a look at — einen Blick werfen auf

▶ Have (got) to: 41a
▶ Have sth. done: 156

'You have a go in ours, and we'll have a go in yours, okay?'

Do *used as a full verb*

56 Forms

infinitive	present tense	past tense	past participle	-ing form
do	I/you/we/they do he/she/it does [dʌz]	did	done	doing

	auxiliary		main verb*		
Fran	does	not	do	much work.	
What	do	you	do	at the weekends?	
What	did	Dan	do	with my keys?	

In the simple present and simple past, we form **negative statements** and **questions** with the **full verb *do*** in the normal way, i.e. by using the auxiliary *do*.

construction set   Baukasten

57 Use

Chris **is doing his best** to get on a TV game show.
Who **did the dishes**? They're not clean.
Has Katie **done the shopping**?
We're doing well with our Web site. It looks good.

Do is a full verb when it means the same as the German *tun, machen, verrichten* or *erledigen*. Like other **activity verbs**, it can be used in both the simple form and the progressive form.

Some common **expressions** with *do*:
do one's best	sein Bestes geben
do business (with)	Geschäfte machen (mit)
do badly	nicht vorankommen, schlechte Leistungen bringen
do damage	Schaden anrichten
do the dishes	abwaschen, spülen
do an exercise	eine Übung machen
do sb. a favour	jemandem einen Gefallen tun
do one's homework	(die) Hausaufgaben machen
do the housework	die Hausarbeit machen
do a job/(some) work	eine Arbeit erledigen
do sb. a service	jemandem einen Dienst erweisen
do the shopping	einkaufen, Einkäufe machen
do well	vorankommen, gute Leistungen bringen
do without sth.	ohne etwas auskommen, auf etwas verzichten

▶ Activity verbs: 69

* We use *main verb* to speak about the function a full verb has in a sentence. (*Full verb* however refers to a verb class.)

58-60 The short forms of the auxiliaries

58 Positive short forms
59 Negative short forms
60 Use

58 Positive short forms

a **Be:**

I'm   'm = am

he's, she's, it's   's = is
here's, there's, that's
what's, when's, where's, who's, why's

you're, we're, they're   're = are

b **Have:**

I've, you've, we've, they've   've = have

he's, she's, it's   's = has
that's
what's, when's, where's, who's, why's

I'd, you'd, he'd, she'd, we'd, they'd   'd = had
who'd

c **Will and would:**

I'll, you'll, he'll, she'll, it'll, we'll, they'll   'll = will
there'll
who'll, what'll

I'd, you'd, he'd, she'd, we'd, they'd   'd = would
there'd
who'd

He's ill.   = He is …   's can mean **is** or **has**.
He's been ill.   = He has been …

I'd already left.   = I had …   'd can mean **had** or **would**.
I'd leave if I could. = I would …

The verb | **41** | **The short forms of the auxiliaries**

59 Negative short forms

a

isn't	= is not	can't	= cannot	
aren't	= are not	couldn't	= could not	
wasn't	= was not	won't [wəʊnt]	= will not	
weren't	= were not	shan't [ʃɑːnt]	= shall not	
don't	= do not	wouldn't	= would not	
doesn't	= does not	shouldn't	= should not	
didn't	= did not	oughtn't to	= ought not to	
haven't	= have not	mightn't	= might not	
hasn't	= has not	mustn't ['mʌsnt]	= must not	
hadn't	= had not	needn't	= need not	

Not has a short form **-n't**.

b

It isn't wrong. = It's not wrong.
I haven't seen her yet. = I've not seen her yet.
We hadn't been invited. = We'd not been invited.

For some auxiliaries there are **two possible negative short forms**:
- abbreviation of *not* to *n't*
- abbreviation of the verb + *not*.

The abbreviation of the verb + *not* is especially frequent with *be*.

60 Use

Beth: I'm sorry I didn't phone you. I couldn't find your new number.
Ben: That's OK. It's 0179/6130977.
Beth: I haven't got any paper. I'll write it on my T-shirt.

Dear Kathy,
Hi! What's new? We've had a pretty busy time here. That's why I haven't written …

'Now that it's all over,' Barney said, 'are we friends?' Kate smiled. 'It's not all over. Nothing's ever all over. That's what keeps me going.'
(Nat Hentoff: *The Day They Came to Arrest the Book.* Cornelsen 1992, p. 133)

We use short forms in **speech** or when we want to represent **spoken English** in writing, e.g. when we write down a conversation.

Short forms are also used in **informal writing**, e.g. in a letter to a friend or in advertisements.

You will also see short forms in **newspaper articles**, **short stories** and **novels** (especially in direct speech).

> **Notes**
>
> **1** Tom's been here. = Tom has been …
>   Our teacher's had an accident. = Our teacher has had …
>
>   We can also use a short form after a proper noun or a noun.
>
> **2** Are you Rachel? – Yes, I am. (**not:** Yes, ~~I'm~~.)
>   I know where she is. (**not:** I know where ~~she's~~.)
>
>   We do not use a positive short form at the end of a sentence.
>
> **3** We have lunch late on Sundays. (**not:** ~~We've~~ lunch …)
>
>   We do not use a short form of *have* when *have* is a full verb.

The verb | **42** | **Full verbs**

61-71 *Full verbs*

    61 Definition
  62-66 Forms
    67 Tense and time
    68 Aspect: the simple form and the progressive form
  69-71 The simple form and the progressive form with different kinds of verbs

61 *Definition*

Jerry **writes** songs.
I **went** on a school exchange programme last year.
Have you ever **done** a bungee jump?
I **think** the school trip will **be** fun.

Most verbs are **full verbs**. They are called *full verbs* because, unlike auxiliaries, they can stand alone without another full verb.

Forms

62 *Summary*

ask, carry, go, see	In English each full verb has five forms:	
	• the **infinitive**	▶ 63
asks, carries, goes, sees	• the **-s form** in the 3rd person singular of the simple present	▶ 64
asking, carrying, going, seeing	• the **-ing form**	▶ 65
asked, carried, went, saw	• the **simple past form**	▶ 66
asked, carried, gone, seen	• the **past participle**.	▶ 66

The verb 43 **Full verbs**

63 The infinitive

stop, talk, go

Go home. (imperative)

I go to a dance class every Monday. (simple present)

The infinitive is the **basic form of the verb**. The imperative and the simple present (except in the 3rd person singular) have the same form as the infinitive.

64 The -s form of the 3rd person singular in the simple present

a **Form:**

infinitive	3rd person singular
forget	he/she forgets
know	he/she/it knows
work	he/she/it works

In the 3rd person singular of the simple present, the full verb ends in **-s**. The **-s** is added to the infinitive.

b **Spelling rules:**

express	he/she/it expresses
finish	he/she/it finishes
watch	he/she/it watches
mix	he/she/it mixes

When the verb ends in a **sibilant** sound, we add **-es**. (Sibilant sounds are spelled e.g. *-ss, -sh, -ch, -x,* or *-z.*)

| tidy | he/she tidies |
| hurry | he/she/it hurries |

When the verb ends in a **consonant + y**, the ending is **-ies**.

but:

| play | he/she/it plays |
| enjoy | he/she/it enjoys |

If the verb ends in a **vowel + y**, we just add **-s**.

⚠️
| go | he/she/it goes |
| do | he/she/it does |

Note the spelling of **goes** and **does**.

c **Pronunciation:**

read [-d]	he/she reads	
come [-m]	he/she/it comes	[-z]
show [-əʊ]	he/she/it shows	

When the verb ends in a **voiced** sound, -s is pronounced [-z].

sleep [-p]	he/she/it sleeps	
take [-k]	he/she/it takes	[-s]
laugh [-f]	he/she/it laughs	

When the verb ends in one of the **voiceless** sounds [-p], [-t], [-k] or [-f], -s is pronounced [-s].

express [-s]	he/she/it expresses	
lose [-z]	he/she/it loses	[-ɪz]
watch [-tʃ]	he/she/it watches	

After the **sibilant** sounds [-s], [-z], [-ʃ], [-tʃ] and [-dʒ], the ending -es is pronounced [-ɪz].

⚠️
| do [duː] | he/she/it does [dʌz] |
| say [seɪ] | he/she/it says [sez] |

Note the pronunciation of **does** and **says**.

▶ Pronunciation of the plural -s: 171 c

65 The -ing form

a Form:

infinitive	-ing form
drink	drinking
go	going

The **-ing form** consists of the infinitive + *-ing*.

b Spelling rules:

stop	stopping
sit	sitting
plan	planning
prefer	preferring
control	controlling

We **double** a single **consonant** (*-p, -b, -t, -d, -g, -m, -n, -l* or *-r*) **at the end of the verb** when the consonant comes after a single vowel in a stressed syllable.

but:

jump	jumping
shout	shouting
open ['– –]	opening
offer ['– –]	offering

We do **not double** if:
- the verb ends in two consonants
- there are two vowels before the consonant
- the verb ends in an unstressed syllable.

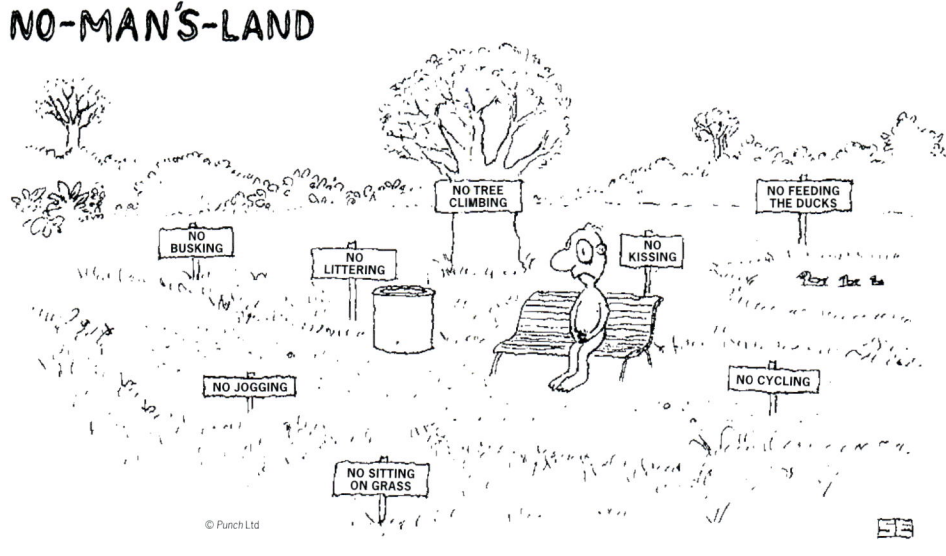

busk Straßenmusik machen
litter Abfall wegwerfen

Note

travel	travelling
dial	dialling

In British English *-l* is doubled even in an unstressed syllable.

smoke	smoking
phone	phoning

When the verb **ends in a silent -e**, we leave it out before *-ing*.

die	dying
lie	lying
tie	tying

Note the spelling of verbs ending in *-ie*.

66 The simple past form and the past participle

a **Form:**

infinitive	simple past	past participle
call	called	called
push	pushed	pushed
drink	drank	drunk
take	took	taken

Some verbs have a regular simple past and past participle, while others are irregular.

With **regular verbs**, we form the simple past and past participle by adding **-ed** to the infinitive.

Irregular verbs have **special forms**.

▶ Irregular verbs: 310

b **Spelling rules for regular verbs:**

infinitive	-ed form
stop	stopped
fit	fitted
plan	planned
prefer	preferred
control	controlled

We **double** a single **consonant** (-p, -b, -t, -d, -g, -m, -n, -l or -r) **at the end of the verb** when the consonant comes after a single vowel in a stressed syllable.

but:

jump	jumped
shout	shouted
open ['– –]	opened
offer ['– –]	offered

We do **not double** if:
- the verb ends in two consonants
- there are two vowels before the consonant
- the verb ends in an unstressed syllable.

smoke	smoked
phone	phoned

When the verb **ends in a silent -e**, we leave it out before -ed.

tidy	tidied
hurry	hurried

When the verb ends in a **consonant + y**, the ending is **-ied**.

but:

play	played
enjoy	enjoyed

If the verb ends in a **vowel + y**, we just add **-ed**.

Note

travel	travelled
dial	dialled

In British English -l is doubled even in an unstressed syllable.

c **Pronunciation of the regular -ed ending:**

live [-v]	lived	
seem [-m]	seemed	} [-d]
play [-eɪ]	played	

When the verb ends in a **voiced** sound, -ed is pronounced [-d].

help [-p]	helped	
laugh [-f]	laughed	} [-t]
wash [-ʃ]	washed	

When the verb ends in one of the **voiceless** sounds [-p], [-k], [-f], [-s], [-ʃ] or [-tʃ], -ed is pronounced [-t].

| need [-d] | needed | |
| paint [-t] | painted | } [-ɪd] |

After [-d] and [-t], -ed is pronounced [-ɪd].

The verb | **46** | **Full verbs**

67 Tense and time

tense	time	
present tense		
present perfect	past (what was)	future (what will be)
past tense		
past perfect	present (what is)	
future		
future perfect		

We have to distinguish between a **grammatical tense** (a form of the verb) and **real time**.

Michael's visiting a friend in Oxford at the moment.
(The present progressive relates to the present time.)
Michael's visiting a friend in Oxford tomorrow.
(The present progressive relates to future time.)

A **grammatical tense** (e.g. the present progressive) can refer to **different times**.

I've known Natalie for over ten years. (present perfect)
Ich kenne Natalie schon seit über zehn Jahren. (Präsens)
Just wait a moment. I'll go with you. (will-future)
    … Ich komme mit dir. (Präsens)

The use of **tenses** in English is **often different** from their use in German.

68 Aspect: the simple form and the progressive form

a
tense	simple form	progressive form
present tense	speak(s)	am/is/are speaking
past tense	spoke	was/were speaking
present perfect	have/has spoken	have/has been speaking
past perfect	had spoken	had been speaking
will-future	will speak	will be speaking

In contrast to German, English verbs have both **simple forms** and **progressive forms**.

b simple form

Ann plays squash.
(Squash is Ann's hobby.)
Rachel works for a computer firm.
(Rachel's job is with a computer firm.)
Dave has watched two videos this evening.
(Dave has finished watching videos.)

The **simple form** expresses the idea that
- someone does something regularly or repeatedly
- an action is long-lasting or permanent
- an action is complete.

progressive form

Ann's playing squash just now.
(Ann is in the squash court right now.)
Rachel's working for a computer firm this summer.
(Rachel has a temporary job with a computer firm this summer.)
Dave has been watching videos for over three hours.
(Dave is still watching videos.)

The **progressive form** expresses the idea that
- an action is in progress at the moment of speaking
- an action is going on for a temporary period
- an action is not yet complete.

I believe what Peter says. (**not:** … am believing …)
Sarah seems to be happy. (**not:** … is seeming …)

Every full verb can be used in the simple form. But it can only be used in the progressive form if it is an activity verb.

▶ Activity verbs: 69

Was darf's denn sein? Benzin oder Wasser für die Blumen?

Mittwoch
8. Januar

2. Kalenderwoche

22.12.–20.1.

Steinbock
Capricorn

The simple form and the progressive form with different kinds of verbs

69 Activity verbs

simple form	progressive form	
Hayley goes to karate classes. I often write e-mails. It always rains on my birthday.	I'm going to my karate class. I'm just writing one to Tim. It's my birthday today – and it's raining.	*Go*, *write* and *rain* belong to the group of verbs which we can use both **in the simple form and in the progressive form**. They refer to activities (*go*, *write*) or events (*rain*). Such verbs are called **activity verbs**.

70 State verbs

a

simple form	
What does 'http' mean? I believe you. Do you like curry? Did you hear that strange sound?	Verbs like *mean*, *believe*, *like* or *hear* are called **state verbs** They refer not to activities or events but to states. That is why we generally use them **only in the simple form**.

b

The most important state verbs are:

be	sein	look	aussehen
belong to	gehören	mean	bedeuten
consist of	bestehen aus	need	brauchen
contain	enthalten	own	besitzen
cost	kosten	possess	besitzen
depend on	abhängen von	seem	scheinen
exist	existieren	sound	klingen, sich anhören
have (got)	haben, besitzen		

- verbs which express **states**, **characteristics** or **possession**

agree	zustimmen	recognize	erkennen
believe	glauben	remember	sich erinnern
disagree	nicht zustimmen	see	verstehen, einsehen
doubt	bezweifeln	suppose	annehmen, vermuten
imagine	sich (etwas) vorstellen	think	meinen, glauben
		understand	verstehen, begreifen
know	wissen	wonder	sich fragen, überlegen
realize	einsehen, merken		

- verbs of **thinking**, **inferring** and **knowing**

dislike	nicht mögen	mind	etwas haben gegen
hate	hassen, gar nicht mögen	prefer	lieber mögen, vorziehen
like	mögen, gern haben	want	wollen, haben wollen
love	lieben, sehr gern mögen	wish	wünschen

- verbs of **liking**, **disliking** and **wishing**.

71 Verbs of perception

simple form	progressive form	
I heard a loud bang in the night.	—	Verbs such as *hear*, *see*, *smell*, *taste* and *feel* are called **verbs of perception** because something can be perceived with the senses. They are used **in the simple form**. But *smell*, *taste* and *feel* can **also** be **activity verbs** – with a different meaning – and so can be used in the **progressive form**.
Who saw what happened?	—	
Dinner smells delicious. What is it? *Das Abendessen riecht köstlich. ...*	I was smelling the roses when a bee stung me. *Ich roch an den Rosen, ...*	
The soup tastes salty. *Die Suppe schmeckt salzig.*	Dad is tasting it. *... probiert sie.*	
I (can) feel a pain in my knee. *Ich spüre einen Schmerz ...*	I'm feeling my knee to see where the pain is. *Ich taste mein Knie ab, ...*	

'I was smelling the roses like the doctor advised and got stung by a bee!'

The verb — **49** — **Full verbs**

Notes

1 Be careful, Tom. – But I *am being careful*.
   … – *Aber ich bin doch vorsichtig.*

If we use *be* + adjective to express temporary behaviour, then we use the progressive form.

2 1a We *have* a flat in Hampstead.
   Wir haben/besitzen eine Wohnung in Hampstead.
   1b Does your sister *have* a boyfriend?
   Hat deine Schwester einen Freund?
   2a I *have a shower* every day.
   Ich dusche jeden Tag.
   2b I *am having a shower*.
   Ich dusche gerade.

When *have* means the same as the German *besitzen* (examples 1a and 1b), we do not use it in the progressive form. But in expressions like *have lunch/a shower/a drink* (examples 2a and 2b), *have* can be used like any other activity verb.

3

activity verb	state verb
You*'re* not *holding* the racket properly. Look, like this. … *hältst* …	Amanda's car only *holds* four, not six. … *fasst* …
Sue*'s measuring* her room for a new carpet. … *misst … aus.*	It *measures* 4 metres by 5. … *misst 4 × 5 m.*
Jane*'s weighing* her suitcase. … *wiegt … (ab).*	Oh dear! It *weighs* more than 20 kilos. … *wiegt mehr als 20 kg.*

Some verbs like *hold*, *measure* and *weigh* can express activities as well as states. As activity verbs they can be used in the simple or the progressive form. As state verbs they are always in the simple form.

▶ Adjectives: 196-202
▶ *Have* as state and activity verb: 54, 55

72-73 Summary: the tenses of the full verbs

72 Present and past

tense	form (a = active, p = passive)	example
present tense	simple a: ask/asks p: am/is/are asked	Tom goes to school on his bike. His mother sometimes takes him by car. My sister knows a lot about sailing. English and French are spoken in Canada. The book describes country life in Devon.
	progressive a: am/is/are asking p: am/is/are being asked	Sorry, I can't come with you now. I'm installing some new computer programs. My room is being painted today.
present perfect	simple a: has/have asked p: has/have been asked	Sarah has applied to three universities. She's been called for two interviews. Kelly has had the same hairstyle for three years.
	progressive a: has/have been asking	Katie has been getting ready for her date since six o'clock.
past tense	simple a: asked p: was/were asked	I bought this camera a year ago. The car was found by the police yesterday. We met some friends in town, went for a hamburger, then looked round the shops.
	progressive a: was/were asking p: was/were being asked	I was playing a computer game when the electricity went off. Jason felt as if he was being watched.
past perfect	simple a: had asked p: had been asked	I lent the video to Dan after I had watched it. When I saw her last, she had been ill for two years. Claire knew why she hadn't been chosen.
	progressive a: had been asking	We had been waiting for an hour when Tom finally arrived.

The verb — 51 — Summary: the tenses

use of tense

• when something happens regularly, often, always or never	▶ : 75a
• when we talk about something permanent	▶ : 75b
• when we talk about texts, films or plays	▶ : 75c
• when an action or event is just now in progress and is not yet complete	▶ : 77a
• when we want to say that something has happened (not when it happened)	▶ : 80a
• when we want to say since when or how long a state has already lasted	▶ : 80b
• when an action or event began in the past and has continued up to (or almost up to) the present	▶ : 82a
• when we want to say when something happened	▶ : 86a
• when we talk about things in the past or tell a story	▶ : 86b
• when a past action or event was in progress at a particular time in the past	▶ : 89a
• when an action or event had already happened before a time in the past or when a state had begun before a time in the past and had lasted up to that time	▶ : 92a
• when an action or event had already begun before a time in the past and had continued up to (or almost up to) that time	▶ : 94

▶ Tenses of the full verbs: 74-94

73 Future

tense	form (a = active, p = passive)	example
will-future	a: will ask p: will be asked	The teachers **will** certainly **be** angry about this mess. We**'ll be punished**. Is the suitcase too heavy? I**'ll carry** it for you.
going to-future	a: am/is/are going to ask p: am/is/are going to be asked	I**'m going to have** a shower. Look at the sky! It**'s going to be** another hot and sunny day. I've forgotten my umbrella. I**'m going to be soaked**.
present progressive	a: am/is/are asking p: am/is/are being asked	We**'re flying** to Rome on Friday. Our house **is being painted** in spring.
simple present	a: ask/asks p: am/is/are asked	The first bus to London **leaves** at 6.20. Their new CD **is released** in February.
future progressive	a: will be asking	This time on Friday we**'ll be flying** to Rome. In a few minutes we**'ll be arriving** at York central station.
future perfect	a: will have asked p: will have been asked	I suppose John **will have left** when we arrive. When she comes back, a huge party **will have been organized**.

'I'll call you back in twenty minutes when the restaurant is crowded.'

The verb — 53 — Summary: the tenses

use of tense

• when we want to make a prediction or an assumption about the future	▶ : 96 a
• when we make a spontaneous decision, an offer or a promise	▶ : 96 b
• when we talk about intentions or plans for the future	▶ : 98 a
• when something will very probably happen because there are already signs of it happening	▶ : 98 b
• when something is definitely planned or arranged for the future	▶ : 99
• when a future event is a fixed part of a timetable, programme, schedule or suchlike	▶ : 100
• when an action or event will be in progress at a point of time in the future	▶ : 102 a
• when something will happen because it normally happens	▶ : 102 b
• when an action or event will be complete at a point of time in the future	▶ : 104

▶ Ways of expressing future time: 95-106

74-94 The tenses of the full verbs

74-75 Simple present
76-77 Present progressive
78 Simple present and present progressive in contrast
79-80 Present perfect (simple form)
81-82 Present perfect progressive
83 Present perfect (simple form) and present perfect progressive in contrast
84 *Since* and *for* with the present perfect
85-86 Simple past
87 Present perfect and simple past in contrast
88-89 Past progressive
90 Simple past and past progressive in contrast
91-92 Past perfect
93-94 Past perfect progressive

Simple present

74 Forms

I	write.
He/She/It	writes.
We/You/They	write.

I do not	
He/She/It does not	write.
We/You/They do not	

Do I	
Does he/she/it	write?
Do we/you/they	

The simple present has the **form of the infinitive**. But in the **3rd person singular** only, we add an **-s**.

Negative statements and **questions** are formed with **do/does**.

▶ -s form in the 3rd person singular: 64
▶ Short forms of the auxiliaries: 59a
▶ Negative statements and questions: 3, 5

75 Use

a I often go to bed after midnight.
Ich gehe oft nach Mitternacht ins Bett.

We go camping every summer.
Wir zelten jeden Sommer.

Hot air rises, doesn't it?
Heiße Luft steigt nach oben, oder?

My brother plays the drums.
Mein Bruder spielt Schlagzeug.

Mike speaks four languages. He even knows some Chinese.
Mike spricht vier Sprachen. Er kann sogar etwas Chinesisch.

b Most young people like trendy clothes.
Die meisten jungen Leute mögen moderne Kleidung.

We use the simple present to say that something happens **repeatedly**, **regularly**, **normally**, **often**, **always** or **never**.
It often occurs with phrases of time such as *always, never, often, sometimes* and *usually,* as well as *every summer, on Fridays, after midnight,* etc.

We also use the simple present to talk about someone's **hobby** or **job**, or to talk about **ability**.

The simple present is used to talk about something **permanent** which is not limited to a particular time.

▶ State verbs: 70

The verb | **55** | **Simple present**

c The novel describes life in an African village.
Der Roman beschreibt das Leben in einem afrikanischen Dorf.

The cover story deals with the election.
Die Titelgeschichte beschäftigt sich mit der Wahl.

In the film Tom Cruise plays a detective who falls in love with a murderess.
In dem Film spielt Tom Cruise einen Detektiv, der sich in eine Mörderin verliebt.

The simple present is used to talk about **texts**, e.g. novels, short stories, newspaper articles, **films** or **plays**.

d How do I get to the station? – First you go along Victoria Street, then you turn left …
… – Zuerst gehen Sie die Victoria Street entlang, dann biegen Sie links ab …

You press this button, you turn this knob, then you adjust the volume here. Easy.
Du drückst auf diesen Schalter, dann drehst du an diesem Knopf, dann stellst du hier die Lautstärke ein. Ganz einfach.

We use the simple present to describe a **series of actions**, e.g. when giving information or instructions.

e We leave London Heathrow at 9.15 and arrive in Munich at 11.30.
Wir fliegen um 9.15 in London Heathrow ab und sind um 11.30 in München.

For **future time** reference using the simple present:
▶ Ways of expressing future time: 100

f Chris will be here when you get back.
          … wenn du zurückkommst.
If Jenny calls, remember to show her your photos.
Wenn Jenny anruft, …

The simple present is used in a **subordinate clause of time** or an **if-clause** referring to the future.

▶ Conditional sentences: 251-257
▶ Adverbial clauses: 267-272

Simple present:
– when something happens regularly, often, always or never
– when we talk about something permanent
– when we talk about texts, films or plays

Present progressive

76 Forms

I am	
He/She/It is	writing.
We/You/They are	

I am not	
He/She/It is not	writing.
We/You/They are not	

Am I	
Is he/she/it	writing?
Are we/you/they	

We form the *present progressive* with **am/is/are + -ing** form.

▶ -*ing* form: 65
▶ Short forms of the auxiliaries: 58, 59

77 Use

a Liz **is washing** her hair (at the moment).
Liz wäscht sich (gerade) die Haare.

I'**m** just **downloading** a file. Hold on!
Ich lade gerade eine Datei herunter. Moment!

The present progressive is used when we want to say that someone is doing something **now/at the moment** or that something is happening as we speak. The action or event is **in progress** and **not yet complete**. Common phrases of time are *at the moment, now, just* and *still*.

▶ **Notes**

1 Bob: I haven't seen you for a couple of days.
Sue: I'm very busy at the moment.
I'**m helping** my parents. We'**re decorating** our living-room.

The present progressive is used for actions which are not yet complete but can be interrupted for a time. Strictly speaking, such interrupted actions are not in progress at the moment of speaking.

2 I'**m always forgetting** my purse.
Ich vergesse dauernd mein Portemonnaie.
You'**re always telling** me the same silly jokes.
Du erzählst mir immer wieder dieselben blöden Witze.

We can use the adverb *always* with the present progressive to say that something happens again and again, although not at regular intervals. Here *always* means *very often* or *too often*. The structure expresses the speaker's annoyance or surprise.

▶ Emphasis: 301 e

b Sally **is working** at a restaurant during her holidays.
Sally arbeitet während ihrer Ferien in einem Restaurant.
John **is walking** to work till the bus strike is over.
John läuft zur Arbeit, bis der Busstreik vorbei ist.

We use the present progressive to express the idea that a repeated action is **temporary**, i.e. it is happening for a limited period of time.

c Shall we go swimming tomorrow evening?
– Sorry, I can't. I'**m meeting** some friends in town.
     ... Ich treffe mich mit ein paar Freunden in der Stadt.

For **future time** reference using the present progressive:
▶ Ways of expressing future time: 99

Present progressive: when an action or event is just now in progress and is not yet complete

78 Simple present and present progressive in contrast

simple present | present progressive

1a Emma works as an illustrator.

1b She is working at her desk (just now).

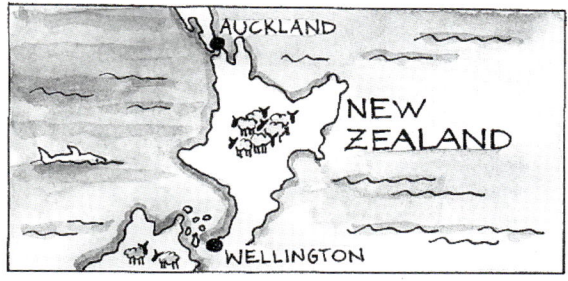

2a Auckland lies north of Wellington, doesn't it?

2b The cat is still lying in its basket.

3a My mother usually does the housework.

3b She is ill, so I am doing her work this week.

The **simple present** is used
- to talk about what happens **repeatedly**, **usually**, **often**, **always** or **never** (examples 1a and 3a).
- to talk about something **permanent** (example 2a).
Typical phrases of time are *usually, often, sometimes, every day, on Monday, at the weekends,* etc.

The **present progressive** is used
- to talk about what is happening **now/at the moment**. The action or event is in progress and **not yet complete** (examples 1b and 2b).
Typical phrases of time are *now, at the moment, today, just* and *still* (examples 1b and 2b).
- to say that a repeated action is **only temporary**, i.e. happening for a limited period of time (example 3b).

Present perfect (simple form)

79 Forms

I have	written.	
He/She/It has	worked.	
We/You/They have		

I have not	written.	
He/She/It has not	worked.	
We/You/They have not		

Have I	written?	
Has he/she/it	worked?	
Have we/you/they		

We form the present perfect with **have/has + past participle**.

▶ Forms of the past participle: 66
▶ Short forms of the auxiliaries: 58, 59
▶ Irregular verbs: 310

 The car has stopped.
Das Auto hat angehalten.
The car has arrived.
Das Auto ist angekommen.

In English we always use **have/has** to form the present perfect. In German either **haben** or **sein** is used to form the *Perfekt*.

80 Use

a A friend of mine has opened a pizza restaurant. We're going there tonight.
Eine Freundin von mir hat eine Pizzeria aufgemacht. …

I've cut my finger. It hurts.
Ich habe mir in den Finger geschnitten. …

Have you ever done a parachute jump?
Bist du schon mal mit dem Fallschirm gesprungen?

Tim's band has given ten concerts so far.
Tims Band hat bis jetzt zehn Konzerte gegeben.

We use the present perfect to say that someone has done something or that something has happened. The **exact time is not important** (or is unknown) and is **not mentioned**. The action or event often has direct consequences for the present or the future.
Some common phrases of time are *already, before, ever, just, never, often, so far, up to now* and *(not …) yet*.

b I've always wanted to go to Hawaii.
Ich habe schon immer nach Hawaii gehen wollen.

Diana has been in Australia since May.
Diana ist seit Mai in Australien.

How long have you had your camcorder?
Wie lange hast du deinen Camcorder schon?

The present perfect is used to express the idea that a **state began in the past** and **is still continuing**.
Some common phrases of time are *always, all my life, all week, since (May)* and *for (two years)*. We also use the present perfect after *how long …?*

 I have known him since 1992.
Ich kenne ihn seit 1992.

I've had this car for two years.
Ich habe dieses Auto seit zwei Jahren.

Note the **German equivalents** of the present perfect in these sentences.

The verb | **59** | **Present perfect (simple form)**

c Look, I've bought a new computer. I bought it at City Comp last Friday. It wasn't even expensive.
… *Ich habe einen neuen Computer gekauft.* …

There has been a further bomb attack in London's West End. In the early hours of the morning a bomb exploded at a West-End cinema. No one was hurt.
Im Londoner West End hat es ein weiteres Bombenattentat gegeben. …

The present perfect is often used when we **begin to talk about a past event**. No point of time is mentioned. When we give further details, such as where and how the event happened, we use the simple past.

Note

BE: Have you ever seen Niagara Falls?
    I've never met Jill's boyfriend.
AE: Did you ever see Niagara Falls?
    I never met Jill's boyfriend.

In American English the simple past is sometimes used instead of the present perfect, especially with *just, already, yet, ever* and *never*.

Present perfect:
– when we want to say that something has happened (not when it happened)
– when we want to say how long a state has already lasted

'Where have you been?'

The verb | **60** | **Present perfect progressive**

Present perfect progressive

81 Forms

I have been	
He/She/It has been	writing.
We/You/They have been	

I have not been	
He/She/It has not been	writing.
We/You/They have not been	

Have I been	
Has he/she/it been	writing?
Have we/you/they been	

We form the present perfect progressive with **have/has been + -ing form**.

▶ -ing form: 65
▶ Short forms of the auxiliaries: 58, 59

82 Use

a I've been standing here for an hour.
Ich stehe hier seit einer Stunde.

Sandra's been working hard the whole afternoon.
Sandra arbeitet schon den ganzen Nachmittag über schwer.

How long have you been playing the keyboard?
Wie lange spielst du schon Keyboard?

The present perfect progressive expresses the idea that an action or event **began in the past** and has **continued up to (or almost up to) the present**.
Some common phrases of time are *all day/all night/…, the whole morning/afternoon/…, since (yesterday)* and *for (an hour)*. We also use the present perfect progressive after *how long …?*.

b I've been running. (That's why I'm out of breath.)
Ich bin gelaufen. …

Sarah and I have been cooking lunch.
(That's why the kitchen is untidy.)
Sarah und ich haben Mittagessen gekocht. …

We use the present perfect progressive when we want to say that an **action in the past** has led to **unintended consequences in the present**. The action usually happened not very long ago.

⚠ They've been arguing for hours now.
Sie streiten jetzt schon seit Stunden.

Note the **German equivalent** of the present perfect progressive.

▶ State verbs: 70

> **Note**
>
> Tom has been playing football since 1997.
> *Tom spielt seit 1997 Fußball.*
> I've been learning French for two years.
> *Ich lerne seit zwei Jahren Französisch.*

The present perfect progressive also refers to interrupted actions which continue up to (or almost up to) the present.

Present perfect progressive:
when an action or event began in the past and has continued up to
(or almost up to) the present

83 *Present perfect (simple form) and present perfect progressive in contrast*

present perfect (simple form)	present perfect progressive
Jill **has drunk** five glasses of cola.	She **has been drinking** cola all evening.
I**'ve done** my homework already. I always do it when I come home.	What **have** you **been doing** all afternoon? – I**'ve been reading** comics.
It **has rained** a lot. Look at those puddles.	It **has been raining** for ten hours now.
We use the **present perfect** (simple form) to say that something has happened before the moment of speaking. The emphasis is on the **result** of the action.	We use the **present perfect progressive** to say that something began in the past and has continued up to (or almost up to) the moment of speaking. The emphasis is on **how long** the event has continued.

⚠️ We**'ve decorated** the living-room.
(result of a past action)
We**'ve been decorating** the living-room.
(action continuing up to the present)

I**'ve known** him for years.
(state)

Activity verbs can be used in the simple form and in the progressive form.

State verbs can be used only in the simple form.

▶ State verbs and activity verbs: 69, 70

'I've been watching you for five minutes, Watson. Well done. One of the straightest paper clips* I've ever seen.'

paper clip Büroklammer

84 Since *and* for *with the present perfect*

Rachel has been in the boutique since two o'clock.
She has been trying on clothes since two o'clock.

Rachel has been in the boutique for two hours.
She has been trying on clothes for two hours.

There are two different ways of saying how long an action or a state has lasted:

- We use **since** with the **point of time** when something began, e.g.:

since ten o'clock	seit zehn Uhr
since Sunday	seit Sonntag
since August 4th	seit dem 4. August
since 1995	seit 1995
since my birthday	seit meinem Geburtstag
since we arrived	seit unserer Ankunft

- We use **for** with the **period of time** that something has lasted, e.g.:

for three hours	seit drei Stunden, (schon) drei Stunden (lang)
for two days	seit zwei Tagen, (schon) zwei Tage (lang)
for a few years	seit ein paar Jahren, (schon) ein paar Jahre (lang)
for a long time	schon lange

 Ich habe meinen neuen Computer seit vier Wochen.
not: I have my new computer for four weeks.
but: I have had my new computer for four weeks.

Ich fahre jetzt schon seit zwei Stunden.
not: I am driving for two hours now.
but: I have been driving for two hours now.

In **German seit** is used mostly with the **present tense** when you want to say how long something has lasted.

Notes

1
Since we arrived, I've been feeling ill.
Seit unserer Ankunft ist mir schlecht.

Since we have been here, I've been feeling ill.
Seitdem wir hier sind, ist mir schlecht.

2 We've been here for ten days. (present perfect)
I was in Australia for six months. (simple past)
Our friends are staying for another week. (present progressive)

Since can also be used as a conjunction.
Used with the simple past, *since* relates to the beginning of a period of time in the past *(the time when we arrived)*.

But *since* used with the present perfect relates to a period of time *(the time we have been here)*. What has happened during this period has continued up to the moment of speaking.

For can not only be used with the present perfect, but also with other tenses.

▶ Adverbial clauses: 267–272

'since' + point of time
'for' + period of time

The verb | **63** | **Simple past**

Simple past

85 Forms

I		wrote.
He/She/It		worked.
We/You/They		

I did not		write.
He/She/It did not		work.
We/You/They did not		

Did I		write?
Did he/she/it		work?
Did we/you/they		

We form the simple past of **regular verbs** by adding **-ed to the infinitive**. But **irregular verbs** have their **own forms**.

We form **negative statements** and **questions** with **did**.

▶ Simple past form: 66
▶ Short forms of the auxiliaries: 59a
▶ Negative statements and questions: 3, 5
▶ Irregular verbs: 310

86 Use

a Tina passed her driving test in 1998.
Tina hat 1998 ihren Führerschein gemacht.

I was a cheerleader from 1999 to 2000.
Ich war von 1999 bis 2000 Cheerleader.

Did Jeff pay for the concert tickets yesterday?
– No, he didn't. He forgot.
Hat Jeff gestern die Konzertkarten bezahlt?
– Nein, er hat es vergessen.

When did you last see Nicole?
Wann hast du Nicole zuletzt gesehen?

We use the simple past to say that something happened at a **particular point of time in the past** (answering the question *when?*) or in a **particular period of time in the past** (which is now over). The point or period of time can be mentioned, or it may be clear from the context. Some common phrases of time are *yesterday, in 1998, last year/month/week, an hour ago*, etc. We also use the simple past (not the present perfect) after *when …?*

Ich habe meine Uhr gestern verloren.
not: I have lost my watch yesterday.
but: I lost my watch yesterday.

Wann bist du weggegangen?
not: When have you left?
but: When did you leave?

In **German**, past events can be reported in the **Perfekt** as well as the **Imperfekt**. But in **English** there are **special rules** for the use of the simple past and present perfect.

b It was late. Penny turned off the TV and went upstairs. Suddenly she heard a noise, a strange, frightening cry …

The simple past is used in **reports** about **past events** and in **stories**.

c There has been an accident in Carlton Street. A van crashed into a bus. The bus stopped abruptly and three people were injured.

We use the simple past when giving more information about a past event we have introduced in the present perfect. The **simple past** is used to give **further details**, e.g. where and how something happened.

The verb | **64** | **Simple past**

d He used to be shy, but he has changed.
Früher war er schüchtern, …
He didn't use to smoke, did he?
Er hat früher nicht geraucht, oder?
Did you use to do sport when you were a child?
Hast du als Kind Sport getrieben?

Used to + infinitive refers to states, habits and regular actions in the past.

⚠️ I am not used/I can't get used to living in a big city.
Ich bin nicht daran gewöhnt/kann mich nicht daran gewöhnen, …

Be careful not to confuse **used to + infinitive** with **be used to/get used to** (+ **-ing** form).

Notes

1 Grandmother would sit at her window for hours, watching the birds.
Großmutter pflegte stundenlang am Fenster zu sitzen und den Vögeln zuzusehen.

To express the idea of regularly repeated actions in the past, we can also use *would* + infinitive (without *to*).

2 It's time we were allowed to do what we want.
Es wird Zeit, dass wir tun dürfen, was wir wollen.
I wish he knew how to solve his problem.
Ich wünschte, er wüsste, …
I wish I were you/I were rich/I weren't here.
Ich wünschte, ich wäre …

The simple past is used in sentences with *I wish* and *it's time* expressing a wish. In such cases the simple past refers to the present or the future and not to the past.

Note the special form *I wish I were …*

▶ *Would* used for typical behaviour: 48

Simple past:
– when we want to say when something happened
– when we talk about things in the past or tell a story

Young Stephen King*

Stephen King   US-Autor von Horrorgeschichten

The verb 65 Present perfect and simple past

87 Present perfect and simple past in contrast

Both the **present perfect** and the **simple past** are used to talk about actions, events and states in the **past**.

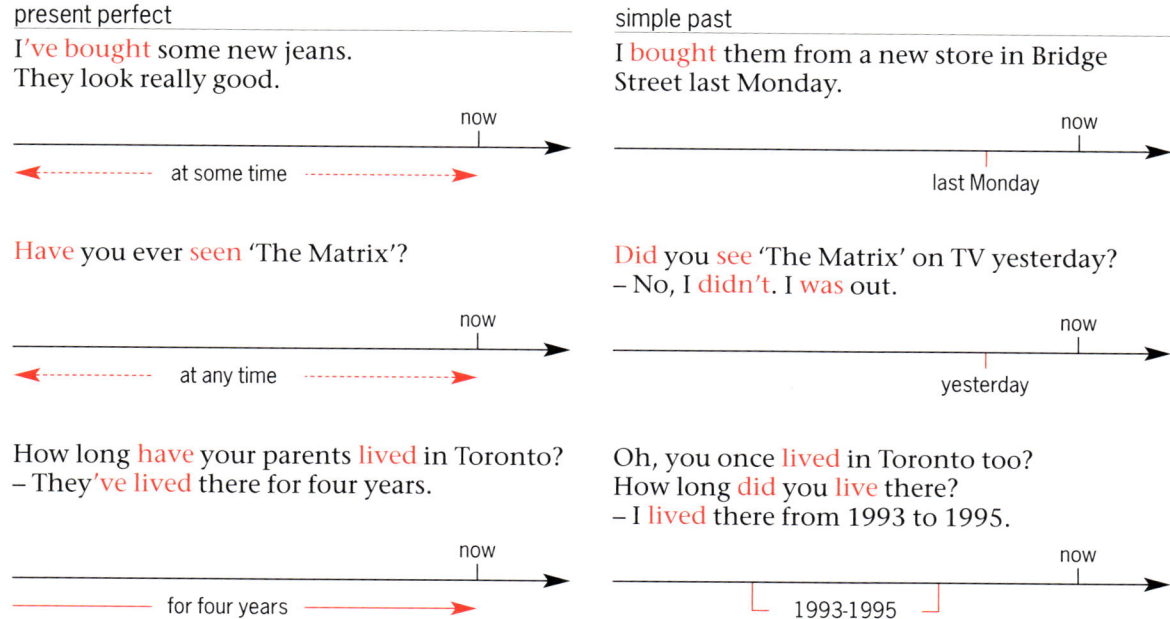

present perfect	simple past
I've bought some new jeans. They look really good.	I bought them from a new store in Bridge Street last Monday.
Have you ever seen 'The Matrix'?	Did you see 'The Matrix' on TV yesterday? – No, I didn't. I was out.
How long have your parents lived in Toronto? – They've lived there for four years.	Oh, you once lived in Toronto too? How long did you live there? – I lived there from 1993 to 1995.

We use the **present perfect**:
- to say that something has happened. The **exact time is not important** (or is unknown) and is **not mentioned**. The action or event often has consequences for the present.
- to express the idea that a state **began in the past** and **is still continuing**.

Some common **phrases of time** with the present perfect are: *all my life, already, before, ever, for ten years, never, just, since 1997, so far, up to now* and *yet*.

We use the **simple past**:
- to say that something happened at a **particular point of time in the past** or in a particular **completed period of time in the past**.

Some common **phrases of time** with the simple past are *yesterday, last night/week/Monday/…, in 1998* and *… ago*. We also use the simple past (not the present perfect) after *when …?*

'I've spent / I spent *twenty-five years making a name for myself and now you want me to CHANGE it?!*'

Choose the correct version of the cartoon caption.

I've spent

Past progressive

88 Forms

I was He/She/It was We/You/They were	writing.

I was not He/She/It was not We/You/They were not	writing.

Was I Was he/she/it Were we/you/they	writing?

We form the past progressive with **was/were + -ing form**.

▶ -ing form: 65
▶ Short forms of the auxiliaries: 59

89 Use

a I tried to call you on your mobile last night, but it was turned off. What were you doing?
– Oh, I was playing squash at the sports centre.
… Was hast du (zu der Zeit) gemacht?
– Oh, ich habe im Sportzentrum Squash gespielt.

At midnight I was driving home from my cousin's.
Um Mitternacht fuhr ich (gerade) von meinem Cousin nach Hause.

The past progressive is used when we want to say that at a **particular time in the past** (e.g. *last night, at midnight*) an action or event was **in progress** and so was **not yet complete**.

b Ricky and Todd were playing cards — when the teacher came in.

The past progressive often refers to **actions** which were **in progress** (*Ricky and Todd were playing cards*), when a **second action began** (*the teacher came in*). The second action is in the simple past.

c It was a terrible night. A strong wind was blowing. It was raining hard. We were lying in our tents. Suddenly someone screamed.
… Ein starker Wind wehte. Es regnete heftig. Wir lagen in unseren Zelten …

The past progressive is used to describe **background activity or accompanying circumstances** in stories or reports.

▶ State verbs: 70

Past progressive:
when an action or event was in progress at a particular time in the past

The verb | **67** | **Simple past and past progressive**

90 Simple past and past progressive in contrast

simple past
We watched TV last night.
I worked on my biology project yesterday.

We use the **simple past** to say that an action or an event happened at a **particular point of time** or in a **particular period of time in the past**. The action or event is **complete**.

past progressive
We were watching TV when you phoned.
I was working on my biology project when Jeff came.

We use the **past progressive** to say that an action or event **was in progress at a particular time in the past**. The speaker expresses the idea that the action **was not yet complete**.

'Ah, there you are, darling. I was just telling / I just told Ken and Angie about your unfortunate* accident.'

Choose the correct version of the cartoon caption.

I was just telling

unfortunate unglückselig

Past perfect

91 Forms

| I had |
| He/She/It had | written. |
| We/You/They had | worked. |

| I had not |
| He/She/It had not | written. |
| We/You/They had not | worked. |

| Had I |
| Had he/she/it | written? |
| Had we/you/they | worked? |

We form the past perfect with **had + past participle**.

▶ Forms of the past participle: 66
▶ Short forms of the auxiliaries: 58, 59
▶ Irregular verbs: 310

⚠ My rucksack had disappeared.
Mein Rucksack war verschwunden.
Someone had stolen it.
Jemand hatte ihn gestohlen.

In English we always form the past perfect with **had**. But in German either **hatte** or **war** is used for the *Plusquamperfekt*.

The verb | **68** | **Past perfect**

92 Use

a
Laura couldn't pay. She had forgotten her purse.
Laura konnte nicht zahlen. Sie hatte ihr Portemonnaie vergessen.

Nina had already left the coffee bar by the time I arrived.
Nina hatte das Café schon verlassen, als ich ankam.

When I visited John in hospital, he had been there for ten days.
Als ich John im Krankenhaus besuchte, war er schon zehn Tage dort.

I had known Marc for years before he moved to Berlin last year.
Ich kannte Marc schon einige Jahre, bevor er letztes Jahr nach Berlin zog.

With the help of the past perfect we can express the idea that one past action followed another. The **action that happened first** is in the past perfect.

The past perfect is also used to refer to a **state**. The state **began before a point of time in the past** and **continued** up to that time.

b
The cat ran out when Joanne opened the door.
Die Katze rannte hinaus, als Joanne die Tür öffnete.
When Tom felt the spider on his face, he screamed.
Als Tom die Spinne auf seinem Gesicht spürte, schrie er auf.

When two or more (short) **actions** in the past **come directly one after the other**, we use the **simple past** for all the actions.

⚠️
               past perfect
When Roy's friends arrived, he had cooked the lunch.
(Roy had already finished cooking when his friends arrived.)

               simple past
When Roy's friends arrived, he cooked the lunch.
(Roy's friends arrived and only then did he begin to cook the lunch.)

We use the **past perfect** for an **action** only when we need to emphasize that it **happened before another action**.

> **Note**
>
> After I had left school | I went to America.
> After I left school |
> *Nachdem ich die Schule verlassen hatte, …*

In a clause with *after* (= *nachdem*), we can use either the past perfect (which is rather formal) or the simple past.

Past perfect:
when an action or event had already happened before a point of time in the past or when a state had begun before a point of time in the past and continued up to that time

Past perfect progressive

93 Forms

I had been He/She/It had been We/You/They had been	writing.

I had not been He/She/It had not been We/You/They had not been	writing.

Had I been Had he/she/it been Had we/you/they been	writing?

We form the past perfect progressive with **had been + -ing form**.

▶ -ing form: 65
▶ Short forms of the auxiliaries: 58, 59

94 Use

Rob **had been travelling** for three months when he ran out of money.
Rob war schon drei Monate auf Reisen gewesen, als ihm das Geld ausging.

We use the past perfect progressive to express the idea that an action or event had **begun before a point of time in the past** and **continued up to (or almost up to) that time**.

▶ State verbs: 70

Past perfect progressive:
when an action or event had begun before a point of time in the past and continued up to (or almost up to) that time

95-106 Ways of expressing future time

95-96 *Will*-future
97-98 *Going to*-future
99 Present progressive
100 Simple present
101-102 Future progressive

103-104 Future perfect
105 Last but not least …
106 Other ways of expressing future time

In English we can use different verb forms to talk about something happening in the future.

Will-*future*

95 Forms

I **will**	
He/She/It **will**	write.
We/You/They **will**	

I **will not**	
He/She/It **will not**	write.
We/You/They **will not**	

Will I	
Will he/she/it	write?
Will we/you/they	

We form the *will*-future with **will + infinitive (without to)**. We usually use the short forms *'ll* and *won't* [wəʊnt]. *Won't* is the short form of *will not*.
In (formal) British English we sometimes use *I/we shall* and *shan't* [ʃɑːnt] (= *shall not*) instead of *I/we will (not)*.

▶ Short forms of the auxiliaries: 58c, 59a
▶ Forms of the modal auxiliaries: 22

96 Use

a I'm sure the weather **will be** hot in Greece.
Es wird mit Sicherheit heiß werden in Griechenland.

I think Emily **will like** it here.
Ich glaube, Emily wird es hier gefallen.

You**'ll** probably **find** the film boring at the beginning.
Du wirst den Film am Anfang wahrscheinlich langweilig finden.

We use the *will*-future to make a **prediction** or an **assumption** about the future. We often use it when talking about things that we cannot control. Here are some common expressions that we use with this structure: *I think, I'm sure, I suppose, I believe, I expect, I hope, perhaps* and *probably*.

b Oh, dear, it's raining. – **I'll lend** you my umbrella.
… – Ich leihe dir meinen Schirm.
Don't worry. I **won't forget** to phone you.
… Ich werde nicht vergessen, dich anzurufen.

We use the *will*-future when making a **spontaneous decision**, especially an **offer** or a **promise**.

▶ *Will* as a modal auxiliary: 27, 43, 44, 46-48
▶ *Will* in conditional sentences: 252a

'Will'-future:
– when we want to make a prediction or an assumption about the future
– when we make a spontaneous decision, an offer or a promise

Going to-*future*

97 Forms

I am He/She/It is We/You/They are	going to write.
I am not He/She/It is not We/You/They are not	going to write.
Am I Is he/she/it Are we/you/they	going to write?

We form the *going to*-future with **am/is/are going to + infinitive**.

'I think your advertising concept is stupid, exploitative* and offensive*. It's going to make us a fortune*!'

exploitative ausbeuterisch
offensive anstößig
make sb. a fortune jd. ein Vermögen einbringen

▶ Short forms of the auxiliaries: 58, 59

98 Use

a I**'m going to be** a pilot when I grow up.
Ich will Pilot werden, wenn ich groß bin.

What **are** you **going to do** tomorrow night?
Was machst du morgen Abend?

We use the *going to*-future to talk about **intentions** or **plans** for the future.

b The plane is losing height. It**'s going to hit** the rocks at any moment.
… Es wird jeden Augenblick auf die Felsen schlagen.

Look at those dark clouds. There**'s going to be** a thunderstorm.
… Es wird ein Gewitter geben.

We use the *going to*-future to say that **something will very probably happen** because there are already **signs** of it happening.

⚠ I**'m going to play** squash.
– Oh, I**'ll come** and watch you.

We use the **going to-future** for **intentions** or **plans**.
But we use the **will-future** for a **spontaneous decision**.

Note

I**'m going** to the school disco tonight.
Are you **coming** with me?

With the verbs *go* and *come* we often use the present progressive instead of *going to*.

▶ Future time reference using the present progressive: 99

'Going to'-future:
– when we talk about intentions or plans for the future
– when something will very probably happen because there are already signs of it happening

Present progressive

99 Use

Could you copy some CDs for me this afternoon?
– Sorry, I'm playing tennis with Mike.
… – Leider spiele ich mit Mike Tennis.

We're having a barbecue on Saturday.
Wir grillen nächsten Samstag.
All my friends are coming.
Alle meine Freunde kommen.

We use the present progressive to say that something is **definitely planned** or **arranged** for the future.
It must be clear from the context or from the use of a phrase of future time (*this afternoon, on Sunday*) that we are talking about the future.

▶ Forms of the present progressive: 76
▶ Short forms of the auxiliaries: 58, 59

Present progressive:
when something is definitely planned or arranged for the future

'Hi, it's me. Listen. It's David's birthday, so a few million of us are going out for a meal. Are you interested?'

Simple present

100 Use

The next train from Dover arrives at 8.25.
Der nächste Zug aus Dover kommt um 8.25 Uhr an.

The new Indian restaurant opens this weekend.
Das neue indische Restaurant wird an diesem Wochenende eröffnet.

We use the simple present to say that a future event is a fixed part of a **timetable**, a **programme** of events, a **schedule** or suchlike (the 'timetable future').
Verbs such as *arrive, open, close, start* or *stop* are often used in this way.

▶ Forms of the simple present: 74

Simple present:
when a future event is a fixed part of a timetable, programme, schedule or suchlike

Future progressive

101 Forms

I will He/She/It will We/You/They will	be writing.

I will not He/She/It will not We/You/They will not	be writing.

Will I Will he/she/it Will we/you/they	be writing?

We form the future progressive with **will be + -ing form**. We usually use the short forms *'ll* and *won't*.

▶ Short forms of the auxiliaries: 58c, 59a

102 Use

a A week today I'll be sitting on the beach.
Heute in einer Woche werde ich am Strand sitzen.

Shall I pick you up at nine?
– Sorry, but we'll be having breakfast then.
..., aber um diese Zeit frühstücken wir.

We use the future progressive for actions or events which will be **in progress at a point of time in the future**. The action or event has begun before the point of time and may possibly continue after it.

Compare:
1 When I get home, my little brother will be watching TV.
2 When I get home, I'll watch TV too.

In example 1 (**future progressive**), his brother will already be in front of the television when the speaker gets home. In example 2 (**will-future**), the speaker will watch television after he gets home.

b We'll be playing golf next weekend. (As usual.)
Wir spielen am nächsten Wochenende Golf. (Wie immer.)

I've got a letter here. Will you be passing the post office?
... Kommst du an der Post vorbei?

We use the future progressive to say that **something will happen because it normally happens**, or that **it will happen in any case, without being specially planned**.

Compare:
I'm seeing Tom tomorrow.
(We've arranged to meet at lunchtime.)

I'm going to see Tom tomorrow.
(I want to ask him something.)

I'll be seeing Tom tomorrow.
(Tom is in my class.)

· **present progressive:** arrangement

· **going to-future:** intention

· **future progressive:** routine

Future progressive:
– when an action or event will be in progress at a point of time in the future
– when something will happen because it normally happens

The verb | **74** | **Future perfect**

Future perfect

103 Forms

I will	have written.
He/She/It will	have worked.
We/You/They will	

I will not	have written.
He/She/It will not	have worked.
We/You/They will not	

Will I	have written?
Will he/she/it	have worked?
Will we/you/they	

We form the future perfect with **will have + past participle**. We usually use the short forms *'ll* and *won't*.

▶ Short forms of the auxiliaries: 58c, 59a
▶ Forms of the past participle: 66
▶ Irregular verbs: 310

104 Use

The last train will have left when we get to the station.
Der letzte Zug wird abgefahren sein, …

I hope you'll have made up your mind by tomorrow.
Ich hoffe, du hast dich bis morgen entschieden.

We use the future perfect for actions or events which will be **complete at a point of time in the future**. The point of time is often mentioned (*when we get to the station, by tomorrow*).

> **Note**
>
> Mike hasn't arrived yet.
> I expect he will have missed the train.
> *… Er wird wohl den Zug verpasst haben.*

The future perfect can also refer to something that we think has happened in the past.

Future perfect:
when an action or event will be complete at a point of time in the future

105 Last but not least …

a We're spending Easter in Edinburgh.
   We're going to spend Easter in Edinburgh.

   One day I'll be rich and famous.
   One day I'm going to be rich and famous.

b I'm sure Liz will come soon.
   Liz kommt sicher bald. / Liz wird sicher bald kommen.

   A week today I'll be lying in the sun.
   Heute in einer Woche liege ich in der Sonne. / … werde ich in der Sonne liegen.

We **cannot always draw exact boundaries** between the different verb forms which are used for the future. In many contexts there is more than one possible form.

English verb forms expressing future time are often equivalent to the **present tense in German**.

106 Other ways of expressing future time

Besides the different verb forms we use for the future, there are other ways of talking about future events.

a I **expect to be** at home at the weekend.
Ich werde am Wochenende wohl zu Hause sein.

We **hope to get** a last-minute flight to Las Palmas in October.
Wir hoffen, im Oktober einen Last-Minute-Flug nach Las Palmas zu bekommen.

Rachel hasn't got much homework, so she **wants to watch** a video this evening.
…, deshalb möchte sie heute Abend ein Video sehen.

I**'d like to have** a Halloween party. Do you think anybody would come?
Ich würde gerne eine Halloween Party machen. …

We can use verbs like **expect to, hope to, want to, would like to, …** (in the present tense) to say what we **think or feel** about the future.

b The President **is to open** the exhibition on April 2nd.
Der Präsident eröffnet die Ausstellung am 2. April.

The players **are to arrive** at the airport at 10.20.
Die Spieler treffen um 10.20 Uhr am Flughafen ein.

Queen **to visit** Russia in June
Queen besucht Russland im Juni

The present tense of **be to** + infinitive expresses the idea that something is **(officially) arranged** for the future.
Be to often occurs in news reports (on television, in newspapers) and is also used in shortened form in news headlines.

c Vicky's got her coat on. She**'s about to leave**.
… Sie ist im Begriff wegzugehen.

Tim is extremely angry. He**'s on the point of doing** something stupid.
… Er ist dabei, eine Dummheit zu begehen.

The present tense of **be about to** + infinitive or **be on the point of** + *-ing* form expresses the idea that something will happen **in the very near future**.

d Amanda's playing well. She**'s certain to win** the match.
… Sie wird das Spiel bestimmt gewinnen.

Valery drives much too fast. She**'s bound to cause** an accident one day.
… Sie wird sicher eines Tages einen Unfall verursachen.

I**'m likely to be** in town tomorrow, so why not come today instead?
Ich bin morgen wahrscheinlich in der Stadt, …

We can use the present tense of **be certain to, be sure to, be bound to, be likely to** and **be unlikely to** + infinitive to say how **certain, probable or improbable** it is that something will happen.

▶ Future time reference using modal auxiliaries: 23 f

107-117 The passive

107 Active and passive
108 Forms of the passive
109 Use
110 Passive sentences with *by*

111-114 The passive with different kinds of verbs
115 The passive infinitive
116 The passive gerund
117 The passive participle

107 Active and passive

active:

Carl Benz **built** the first car with a petrol engine.

passive:

This car **was built** in Mannheim in 1885.

When we talk about something happening, we use either an active or a passive sentence. The choice of active or passive depends on our point of view.

- In the **active**, the subject (here: *Carl Benz*) does the action. The example sentence says something about Carl Benz (he built the first car with a petrol engine).

- In the **passive**, something is done to the subject (here: *This car*). The example sentence says something about the car (where and when it was built).

108 Forms of the passive

a

tense	form of *be*	past participle	
simple present:	Letters are	written.	The passive is a **form of *be* + past participle**. In German the passive is a form of *werden* + past participle.
	… *werden geschrieben.*		
simple past:	… were	written.	
	… *wurden geschrieben.* /		The rules about when to use the different tenses are the same as in the active.
	… *sind geschrieben worden.*		
present perfect:	… have been	written.	
	… *sind geschrieben worden.*		
past perfect:	… had been	written.	
	… *waren geschrieben worden.*		
will-future:	… will be	written.	
	… *werden geschrieben (werden).*		

The verb | **77** | **The passive**

b

tense	form of *be*	past participle
present progressive:	Letters are being	written.
	… werden (gerade) geschrieben.	
past progressive:	… were being	written.
	… wurden (gerade) geschrieben.	

We form the **passive progressive** with *being*:
- *are being written* (present progressive passive)
- *were being written* (past progressive passive).

As in the active, the progressive form expresses the idea of an action in progress.

c

	modal + form of *be*	past participle
modal auxiliary:	Letters should be	written.
	… sollten geschrieben werden.	
	… must have been	written.
	… müssen geschrieben worden sein.	

In sentences with a modal auxiliary, *be* is used in the present infinitive (*be*) or the perfect infinitive (*have been*).

▶ Use of tenses: 72, 73
▶ Passive infinitive/gerund/participle: 115-117
▶ Forms of the infinitive: 120

⚠️ *Probleme werden in unseren Versammlungen diskutiert.*
Problems are discussed at our meetings.
(simple present: passive)

Wir werden am Montag einige neue Probleme diskutieren.
We will discuss some new problems on Monday.
(*will*-future: active)

Be careful: in German **werden** is used not only to form the **passive** but also the **future**.

Notes

1 All the classroom windows were shut before the storm.
… wurden … geschlossen.

The classroom was hot because all the windows were shut.
… geschlossen waren.

The passive can express both an action and a state. If the passive expresses an action, in German we use a form of *werden* ('Vorgangspassiv').

If the passive expresses a state, i.e. the result of an action, then in German we use a form of *sein* ('Zustandspassiv').

2 It was too late. Nothing could be done.
… *Man* konnte nichts tun. / … *Es* konnte nichts getan werden.

Passive sentences in English sometimes correspond to active sentences in German with the word *man*.

3 Three people got killed in the accident.
Drei Menschen wurden bei dem Unfall getötet.

In informal English we can use a form of *get* instead of *be*, especially when something happens suddenly and unexpectedly (e.g. in an accident).

4 We got dressed quickly.
Wir zogen uns schnell an.
Tom and Sue are planning to get married in May.
… zu heiraten.

Get is also used in some fixed phrases:
get divorced — sich scheiden lassen
get dressed — sich anziehen
get married — heiraten

The passive: form of 'be' + past participle

The verb 78 The passive

109 Use

a
1. Lasers are used in CD players and videodisc systems. Holograms are also produced with the help of lasers.
2. A cyclist was injured in an accident in Wembley Park Road yesterday. The 17-year-old youth was taken to hospital, where he was treated for shock and minor cuts. It seems that the accident was nobody's fault.
3. The worst earthquake in California was in 1906, when San Francisco was almost completely destroyed. More than 2000 people were killed. Widespread fires which broke out after the quake could not be put out for three days.

As in German, we use the passive to say **what is done** or **what happens to something or someone**. Who does the action is normally
- **unknown** or **unimportant** (examples 1 and 2)
- **obvious** (example 3).

The passive is often found
- in technical or scientific writing (example 1)
- in reports of accidents or crimes (example 2)
- in reports of natural disasters (example 3).

In such cases the agent (who or what does the action) is not mentioned. This may be because we can't, don't want to or don't need to identify it. In this way the passive acquires an impersonal and neutral tone.

Note

1. English spoken here (= English is spoken here.)
2. Baby kidnapped from hospital (= A baby has been kidnapped …)

On signs or notices (example 1) and in newspaper headlines (example 2), the passive is often used in a shortened form, without *be*.

b
1. This house is very old. It was built in 1683.
2. Ann: Did Ford build the first car with a petrol engine?
   Sue: No. The first one was built by Benz in 1885.
   Ann: And what about the Model T?
   Sue: Yes, the Model T was designed by Ford, but that was a few years later, wasn't it?

The first part of a sentence very often contains information that is already known, or it refers back to information already known (example 1: *This house … / It …*). The new or interesting information, on the other hand, usually comes at the end of the sentence (*… is very old / … was built in 1683*).

This principle of **information structure** (**'from the given to the new'**) is often the reason for using the passive.

110 Passive sentences with by

Tutankhamun's tomb was found by Howard Carter in 1922.
Tutanchamuns Grabmal wurde 1922 von Howard Carter entdeckt.

Our car was damaged by falling rocks.
Unser Auto wurde durch fallende Steine beschädigt.

The new information can be the agent (**who** or **what** does the action). If we want to, we can add this information after the preposition **by** (*by Howard Carter, by falling rocks*).

The passive with different kinds of verbs

111 Verbs with one object

a

		subject		(direct) object
1	active:	The police	questioned	everybody.

		subject	
	passive:	Everybody	was questioned.
		Jeder wurde befragt. / Alle wurden befragt.	

2 active: They told me to leave at once.

   passive: I was told to leave at once.
   Man befahl mir, sofort zu gehen. / Es wurde mir befohlen, sofort zu gehen.

3 active: People will talk about this scandal for years.

   passive: This scandal will be talked about for years.
   Man wird über diesen Skandal noch jahrelang sprechen.

In English we can form the passive with almost all verbs which in the active are followed by an object – either direct or indirect (examples 1-3). The **subject of the passive sentence** corresponds to the **object of the active sentence**.

But in German the passive can be formed only with transitive verbs, i.e. verbs which in the active are followed by a direct object. The passive is therefore used less often in German than in English.
For more details about the different uses of the passive in English and German, see below.

b

			(direct) object	
1	active:	People advised	me	to go to art school.

		subject	
	passive:	I	was advised to go to art school.

Mir (= dative object) wurde geraten, auf die Kunsthochschule zu gehen. / Es wurde mir geraten, auf die Kunsthochschule zu gehen. / Man riet mir, auf die Kunsthochschule zu gehen.

(The Princess died in 1997.)
2 active: People will remember her for a long time.

   passive: She will be remembered for a long time.
   Man wird sich noch lange Zeit an sie erinnern.

Unlike their German equivalents, the following English verbs can be used in passive sentences, usually with a person as the subject (**'persönliches Passiv'**):

advise sb.	jemandem (etwas) raten
allow sb.	jemandem (etwas) erlauben
answer sb.	jemandem antworten
follow sb.	jemandem folgen
help sb.	jemandem helfen
join sb.	sich jemandem anschließen
remember sb./sth.	sich an jd./etwas erinnern
thank sb.	jemandem danken

The corresponding German verbs cannot be used in the passive because they are intransitive, i.e. in the active they are followed by a dative object (example 1: *mir*) or a prepositional object (example 2: *an sie*). They can only be used in constructions with *man* or in passive constructions with *es* (Beispiel 1: *Mir wurde geraten … / Es wurde mir geraten …*).

The verb | 80 | The passive

112 Verbs with two objects

		indirect object	direct object
active:	The agency offered	Kelly/her	a TV role.

subject: The agency offered Kelly/her

passive: **Kelly/She** was offered a TV role.
Kelly/Ihr wurde eine Fernsehrolle angeboten. / Man bot Kelly/ihr eine Fernsehrolle an.

She was promised a film part too.
Ihr wurde auch eine Filmrolle zugesagt. / Man sagte ihr auch eine Filmrolle zu.

In the active, verbs like *give*, *offer*, *promise*, *show* and *tell* are usually followed by **two objects**: an indirect object and a direct object.

When a verb has two objects, the **indirect object of the active sentence** (the person: *Kelly/her*) usually becomes the **subject of the passive sentence** (*Kelly/She*). This structure (**'persönliches Passiv'**) is not used in German. The indirect dative object of the active sentence (*ihr*) does not change in the passive.

		indirect object	direct object
active:	The agency offered	Kelly/her	a TV role.

subject:

passive: **A TV role** was offered to Kelly/her.
A film part was promised to her too.

The **direct object of the active sentence** (*a TV role, a film part*) can also become the **subject of the passive sentence**. Whether we choose a person or a thing as the subject of the passive sentence depends on the context and the information structure.

▶ Verbs with two objects: 20

Note

A TV role was offered (to) Kelly/her.
A film part was promised (to) her too.

When the subject of the passive sentence is a thing, we can leave out the preposition *to* before the indirect object.

113 Prepositional verbs and fixed phrases

		verb + preposition	object
active:	Someone	has broken into	the video shop.

subject: The video shop | verb + preposition: has been broken into

passive: The video shop has been broken into.
In den Videoladen ist eingebrochen worden. / Man ist in den Videoladen eingebrochen.

We can form the passive of many **verb + preposition** combinations (e.g. *break into, look after, talk about, think of*). As in an active sentence, the preposition comes right after the verb.

		verb + noun + preposition	object
active:	They	made fun of	Tahira's accent.

subject: Tahira's accent | verb + noun + preposition: was made fun of

passive: Tahira's accent was made fun of.
Man lachte über Tahiras Akzent.

There are also **fixed phrases** consisting of a verb + noun + preposition. Here too, in the passive the preposition stays right after the noun. Such phrases include:

make fun of	sich lustig machen über
pay attention to	beachten
take care of	aufpassen auf, sich kümmern um
take notice of	(einer Sache) Beachtung schenken

▶ Prepositions in questions: 5e
▶ Prepositional verbs: 164-166

The verb | **81** | **The passive**

114 Verbs of speaking and thinking

active: People say that the President is seriously ill.

passive: 1 It is said that the President is seriously ill.
Man sagt, dass der Präsident schwer krank sei.

2 It is thought that he has gone to hospital.
Man glaubt, er sei ins Krankenhaus gegangen.

3 The President is said to be seriously ill.
Der Präsident soll (angeblich) schwer krank sein. /
Man sagt/berichtet, dass der Präsident schwer krank sei.

4 He is thought to have gone to hospital.
Er soll ins Krankenhaus gegangen sein. /
Man glaubt/nimmt an/vermutet, er sei ins Krankenhaus gegangen.

With verbs of speaking and thinking (e.g. *believe, consider, expect, know, report, say, suppose* and *think*), there are two different passive structures in English:
- *it* as subject (**'unpersönliches Passiv'**):
 it + passive verb + *that*-clause (examples 1 and 2)
- a person as subject (**'persönliches Passiv'**):
 subject + passive verb + *to*-infinitive (examples 3 and 4).

These passive structures are often used in newspaper reports to avoid naming the source of the information.
In German: *Man sagt/glaubt … / Es heißt … / Angeblich ist/soll …*

'It is said that Reinhold Messner has been seen around here again.'
–'Don't be stupid. You don't really believe he exists, do you?'

Reinhold Messner Bergsteiger und Autor, z.B. von „Yeti – Legende und Wirklichkeit"

> **Note**
>
> In order to make clear the formation of the passive, in sections 111-114 each passive sentence is shown with its active equivalent. In normal usage, however, passive sentences are not formed from active ones, but are used independently. The decisive factor in the choice of active or passive is the context, the information structure, etc. (▶ 109).
> It often happens that in a particular text a passive sentence is the only possible (stylistically correct) choice and cannot be replaced by an active one (and vice versa).

verbs that can be passive: all those with an object in the active

The verb | **82** | **The passive**

115 The passive infinitive

1. I want to **be left** alone.
   Ich will in Ruhe gelassen werden.

2. I think Luke should **be asked** too.
   Ich glaube, Luke sollte auch gefragt werden.

3. Luke should **have been asked** much earlier.
   Luke hätte viel früher gefragt werden sollen.

The passive infinitive (with or without *to*) can be **present** (examples 1 and 2) or **perfect** (example 3). The passive infinitive can follow the same verbs as the active infinitive.

▶ Infinitive: 120 a/c

Note

The boss **wanted the letters** (to be) **written** as soon as possible.
Die Chefin wollte, dass die Briefe so bald wie möglich geschrieben werden. / Die Chefin wollte die Briefe ... schreiben lassen.

Would you **like the brakes** (to be) **checked**?
Sollen die Bremsen überprüft werden?

In the structure *want/would like* + object + passive infinitive, we often leave out *to be* and use only the past participle.

▶ Have sth. done: 156

116 The passive gerund

1. I don't like **being called** 'stupid'.
   Ich mag es nicht, „Dummkopf" genannt zu werden/ wenn man mich „Dummkopf" nennt.

2. Sue remembered **having been beaten** in her first match.
   Sue erinnerte sich daran, dass/wie sie in ihrem ersten Spiel geschlagen wurde.

The passive gerund can be **present** (example 1) or **perfect** (example 2). The passive gerund can follow the same verbs, prepositions, etc. as the active gerund.

▶ Gerund: 136

Note

The lawn **needs mowing** (= needs to be mowed).
Der Rasen muss gemäht werden.

The car **wants cleaning**.
Das Auto muss gewaschen werden.

This book is certainly **worth reading**.
Dieses Buch ist auf jeden Fall lesenswert/wert, gelesen zu werden.

After the verbs *need* and *want* and the adjective *worth*, we use the active gerund even though it has a passive meaning.

117 The passive participle

1. Have you ever watched an operation **being done**?
   Hast du schon mal gesehen, wie eine Operation durchgeführt wird?

2. **Having been beaten** several times, Sue decided to take her tennis training more seriously.
   Nachdem sie mehrmals geschlagen worden war, entschied sich Sue, ihr Tennistraining ernster zu nehmen.

The passive participle can be **present** (example 1) or **perfect** (example 2).

▶ Participle: 151

118 Non-finite forms of the verb

118 Finite and non-finite forms of the verb

In English every full verb has **finite** and **non-finite** forms.

a Tom: I take Spanish at school.
(1st pers. sing., simple present)

My friend takes Spanish too.
(3rd pers. sing., simple present)

We took a course in Barcelona last year.
(1st pers. pl., simple past)

A **finite** verb can have different forms. The finite forms tell us something about person, number and tense.

b It's easy to find penfriends on the Internet. (infinitive)
I like getting up early. (gerund)
I know a lot of people learning taekwondo.
(present participle)
Have you taken your driving test yet? (past participle)

Rachel has to learn biology for tomorrow's test.
Last week I had to learn chemistry and maths.

The **infinitive**, the **-ing form** (gerund or present participle) and the **past participle** are **non-finite** forms of the verb. They do not change their form and they tell us nothing about person, number or tense.

Information about person, number or tense can be given by means of auxiliaries (e.g. has, had).

c 1 a The best thing would be to take a computer course.
(infinitive)
Es wäre das Beste, einen Computerkurs zu machen.
   b The best thing would be for you to take a computer course.
Es wäre das Beste, wenn du einen Computerkurs machen würdest.

2 a Carol hated playing the guitar. (gerund)
Carol hasste es, Gitarre zu spielen.
   b Carol hated him playing the guitar.
Carol hasste es, wenn er Gitarre spielte.

3 a Having finished, the girls went home. (past participle)
Als die Mädchen fertig waren, gingen sie nach Hause.
   b The ballet lesson having finished, the girls went home.
Als der Ballettunterricht zu Ende war, gingen die Mädchen nach Hause.

Non-finite constructions can be **without their own subject** (examples 1a, 2a and 3a), or they can have **their own subject** (examples 1b, 2b and 3b: you, him, the ballet lesson).

▶ Subject in infinitive constructions: 127
▶ Subject in gerund constructions: 149
▶ Subject in participle constructions: 162

'Until we get some reaction to the campaign, Fenton, I want you to pretend* it's your idea.'

pretend so tun, als ob

The infinitive

119 Summary
120 Forms
121 Functions
122-130 The *to*-infinitive
131-134 The infinitive without *to*

119 Summary

Phil has decided to move to Berlin.
Phil hat sich entschlossen, nach Berlin zu ziehen.
I really must catch the last bus home.
Ich muss unbedingt den letzten Bus nach Hause bekommen.

Every full verb has a basic form, the infinitive. This can be:
- a **to-infinitive**
- an **infinitive without to** (a bare infinitive).

▶ Full verbs: 61-71

⚠ I mustn't forget to give Mike his CDs back.
Ich darf nicht vergessen, Mike seine CDs wiederzugeben.

In English we do **not use a comma** before the infinitive.

120 Forms

a

I should write an article for the school magazine.
    ... *schreiben.*

It should be written in a funny tone.
    ... *geschrieben sein.*

I should have written more regularly for the magazine.
    ... *hätte ... schreiben sollen.*

In fact, the article should have been written weeks ago.
    ... *geschrieben worden sein.*

These are the **forms of the infinitive**:
- present active infinitive
- present passive infinitive
- perfect active infinitive
- perfect passive infinitive.

▶ Forms of the passive: 108 c

Note

The keys were nowhere to be found.
Die Schlüssel waren nirgends zu finden.

His behaviour leaves much to be desired.
Sein Verhalten lässt viel zu wünschen übrig.

That remains to be seen.
Das bleibt abzuwarten.

In contrast to German, the passive infinitive can be used after the verbs *be*, *leave* and *remain*.

The verb | **85** | **The infinitive**

b
Dave's taken his sports bag. He must be playing squash.
… *Er wird (wohl gerade) Squash spielen.*

Emma looked very tired yesterday. She must have been working hard.
… *Sie muss (wohl) hart gearbeitet haben.*

The infinitive also has **progressive forms**:
- *(to) be* + *-ing* form (the present progressive infinitive)
- *(to) have been* + *-ing* form (the perfect progressive infinitive).

c The teacher advised us not to write a long text.

In the **negative infinitive**, *not* comes before the infinitive.

> **Note**
>
> **Compare:**
> Jane's sorry not to have left school.
> *Jane bedauert es, dass sie die Schule nicht verlassen hat.*
> (She has not left school.)
> Jane's not sorry to have left school.
> *Jane bedauert es nicht, dass sie die Schule verlassen hat.*
> (She has left school.)

A change in the position of *not* can change the meaning of the sentence.

121 Functions

a

The infinitive is partly like a noun and partly like a verb. This means that it can fulfil different functions.

Like a **noun**, it can be used in the following ways:

subject
To understand is to forgive.

- as a subject (This occurs mainly in fixed expressions and proverbs and is not very frequent. A gerund is usually preferred.)

object
Debbie has promised to come.

- as an object

subject complement
The aim is to arrive on time.

- as a subject complement

adverbial
Marc left at twelve to catch the last train.

- as an adverbial.

b
Joe asked me yesterday to phone him.
Don't forget to read the article carefully.
Barbara wants to travel to New Zealand.

Like a **verb**, it can be followed by various elements:
- by an object (e.g. *him*)
- by an adverb (e.g. *carefully*)
- by an adverbial phrase (e.g. *to New Zealand*).

The to-infinitive

122 Verb + to-infinitive

We decided to meet again on Friday.
Wir beschlossen, uns am Freitag wieder zu treffen.

Didn't Oliver promise to wash the car?
Hat Oliver nicht versprochen, das Auto zu waschen?

Sarah simply refuses to listen to anybody's advice.
Sarah weigert sich einfach, auf den Rat von irgendjemandem zu hören.

'Should we walk upright*? Should we continue to live in trees? Should we try to make things? Decisions, decisions!'

upright   aufrecht

You ought to go out more often.
Du solltest öfter ausgehen.
Sorry I have to leave early.
Tut mir Leid, dass ich so früh gehen muss.

The **to-infinitive** often corresponds to a German infinitive with *zu*. It comes **after certain verbs**, e.g.:

agree	zustimmen
arrange	vereinbaren
choose	beschließen
decide	sich entschließen
expect	erwarten, damit rechnen
hope	hoffen
learn	lernen
offer	anbieten
plan	planen, vorhaben
promise	versprechen
refuse	sich weigern
seem	scheinen
try	versuchen
want	(tun) wollen
would like/love	möchte(n) gern, gern (tun) wollen

Note also:

ought to do	tun sollen
be able to do	tun können
be allowed to do	tun dürfen
have to do	tun müssen

▶ Forms of the *going to*-future: 97
▶ Verb + *to*-infinitive or *-ing* form: 139 b/c
▶ *Be to*, *be supposed to*: 42 c/d, 106
▶ *Used to*: 86 d
▶ *Ought to*: 23 a

Notes

1 Don't try to lift the TV on your own. /
Don't try and lift the TV on your own.
Versuch nicht, den Fernseher allein hochzuheben.

2 Try turning the key the other way.
I've already tried to open the door this way, but it won't open.

A verb coming after *try* can have *and* instead of *to* (mainly in informal English). *Try and …* is especially frequent in imperatives.

Try and a number of other verbs can be followed by either a *to*-infinitive or an *-ing* form.

▶ Verb + *to*-infinitive or *-ing* form (with a difference in meaning): 139 c

The verb | **87** | **The infinitive**

123 Verb + object + to-infinitive

a

	verb	object + to-infinitive	
1 Mr Hill	asked	Kevin to be	quiet.
2 He didn't	allow	the class to use	a dictionary.
3 And he	warned	us not to waste	time.

1 Mr Hill bat Kevin, leise zu sein.
2 Er erlaubte der Klasse nicht, ein Wörterbuch zu verwenden.
3 Und er warnte uns, keine Zeit zu vergeuden.

After **certain verbs** we can use an **object with a *to*-infinitive**. The German equivalent usually has an infinitive with *zu*. Examples:

advise	raten
allow	erlauben
ask	bitten
encourage	ermutigen
force	zwingen
help	helfen
invite	einladen, auffordern
remind	daran erinnern
teach	lehren, beibringen
warn	ermahnen, warnen

Notes

1 Sue, please help me (to) repair my bike.
Sue, hilf mir bitte, mein Fahrrad zu reparieren.

2 We warned her not to jump into the water.
Wir warnten sie davor, ins Wasser zu springen.

To is often left out after *help* + object, especially in American English.

Warn sb. not to do sth. means the same as the German *jd. davor warnen, etwas zu tun.*

b

1 Mr Hill expected his pupils to work hard.
Mr Hill erwartete, dass seine Schüler hart arbeiteten.

2 He didn't want them to get nervous.
Er wollte nicht, dass sie Angst bekamen.

3 He said, 'I would like you all to get good marks in the exam.'
Er sagte: „Ich möchte, dass ihr alle in der Prüfung gute Noten bekommt."

We can also use an **object and a *to*-infinitive** after the following verbs:

cause	verursachen, dass
expect	erwarten, dass
tell	sagen, dass (… soll)
want	wollen, dass
would like/love	möchte(n) gern, dass

Personal pronouns have the **object form** (example 2: *them*).
In contrast to the verbs listed in 123a, in German a clause with *dass* is used and not an infinitive.

⚠️ *Die Parkers möchten gern, dass Tom bei einer Bank arbeitet.*
not: The Parkers would like ~~that Tom works~~ …
but: The Parkers would like Tom to work in a bank.

Sie wollen, dass er sich sofort bewirbt.
not: They want ~~that he applies~~ at once.
but: They want him to apply at once.

Note that in English *want* and *would like* or *would love* are **not** followed by a **that-clause**.

Note

Tom wants to help his sister. (Here Tom wants to help.)
Tom wants his sister to help. (Here his sister is supposed to help.)

A change in the position of the object can change the meaning of a sentence.

c 1 I believe that to be complete nonsense.
      Ich glaube, dass das völliger Unsinn ist.

   2 We know Johnson to be a man of his word.
      Wir wissen, dass Johnson zu seinem Wort steht.

   3 We all consider Jill (to be) a computer expert.
      Wir alle halten Jill für eine Computerexpertin.

In formal English the structure **object + to be** is often used after some **verbs of speaking and thinking** (e.g. *believe, consider, declare, imagine, know, suppose*). After *consider* we can leave out *to be*. Instead of this structure, a *that*-clause is normally used in informal English (example 2: *We know **that** Johnson is a man of his word.*).

124 Adjective + to-infinitive

The lyrics of the song are difficult to understand.
It's more important to finish your essay than your comic.
Which of these French books is (the) easiest to read?

We can use a *to*-infinitive **after an adjective** and its **comparative forms**.

The adjective can occur in various structures, e.g.:

The problem is easy to solve.
- after a noun or pronoun + a form of *be*

It was an easy problem to solve.
   … ein leicht zu lösendes Problem.
- before a noun

The problem was easy enough to solve.
The question is too difficult to answer.
- with *too* and *enough*.

▶ Comparison of adjectives: 197-200

'Yes, of course it's important enough to disturb* him.'

disturb stören

Note

He's unlikely to pass the test.
Er wird den Test wahrscheinlich nicht bestehen.
The team is certain/sure to lose the match.
Die Mannschaft wird das Spiel ganz bestimmt verlieren.

Infinitive constructions after the adjectives *likely/unlikely, certain* and *sure* are usually expressed in German by means of adverbs such as *wahrscheinlich* or *bestimmt*.

125 The first, the last, the next, the only + to-infinitive

The captain was the last (person) to leave the ship.
       … the last (person) who left …

Liverpool is the only English city to have two cathedrals.
       … the only English city that has …

The *to*-infinitive can come **after *the first*, *the last*, *the next*** or **the only** (+ noun or *one*). In this structure it replaces a relative clause.

▶ Relative clauses: 258-266

The verb | 89 | **The infinitive**

126 Noun + to-infinitive

a   It's **time to go**.
    Es ist Zeit zu gehen.

    Did you know about Katie's **plans to work** in India?
    Wusstest du von Katies Plänen, in Indien zu arbeiten?

| | The *to*-infinitive can come **after a noun**. It often corresponds to a German infinitive with *zu*. |

b   We've got some **work** | **to do**.
                            | that we must do.

    Is he a **man** | **to rely on**?
                    | (who) we can rely on?

The *to*-infinitive often comes **after a noun** and **replaces a relative clause** containing a modal auxiliary.

A preposition comes in the same position as it would in the relative clause (*rely on*).

c   There's **nobody** | **to ask** for advice.
                        | (who) I could/might ask for advice.

    There is **nothing** | **to be done**.
                          | that we can do.
                          | that can be done.

A *to*-infinitive construction can also replace a relative clause **after somebody, anybody, something, anything, nobody, nothing**, etc.

127 The subject in infinitive constructions

a   1 My parents **wanted to be** home by ten.
       Meine Eltern wollten um zehn zu Hause sein.

    2 My parents **wanted Paul to be** home by ten.
       Meine Eltern wollten, dass Paul um zehn zu Hause ist.

    3 My parents **wanted him to be** home by ten.
       Meine Eltern wollten, dass er um zehn zu Hause ist.

The *to*-infinitive can be **without its own subject** (example 1), or it can have **its own subject** (examples 2 and 3). This changes the meaning of the sentence.
In all the examples, *my parents* is the subject of the whole sentence. In example 1, the *to*-infinitive is without a subject of its own. In this case the subject of the whole sentence is understood as the subject of the infinitive.
In examples 2 and 3, the *to*-infinitive does have its own subject. This is the 'notional subject', the **person who carries out the action** of the *to*-infinitive: *Paul/him*. In this construction a personal pronoun has the object form (example 3: *him*).

b   1 The book is too **difficult for a little boy to understand**.
       Das Buch ist für einen kleinen Jungen (zu) schwer zu verstehen.

    2 I brought along a **comic for her to read** on the trip.
       Ich brachte einen Comic mit, den sie auf der Fahrt lesen konnte.

When the *to*-infinitive comes after an adjective or noun, we can use a subject in the construction **for** + **noun** or **pronoun** (in the object form).

▶ Finite and non-finite forms of the verb: 118c

c   She has **arranged for her cousin to collect** her suitcase at the airport.
    Sie hat es so organisiert, dass ihre Cousine ihren Koffer am Flughafen abholt.

    We **waited for them to get dressed**.
    Wir warteten, bis sie angezogen waren.

After the verbs **arrange for**, **wait for**, etc., which normally combine with *for*, the *to*-infinitive can have the construction *for* + noun or pronoun in front of it.

128 Question word + to-infinitive

We didn't know | who to ask.
 | who we should/could ask.
 | …, wen wir fragen sollten/könnten.

Can you tell me | how to get to the library?
 | how I can get to the library?
 | …, wie ich zur Bücherei komme?

Helen wondered | whether to stay or to leave.
 | whether she should stay or leave.
 | …, ob sie bleiben oder gehen sollte.

The *to*-infinitive can come **after a question word** (e.g. *who, how, what, where, when*) as well as after **whether** (= *ob*). This construction is often used in preference to a subordinate clause with a modal auxiliary such as *can, could, should, might* or *must*. To express the same thing in German, a subordinate clause is always used after the question word.

129 The to-infinitive to indicate the purpose of an action

I left at ten to catch the last bus.
Ich ging um zehn, um den letzten Bus zu erwischen.

They arrived early in order to get good seats.
Sie kamen früh, um gute Plätze zu bekommen.

I got up at six in order not to be late for the exam.
Ich stand um sechs Uhr auf, um nicht zu spät zur Prüfung zu kommen.

We often use the *to*-infinitive to express the **aim** or **purpose** of an action. We can also use *in order to* or *so as to* instead of *to*.

In the negative we use either *in order not to* or *so as not to*.

The equivalent in German of this kind of *to*-infinitive is *um (nicht) … zu* + infinitive.

130 Special features

a 1 We're going to have a barbecue on Saturday. Would you like to come? – Yes, I'd like to. What time?

   2 Rick was asked to go to an art exhibition, but he didn't want to.

To avoid repetition, we often use **to on its own**:
- instead of a *to*-infinitive (example 1)
- instead of a *to*-infinitive and its complementation (example 2).

b It's difficult to fully understand the meaning of this poem.
(It's difficult to understand fully the meaning of this poem.)

We can also use an **adverb between to** and the **infinitive**, especially if we want to emphasize the verb rather than the adverb. This is called a 'split infinitive'. (It is often better to use a split infinitive than to put the adverb between the verb and the object.)

'to'-infinitive:
– after certain verbs
– after a verb + object
– after an adjective, a noun, 'the first', etc.
– after 'for' + noun/pronoun
– after a question word
– to indicate the purpose of an action

The verb | **91** | **The infinitive**

The infinitive without to

131 Auxiliary + infinitive without to

Simon can ride.
You should practise speaking English more.

Tim's girlfriend doesn't like discos.

The **infinitive without to** comes:
- after a **modal auxiliary** (but: *ought to*)

- after the auxiliary **do/does/did**.

132 Fixed phrases + infinitive without to

The infinitive without *to* comes **after fixed phrases** like:

You'd better go to the police.
Du solltest besser zur Polizei gehen.

- had better ('d better)

I'd rather not talk about this problem.
Ich möchte lieber nicht über dieses Problem sprechen.

- would rather ('d rather)
- would sooner ('d sooner)

We decided to buy Mariah Carey's new CD rather than pay for concert tickets.
Wir entschieden uns, lieber die neue Mariah Carey CD zu kaufen, als für Konzertkarten zu bezahlen.

- rather than

Why not ask your parents, Susan?
Warum fragst du nicht deine Eltern, Susan?

- why not …?

Let's meet at two o'clock.
Treffen wir uns (doch) um zwei Uhr.

- let's …

133 Let/Make + object + infinitive without to

	verb	object + infinitive	
1 Miss Jones	lets	us talk	in class.
2 But she	doesn't let	us eat or drink.	
3 Before exams she	makes	us work	hard.

After the verbs **let** and **make**, the **object** + **infinitive** structure is **without to**. Let and make have different meanings:

let = (zu)lassen, erlauben
make = (veran)lassen, dazu bringen, zwingen

1 *Miss Jones lässt uns während des Unterrichts reden.*
2 *Aber sie lässt uns nicht essen oder trinken.*
3 *Vor Prüfungen zwingt sie uns, hart zu arbeiten.*

'What exactly makes you think your brother bribed* the piercer?'

bribe bestechen

134 *Verbs of perception + object + infinitive without* to

1 We heard Tom say something.
   Wir hörten, dass Tom etwas sagte.

2 I saw the police car drive round the corner and stop in front of our house.
   Ich sah den Polizeiwagen um die Ecke biegen und vor unserem Haus anhalten.

3 We watched Ann put her luggage into the car, get in and drive away.
   Wir sahen zu, wie Ann ihr Gepäck im Wagen verstaute, einstieg und wegfuhr.

but:
We watched Ann putting her luggage into the car.
Wir sahen, wie Ann ihr Gepäck im Wagen verstaute.

After **verbs of perception** like *feel, hear, listen to, notice, see, smell* and *watch* we can use an **object** + **infinitive without** *to* (e.g. *heard Tom say*). The equivalent in German can also be an infinitive, or it can be a clause with *dass* or *wie*. We use the infinitive mainly to express the idea that
- an action has finished (examples 1 and 2)
- the whole event was perceived (from start to finish) (example 3).

Instead of the infinitive, we use the present participle when the event is still in progress (i.e. not yet finished) at the time it is perceived.

▶ Verbs of perception: 71
▶ Forms of the participle: 151
▶ Verbs of perception + object + participle: 154

'But are you absolutely sure you saw him take something, because if you're wrong …'

Infinitive without 'to':
– after a modal auxiliary or 'do/does/did'
– after phrases like 'had better', 'would rather', etc.
– after 'let' and 'make' + object
– after a verb of perception + object

The verb | 93 | **The -ing form**

135 The -ing form

135 Summary

a

infinitive	-ing form
wait	waiting
swim	swimming
be	being

Every full verb (including *be*) has an **-ing form**.

▶ *-ing* form: 65
▶ Full verbs: 61

b

Working isn't Joe's favourite activity.
Arbeiten ist nicht Joes Lieblingsbeschäftigung.

Katie's just got a job, so she's a working mother now.
Katie hat gerade einen Job gefunden, also ist sie jetzt eine berufstätige Mutter.

Depending on its function in the sentence, the *-ing* form is either:
· a **gerund**
▶ 136-150

· a **present participle**.
▶ 151-163

> **Note**
>
> The Tower of London is very interesting. (adjective)
> It's a very old building. (noun)

Not all words ending in *-ing* are *-ing* forms. There are adjectives and nouns with an *-ing* ending.

get stuck hängen bleiben

The verb | 94 | **The gerund**

136-150 The gerund

136 Forms
137 Functions
138 The gerund as subject
139 The gerund as object

140-144 The gerund after prepositions
145-148 The gerund after certain words and phrases
149 The subject in gerund constructions
150 Other constructions instead of a gerund

136 Forms

a

driving
being driven
having driven
having been driven

There are four **forms of the gerund**:
- the present active gerund (example 1)
- the present passive gerund (example 2)
- the perfect active gerund (example 3)
- the perfect passive gerund (example 4).

1 Simon likes driving his old van.
 Simon mag es, mit seinem alten Laster zu fahren.

2 He also enjoys being driven in his girlfriend's Ferrari.
 Er genießt es auch, im Ferrari seiner Freundin herumgefahren zu werden.

3 He's proud of having driven for a year without an accident.
 Er ist stolz darauf, ein Jahr unfallfrei gefahren zu sein.

4 He denies having been driven by his girlfriend for most of that time.
 Er streitet es ab, die meiste Zeit von seiner Freundin herumgefahren worden zu sein.

The present active gerund (e.g. *driving*) is the most common form.

▶ Forms of the participle: 151

'I believe in paying my employees* as much as they need. Since you'll be working 90 hours a week, you won't need much.'

employee Angestellte(r)

b In his holidays John enjoys not having to get up before nine.
 John genießt es, in seinem Urlaub nicht vor neun aufstehen zu müssen.

We form the **negative** by putting *not* before the gerund.

137 Functions

a

subject
Reading is fun.
(Books are fun.)

object
Do you like reading?
(Do you like books?)

preposition + gerund
I get a lot of pleasure from reading.
(I get a lot of pleasure from books.)

subject complement
Jenny's hobby is reading.

The gerund **functions as a noun** (e.g. *books*).
It can be used:
- as a subject
  ▶ 138
- as an object
  ▶ 139
- after a preposition
  ▶ 140-144
- as a subject complement (after *be*).

b

Reading detective stories is fun.
Reading in bed is fun.

Like a **verb**, the gerund can be followed by various elements:
- by an object (e.g. *detective stories*)
- by an adverbial phrase (e.g. *in bed*).

'Visiting your health club's Web site is a start, but I'd prefer you to actually go there and exercise.'

138 The gerund as subject

a Canoeing can be dangerous.
Kanufahren kann gefährlich sein.

Canoeing in bad weather can be dangerous.
Kanufahren bei schlechtem Wetter kann gefährlich sein.

The gerund can be the **subject of a sentence**.

b Repairing the old bike was hard work.
*Das alte Fahrrad zu reparieren, war harte Arbeit. /
Das Reparieren des alten Fahrrads war harte Arbeit.*

The gerund often corresponds to an **infinitive** in **German**.

139 The gerund as object

a

Kim **enjoys skating**.
Kim skatet sehr gern.

I **miss seeing** my friends every day.
Ich vermisse es, täglich meine Freunde zu sehen.

'You must stop wearing flip-flops.'

The gerund comes **after certain verbs**, e.g.:

admit	zugeben
avoid	(es) vermeiden
carry on/go on	weiter(machen)
consider	in Betracht ziehen
delay	aufschieben
deny	leugnen, abstreiten
dislike	sehr ungern tun, (es) nicht mögen
enjoy	sehr gern tun, genießen
finish	beenden, aufhören (mit)
give up	aufgeben, aufhören (mit)
imagine	sich (etwas) vorstellen
include	einschließen
involve	mit sich bringen, umfassen
justify	rechtfertigen
keep	weiter(machen); immer wieder tun
mention	erwähnen
mind	etwas dagegen haben
miss	(es) verpassen; (es) vermissen
practise	üben
risk	(es) wagen, riskieren
stop/quit	aufhören (mit)
suggest	vorschlagen

 Emma **dislikes going** to parties alone.
Emma mag es nicht, alleine auf Partys zu gehen.

Imagine having dinner with your favourite star.
Stell dir vor, mit deinem Lieblingsstar essen zu gehen.

In German most of these verbs are followed by an infinitive. But in **English** we do **not put an infinitive** after them.

▶ Verb + *to*-infinitive: 122

Note

Your hair **needs cutting**.
　　… muss geschnitten werden.
I think this article **requires** careful **reading**.
　　… muss sorgfältig gelesen werden.
The car **wants washing**.
　　… muss gewaschen werden.

We use a gerund after the verbs *need* and *require* (and also after *want* in informal English). In these structures the active form has a passive meaning.

b Beth **hates** | **going** / **to go** | to the hairdresser's.
Beth hasst es, zum Friseur zu gehen.

I **love** | **meeting** / **to meet** | unusual people.
Ich finde es toll, ungewöhnliche Leute zu treffen.

There is a group of verbs after which we can use either the **-ing form or the to-infinitive**. Both forms have the same meaning. These verbs include:

begin/start	anfangen
continue	weiter(machen)
hate	sehr ungern tun, (es) hassen
like	gern tun
love	sehr gern tun, (es) toll/gut finden
prefer	lieber tun

The verb 97 The gerund

⚠️ I **would like to see** Will Smith's new film.
Would you **like to see** it too?
– Yes, I **'d love to** (see it).

but: I like | to see / seeing | new films.

After *would hate, would like, would love* and *would prefer* (short form: *'d hate,* etc.) we use **only the *to*-infinitive** and not the *-ing* form.

But after *like* either the **to-infinitive or the -ing form** is possible.

c

Some **verbs** have **different meanings**, depending on whether they are followed by a gerund or a *to*-infinitive. These verbs include:

forget
forget doing sth. = vergessen, dass man etwas (in der Vergangenheit) getan hat

I'll never **forget going** to the dentist's for the first time.
Ich werde nie vergessen, wie ich das erste Mal beim Zahnarzt war.
I mustn't **forget to go** to the dentist's this afternoon.
Ich darf nicht vergessen, heute Nachmittag zum Zahnarzt zu gehen.

forget to do sth. = vergessen, (später) etwas zu tun

remember
remember doing sth. = sich daran erinnern, dass man (in der Vergangenheit) etwas getan hat

I **remember locking** the door when I went to bed.
Ich erinnere mich, die Tür abgeschlossen zu haben, als ich ins Bett ging.
Remember to lock the door when you go to bed.
Denk daran, die Tür abzuschließen, wenn du ins Bett gehst.

remember to do sth. = daran denken, (in der Zukunft) etwas zu tun

stop
stop doing sth. = aufhören, etwas zu tun

Tom has **stopped talking** to Jerry. They had a quarrel.
Tom hat aufgehört, mit Jerry zu reden. Sie hatten Streit.
Where's Tom? – I think he **stopped to talk** to Jerry.
Wo ist Tom? – Ich glaube, er hat angehalten, um mit Jerry zu reden.

stop to do sth. = anhalten, um etwas (anderes) zu tun

go on
go on doing sth. = etwas (dasselbe) weiterhin tun

Mr Jones **went on talking** about his son for hours.
Mr Jones fuhr fort, stundenlang über seinen Sohn zu reden.
Then he **went on to talk** about his daughter.
Dann redete er über seine Tochter.

go on to do sth. = etwas (anderes) als Nächstes tun

try
try doing sth. = etwas ausprobieren („herumprobieren")

If the door won't open, **try kicking** it.
Wenn die Tür nicht aufgeht, versuch mal, dagegen zu treten.
I **tried to kick** the door open, but I hurt my foot.
Ich habe versucht, die Tür aufzutreten, …

try to do sth. = sich bemühen, etwas zu tun

mean
that means doing sth. = das bedeutet/heißt, dass etwas getan werden muss

The last bus has gone. That **means taking** a taxi.
… Das heißt, wir müssen ein Taxi nehmen.
We **meant to take** a taxi, but we didn't have enough money.
Wir hatten vor, ein Taxi zu nehmen, …

mean to do sth. = etwas zu tun beabsichtigen

▶ Verb + *to*-infinitive: 122

We use the gerund:
– as a subject
– as an object after certain verbs.

The gerund after prepositions

140 Summary

Tim is interested in parasailing.
What's your reason for wanting to go to Zimbabwe?
I decided against applying to an American university.
Sue ran across the road without looking.

Verbs which come after a **preposition** take the form of a gerund. The preposition can be

- linked to an **adjective**
- linked to a **noun**
- linked to a **verb**
- **on its own**.

141 Adjective + preposition + gerund

Daniel is good at acting.
Daniel ist ein guter Schauspieler.

We're tired of waiting.
Wir haben es satt zu warten.

'I'm sick and tired of making you endless cups of tea.'

Here are some common **adjective** + **preposition** combinations which can be followed by a gerund:

be afraid of	Angst haben vor
be angry about/at	böse sein über
be bad/good at	schlecht/gut sein in, (etwas) schlecht/gut können
be clever at	gut/geschickt sein in
be crazy about	verrückt sein nach
be disappointed about/at	enttäuscht sein über
be excited about	aufgeregt sein wegen
be famous for	berühmt sein für
be glad about	froh sein über
be interested in	interessiert sein an, sich interessieren für
be keen on	begeistert sein von
be proud of	stolz sein auf
be sick/tired of	genug haben von, es satt haben zu, es leid sein zu
be sorry about/for	(jemandem) Leid tun, dass
be used to	gewöhnt sein an, etwas gewohnt sein
be worried about	besorgt sein wegen

Note

Tony is used to travelling abroad.
Tony ist daran gewöhnt, ins Ausland zu reisen.

He used to travel all over the world on business.
Früher machte er Geschäftsreisen auf der ganzen Welt.

In the expression *be used to*, the word *to* is a preposition. So when it is followed by a verb, the verb is a gerund and not an infinitive.

Used to is a verb form expressing past time. The verb after *used to* is an infinitive.

▶ Used to: 86 d

The verb | **99** | **The gerund**

142 Noun + preposition + gerund

Is there any danger of losing the money we invested?
Besteht die Gefahr, das Geld zu verlieren, das wir investiert haben?

There is still hope of winning the match.
Es besteht immer noch Hoffnung, das Spiel zu gewinnen.

I like the idea of giving a surprise party for Kate.
Ich finde die Idee gut, eine Überraschungsparty für Kate zu geben.

How serious is the risk of losing your job?
Wie groß ist das Risiko, dass du deinen Job verlierst?

Here are some common **noun + preposition** combinations which can be followed by a gerund:

advantage of	Vorteil (des/von)
chance of	Chance, (günstige) Gelegenheit, Aussicht (zu)
choice between	(Aus-)Wahl zwischen/aus
danger of	Gefahr (zu)
difficulty (in)	Schwierigkeit(en) (zu)
doubt about	Zweifel an
hope of	Hoffnung (zu/auf)
idea of	Vorstellung, Einfall (zu)
interest in	Interesse an
opportunity of	Gelegenheit zu
possibility of	Möglichkeit (zu)
problem of	Problem (zu)
reason for	Grund für
risk of	Risiko (zu)
trouble (in)	Schwierigkeit(en) (zu/mit)
way of	Art und Weise, Weg (zu)

> **Note**
>
> We had difficulty/trouble (in) getting visas for Russia.
> *Wir hatten Schwierigkeiten, Visa für Russland zu bekommen.*
>
> When we use *difficulty (in)* and *trouble (in)*, the preposition *in* is often left out.

143 Verb + preposition + gerund

We apologized for arriving two hours late.
Wir entschuldigten uns dafür, zwei Stunden zu spät gekommen zu sein.

Don't complain about having so much work. Just do it!
Beklage dich nicht darüber, so viel Arbeit zu haben. Erledige sie einfach!

We decided against going to Iceland. It's too expensive.
Wir haben uns dagegen entschieden, nach Island zu fahren. Es ist zu teuer.

I feel like going out and having a good time.
Ich habe Lust, auszugehen und Spaß zu haben.

Here are some common **verb + preposition** combinations which can be followed by a gerund:

agree with	einverstanden sein mit
apologize for	sich entschuldigen für
believe in	glauben an
complain about	sich beklagen über
decide against	sich entscheiden gegen
depend on	abhängen von
dream of/about	träumen von
feel like	Lust haben auf/zu
insist on	bestehen auf
look forward to	sich freuen auf
rely on	sich verlassen auf
specialize in	sich spezialisieren auf
succeed in	Erfolg haben bei/mit
talk about/of	sprechen über, reden von
think of	denken an, in Betracht ziehen
worry about	sich Sorgen machen wegen/um

Ich freue mich darauf, dich am Samstag zu sehen.
not: I look forward ~~to see~~ you on Saturday.
but: I look forward to seeing you on Saturday.

In the expression **look forward to**, the word *to* is a preposition. So when it is followed by a verb, the verb is a gerund and not an infinitive.

The verb 100 **The gerund**

> **Note**
>
> Joe **spends all his money on** cart-racing.
> *Joe gibt sein ganzes Geld für Cartfahren aus.*
> I **thanked her for being** so helpful.
> *Ich dankte ihr dafür, dass sie mir so viel geholfen hatte.*

Verbs like *spend … on* or *thank … for* have an object (e.g. *money*, *her*) between the verb and the preposition (*on*, *for*).

144 *Preposition + gerund*

1 **After having** breakfast he made a few phone calls.
  Nach dem Frühstück …

2 **Before getting up** he thought about what he would say at the interview.
  Vor dem Aufstehen …

3 How did you pass the exam? – **By working** hard.
  … – Mit harter Arbeit.

4 Dad gave me extra pocket money **for cleaning** his bike.
  …, weil ich sein Fahrrad geputzt hatte.

5 We weren't the first guests **in spite of arriving** at the party early.
  …, obwohl wir früh auf die Party gekommen waren.

6 **On hearing** the good news Dave started jumping up and down wildly.
  Als er die gute Nachricht hörte, …

7 **Instead of sleeping** Tim was reading comics in bed.
  Anstatt zu schlafen, …

8 We watched the film from beginning to end **without speaking**.
  …, ohne zu sprechen.

After a **preposition on its own**, the verb takes the form of a gerund.
German normally uses a different structure: a preposition + noun (examples 1-3), a subordinate clause (examples 4-6) or an infinitive construction (examples 7 and 8).

After a preposition a verb is always in the '-ing' form.

> **Note**
>
> **enjoy** /ɪnˈdʒɔɪ/ *verb* **1** to get pleasure from sth: [VN] *We thoroughly enjoyed our time in New York.* ◊ *Thanks for a great evening. I really enjoyed it.* ◊ [V-ing] *I enjoy playing tennis and squash.*
>
> **look ˈforward to sth** to be thinking with pleasure about sth that is going to happen (because you expect to enjoy it): *I'm looking forward to the weekend.* ◊ [+ -ing] *We're really looking forward to seeing you again.*
>
> **prom·ise** /ˈprɒmɪs; AmE ˈprɑːm-/ *verb, noun*
> ■ *verb* **1** ~ sth (to sb) | ~ sb sth to tell sb that you will definitely do or not do sth, or that sth will definitely happen: [V to inf] *The college principal promised to look into the matter.* ◊ [V to inf, V]

Reproduced by permission of Oxford University Press from the *Oxford Advanced Learner's Dictionary* Sixth Edition, Copyright © Oxford University Press 2000

When you use English verbs in structures like these, you need to know (or find out from a dictionary) whether a following verb should be a gerund or an infinitive, or whether you need to use a preposition + gerund.

The gerund after certain words and phrases

145 *Adjective + gerund*

It's hopeless trying to convince her.
Es ist aussichtslos zu versuchen, sie zu überzeugen.

Dave's busy organizing the next concert for his band.
Dave ist damit beschäftigt, das nächste Konzert für seine Band zu organisieren.

Some **adjectives** (such as *hopeless*, *busy*, *hard* or *worth*) can be followed **directly** by a gerund.

▶ Adjective + preposition + gerund: 141

'It must be hard living in a country where the rich and powerful completely ignore the needs of the less fortunate*.'

the less fortunate die weniger (vom Glück) Begünstigten

The new Tom Hanks film is well worth seeing.
Der neue Tom Hanks Film ist es wert, angesehen zu werden.

After the adjective **worth** we use the active form of the gerund. However, it has a passive meaning.

▎ Note

It was awful watching the team lose like that.
or: It was awful to watch …
It's wonderful seeing you again.
or: It's wonderful to see …

After the frequently used structure *it is/was* + adjective, we can use either an infinitive or a gerund. An infinitive is usually preferred.

146 *Noun + gerund*

It was bad luck missing the train by only a few seconds.
Es war Pech, den Zug nur um ein paar Sekunden zu verpassen.

It wasn't much fun standing in the rain for an hour.
Es war nicht gerade ein Vergnügen, eine Stunde im Regen zu stehen.

We can use a gerund **after certain nouns** such as *luck*, *fun* and *a hard time*.

The verb | **102** | **The gerund**

147 Fixed phrases + gerund

We use the gerund **after** certain **fixed phrases**, e.g.:

We **couldn't help laughing** when Jeff split his pants.
Wir mussten einfach lachen, …

- *can't help* or *couldn't help*

How about buying a fitness video?
Wie wäre es, ein Fitness-Video zu kaufen?

- *how about …?* or *what about …?*

It's no use/no good pretending you didn't know about the money you owe her.
Es hat keinen Zweck, so zu tun, …

- *it's no use* or *it's no good*

There's no denying the fact that my school marks could be better.
Es lässt sich nicht bestreiten, dass …

- *there's no*

There's no point telling me what to do, because I won't do it.
Es ist zwecklos, mir zu sagen, was ich tun soll, …

- *there's no point (in).*

148 Determiner + gerund

We can use the gerund **after** certain **determiners**, e.g.:

I'm enjoying the computer course, but all **the learning** makes me tired.
…, aber das ganze Lernen macht mich müde.

- *the*

I hate **this arguing**. Let's be friends.
Ich hasse diese Streitereien. …

- *this*

Sorry – **no parking** on this side of the road.
Tut mir Leid, aber Parken ist auf dieser Seite der Straße verboten.

- *no.*

> **Note**
>
> *Das dauernde Lernen neuer Rollen macht ihn aggressiv.*
> **not:** The constant ~~studying new roles~~ …
> **but:** The constant **studying of new roles** makes him aggressive.

When a determiner + gerund has an object, we usually use *of*.

149 The subject in gerund constructions

1 John imagined living in Florida.
   John stellte sich vor, in Florida zu leben.
2 John imagined his family living in Florida.
   John stellte sich vor, dass seine Familie in Florida lebte.
3 John imagined them living in Florida.
   John stellte sich vor, dass sie in Florida lebten.

A gerund construction can be **without its own subject** (example 1), or it can have **its own subject** (examples 2 and 3). The meaning of the sentence is different in each case.

In all three examples *John* is the subject of the whole sentence. In example 1 the gerund does not have its own subject. Therefore the subject of the whole sentence is understood as the subject of the gerund *living*. In examples 2 and 3 the gerund does have its own subject. This is the 'notional subject', **the person who carries out the action** of the gerund: *family/them*. *Living* relates to these subjects (and not to *John*). In this construction a personal pronoun has the object form (example 3: *them*).

▶ Finite and non-finite forms of the verb: 118 c
▶ Object form of the personal pronoun: 227 a

Note

1 a We're happy about our son/him passing the test.
  b We are pleased about our son's passing the test.
  c We are pleased about his passing the test.

2 a Do you mind me leaving early?
  b Do you mind my leaving early?

When we introduce such a 'notional subject', in informal English we normally use a noun or a personal pronoun in the object form (examples 1 a and 2 a). Formal English, on the other hand, prefers the possessive form of a noun (example 1 b) or a possessive determiner (examples 1 c and 2 b).

150 Other structures instead of a gerund

Cathy was happy about getting a new camera. (gerund)
Cathy was happy with her new camera.
Cathy was happy to get a new camera.
Cathy was happy when she got a new camera.

The reason for Gary behaving badly couldn't be explained. (gerund)
The reason for Gary's bad behaviour …
The reason why Gary behaved badly …

Leo didn't mention leaving the disco early. (gerund)
Leo didn't mention the fact that he'd left …
Leo didn't mention why he'd left …

Although there are certain contexts where we often use gerunds, it is not always necessary to do so. For example, after an adjective, noun or verb (+ preposition), we can use **other structures** than the gerund.

The participle

151-163

151 Forms
152 Use
153 Participles with a noun
154-156 Participles with certain kinds of verbs
157-161 Participles expressing time, reason, etc.
162 The subject in participle constructions
163 Fixed phrases with participles

151 Forms

a

infinitive	present participle	
wait	waiting	wartend
write	writing	schreibend
swim	swimming	schwimmend

infinitive	past participle	
wait	waited	gewartet
write	written	geschrieben
swim	swum	geschwommen

There are two kinds of participles:

- The **present participle** is formed by adding **-ing** to the infinitive of a verb. This *-ing* form is the same as a gerund.

- The **past participle** of regular verbs has an **-ed** ending. **Irregular verbs** (e.g. *write*, *swim*) have their own forms.

▶ *-ing* form: 65
▶ Forms of the gerund: 136a
▶ Forms of the past participle: 66
▶ Irregular verbs: 310

typist Schreibkraft

b The test being written is not difficult.
Der Test, der gerade geschrieben wird, ist nicht schwer.

Having written similar tests before, Don had no problems.
Da Don schon früher ähnliche Tests geschrieben hatte, hatte er keine Probleme.

The test having been written, the pupils agreed that it had been easy.
Nachdem der Test geschrieben worden war, stimmten die Schüler überein, dass er leicht gewesen war.

We also use the **past participle** in **compound forms**. These are formed with *be* or *have*.

152 Use

a Claire **is writing** job applications.
Was she **doing** that this morning too?
– Yes, she**'s been writing** applications all day.

I**'ve written** thirty invitations to my party.
I **had made** a guest list, so it didn't take me long.
– When **will** they all **be sent off**?

We use the **present participle** in all the progressive forms of the verb.

We use the **past participle** in:
• the present perfect
• the past perfect
• all the passive forms.

▶ Tenses of the full verbs: 72-73
▶ Use of the progressive form: 68
▶ Forms of the passive: 108

b There were lots of **complaining passengers**.
The passengers complaining about their missing luggage were asked to fill in forms.

A participle can come **before** or **after a noun**.

▶ 153

c The crowd **saw** the police **arriving**.
Mike **remained seated** throughout the whole performance.
She is **having** her eyes **tested**.

We can use a participle **with certain verbs**.

▶ 154-156

d **Entering** the house, I noticed a strange smell.
When I entered the house, …
Not knowing any of the answers, John handed in his test at once.
As he didn't know any of the answers, …
Unless questioned, don't say anything.
If you aren't questioned, …

We can use a participle instead of an adverbial clause to **express time**, **reason**, **etc**.

▶ 157-160

be better off besser dran sein

The verb 106 **The participle**

153 Participles used with a noun

a

The young prince was greeted by thousands of screaming girls.
… von schreienden Mädchen …
When I was a child, I believed in flying saucers.
… fliegende Untertassen.

Participles are sometimes used to **modify a noun**.
The **present participle** has an **active meaning**: *screaming girls = girls who are screaming.*

The damaged car was photographed by the police.
Das beschädigte Auto …
Dissatisfied customers can get their money back.
Unzufriedene Kunden …

The **past participle** usually has a **passive meaning**: *the damaged car = the car that was damaged.*

▸ Note

It was a rather exciting experience to travel to New York by ship. But it was an even more exciting experience to be sitting in the cockpit on a flight to New York.

A number of participles have become true adjectives. They can therefore be modified by words like *rather* or *very*, and we can form their comparative and superlative with *more/most*. Such adjectives include:

amazing   amazed
boring   bored
disappointing   disappointed
exciting excited
interesting   interested

 „Kit's Wilderness" ist ein interessantes Buch.
not: 'Kit's Wilderness' is an ~~interested~~ book.
but: 'Kit's Wilderness' is an interesting book.

Helen was very interested in it.
… interessiert …

Be careful **not to confuse** the **forms with -ing** and those **with -ed**.

 The police are looking for the escaped criminals.
… nach den geflohenen Verbrechern.
After the storm the ground was covered with fallen leaves.
… mit abgefallenen Blättern.

A few intransitive verbs have a **past participle** with an **active meaning**: *escaped criminals = criminals who have escaped.*

b Have you ever been to an English-speaking country?
… einem englischsprachigen Land …

Jeff has a well-paid job as an audio engineer.
… einen gut bezahlten Job …

A participle can form a **compound with another word**.

c The boy | talking to Ed is Rob Williams.
        | who is talking to Ed …
        …, der sich mit Ed unterhält, …

'Imagine' is a ballad | written by John Lennon.
                     | which was written …
                     …, die … geschrieben wurde.

A participle must come **after the noun** it relates to when the participle has **an object or an adverbial** after it. These participle constructions have the same function as a **relative clause**. They are used more in writing than in speech.

The verb | **107** | **The participle**

 The number of accidents caused by teenagers on motorbikes is highest in summer.
Die Zahl der von Jugendlichen auf Motorrädern verursachten Unfälle ist im Sommer am höchsten.

All students arriving from non-EU countries will be met at Heathrow Airport.
Alle nicht aus Ländern der EU stammenden Studierenden werden am Flughafen Heathrow empfangen.

In contrast to German, the participle **cannot come before the noun** when it has **an object or adverbial** after it.

 Die diskutierten Probleme …
not: The ~~dicussed problems~~ …
but: The problems discussed …

Even when the participle is **on its own** (without an object or adverbial), often it **cannot come before the noun**. There are no fixed rules about which participles can come in this position.

d 1 Sue likes cars | designed for speed, not comfort.
                    | that are designed …
                    | that were designed …
                    | that have been designed …

   2 There were ten pupils | working on the eco-project.
                            | who worked on …
                            | who were working on …

A participle can replace
• **different tenses** (example 1)
• a **simple** or a **progressive form** (example 2).
Using a participle makes a sentence shorter and also helps to avoid mistakes. But remember that it can sound unnatural to use too many participle constructions.

Notes

1

'Kit's Wilderness' is a story involving people of all age groups.
… is a story which involves …
… ist eine Geschichte, die … einbezieht.

We can also form present participles from verbs that are not normally used in the progressive form. These participles are often used in written texts such as reports or in scientific writing. Some examples are:

… problems <u>arising</u> from …   … Probleme, die durch … entstehen …
… decisions <u>concerning</u> …   … Entscheidungen, die … betreffen …
… text <u>consisting of</u> …   … Text, der aus … besteht …
… statement <u>containing</u> …   … Erklärung, die … enthält …
… story <u>involving</u> …   … Geschichte, die … einbezieht …

2

The Emancipation Proclamation based on the Declaration of Independence set all slaves free.
…, which was based on …
Die „Emancipation Proclamation", die auf der … beruhte …

Past participles are also often used in explanatory texts or scientific writing. Some examples:

… book <u>based on</u> …   … Buch, das auf … beruht …
… damage <u>caused by</u> …   … Schaden, der durch … verursacht wurde …
… people <u>concerned with</u> …   … Menschen, die mit … beschäftigt sind …
… dialogue <u>taken from</u> …   … Dialog, der aus … entnommen wurde …

A participle which is followed by an object or an adverbial always comes after the noun.

Participles with certain kinds of verbs

154 Verbs of perception + object + present participle

a

	verb	object	present participle
1 Tina	saw	a crowd	waiting on the street.
2 She	heard	the people	shouting.
3 She	noticed	U2	coming out of the hotel.
4 She	watched	them	getting into a car.
5 She	felt	her heart	beating with excitement.

1 Tina sah eine Menschenmenge auf der Straße warten.
2 Sie hörte die Menschen schreien.
3 Sie bemerkte, wie U2 aus dem Hotel kam.
4 Sie beobachtete, wie sie in ein Auto stiegen.
5 Sie spürte, wie/dass ihr Herz vor Aufregung schlug.

After **verbs of perception** like *feel, hear, listen to, notice, see, smell* and *watch* we can use an **object** + **present participle** (e.g. *saw a crowd waiting*).

The equivalent structure in German is an infinitive (examples 1 and 2) or a subordinate clause with *wie* or *dass* (examples 3-5).

▶ Verbs of perception: 71

'I can't smell anything burning. Are we eating out tonight?'

b Tina noticed U2 pick up their instruments. She heard them say goodbye to the manager.
Then she saw them leave the hotel with their bodyguards. They drove round the corner.
but:
Tina saw U2 leaving the hotel with their bodyguards, when they were suddenly attacked by a madman.

After a verb of perception we can also use an **infinitive** (**without to**). The infinitive expresses the idea that the complete action is perceived from beginning to end.

The **present participle**, on the other hand, expresses the idea that we perceive an action which is in progress and so not yet complete.

▶ Verbs of perception + object + infinitive without *to*: 134

155 Verbs of rest and movement + present participle

a The class stood staring at the French teacher, who had grown a beard.
Die Klasse stand da und starrte den Französischlehrer an, …

We all sat waiting for the lesson to end.
Wir alle saßen da und warteten darauf, dass …

Sarah's two dogs came running up to me.
Sarahs zwei Hunde kamen auf mich zu gelaufen.

A **present participle** comes **after verbs of rest** (e.g. *lie, remain, sit, stand* and *stay*) and after **verbs of movement** (e.g. *come* and *go*).
Note the different ways of translating this structure into German.

b I don't think I can get the stereo working again.
Ich glaube nicht, dass ich die Stereoanlage wieder zum Laufen bringe.

Sue kept her ex-boyfriend waiting outside.
Sue ließ ihren Exfreund draußen warten.

A present participle can also come **after** a number of **other verbs**, e.g. *catch, find, get, have, keep, leave* and *send*.

156 Have something done

	have	object	past participle
1 We often	have	a pizza	delivered.
2 Did you	have	your fortune	told?
3 Mr Fox	is having	his car	resprayed.
4 I	've had	my ears	pierced.

1 *Wir lassen uns oft eine Pizza kommen.*
2 *Haben Sie sich die Zukunft vorhersagen lassen?*
3 *Mr Fox lässt gerade sein Auto neu lackieren.*
4 *Ich habe mir Ohrlöcher stechen lassen.*

We use the **past participle after *have*** + **object** to express the idea that we arrange for someone to do something for us rather than doing it ourselves.

 Lisa usually has her hair dyed at an expensive hairdresser's in town.
Lisa lässt sich normalerweise die Haare bei einem teuren Frisör in der Stadt färben.

Emily has dyed her hair. Now it's pink.
Emily hat sich die Haare gefärbt. …

she has her hair dyed =
simple present of *have* (+ object + *dyed*)
(Someone does it for her.)

she has dyed her hair =
present perfect of *dye*
(She has done it herself.)

Notes

1 When did you have your computer repaired? / When did you get your computer repaired?
Wann hast du deinen Computer reparieren lassen?

In informal English *get* is often used instead of *have*.

2 Sophie has had her bike stolen.
Sophie wurde das Fahrrad gestohlen.

Marc got his left hand broken in a fight.
Marc hat sich bei einem Kampf die linke Hand gebrochen.

We also use *have* or *get* + object + past participle to express the result of an event, usually something unpleasant.

The verb 110 **The participle**

157 Participles expressing time, reason, etc.

1 **Seeing** the parcel on the table, she immediately opened it.
When she saw the parcel …

2 Cheryl cut her finger **emptying** the dishwasher.
While she was emptying the dishwasher, …

3 **Asked** to stop smoking, the passenger reacted angrily.
When the passenger was asked to stop smoking, …

A participle phrase can be the equivalent of **an adverbial clause of time**, **reason**, **etc**. The participle construction and the main clause have the same subject (example 1: *she*). But this subject appears only in the main clause. These participle constructions are typical of **written English**, especially when they come before the main clause. In spoken English an adverbial clause is preferred.

▶ Subject in participle constructions: 162

158 Participles expressing time

1 **Hearing** the good news, we decided to have a celebration party.
When we heard …

2 **Travelling** around the world, you meet some very interesting people.
While you are travelling …

3 **Having arrived** at the station, I realised that I had forgotten my ticket.
After I had arrived at the station, …

4 **(Having been) Told** to wait his turn, the customer went red in the face.
After the customer had been told to wait his turn, …

The **present participle** (examples 1 and 2) and the **past participle** (examples 3 and 4) can both be used as equivalents of an **adverbial clause of time**.

Having + **past participle** corresponds to an **adverbial clause of time**, usually a clause beginning with **after**. The participle phrase expresses the idea of something happening earlier.

We can leave out *having been* without changing the meaning.

159 Participles expressing reason

1 **Being** a doctor, Simon knows what to do in an emergency.
As he is a doctor, …

2 **Not having** a map with us, we had to ask the way three times.
Since we didn't have a map with us, …

3 **Having seen** the film at the cinema, we didn't watch it again on TV.
Since we had seen the film at the cinema, …

The **present participle** and the **past participle** can both be used as equivalents of an **adverbial clause of reason**. Especially common in this structure are state verbs, which are not normally used with the *-ing* form.

We use *having* + **past participle** to say that the **reason** for something **lies in the past**.

▶ State verbs: 70

Note

Concentrating on my work, I don't think about my problems.
Wenn ich mich auf meine Arbeit konzentriere, …
Da ich mich auf meine Arbeit konzentriere, …

When/While concentrating on my work, …

A participle construction does not always have a single meaning. In the example sentence, it can express time *(when)* as well as reason *(because)*.

If we use a conjunction of time *(when* or *while)*, we can prevent the participle construction being understood as expressing reason.

The verb | **111** | **The participle**

160 Participles expressing accompanying circumstances

1 Jane rushed out of the house, forgetting her keys.
  … wobei …
2 Feeling like the king of the world, Jason drove off on his new motorbike.
  … und …
3 The tennis star entered the TV studio accompanied by his coach and his manager.
  … begleitet von … / … Er wurde begleitet von …

We often use the **present participle** – or less often the past participle – to describe the **accompanying circumstances of an action**. In German we use:
- a subordinate clause beginning with *indem* or *wobei* (example 1)
- a clause linked by *und* (example 2)
- also a participle (example 3)
- two separate sentences (example 3).

161 Participle constructions introduced by conjunctions

a Kim noticed a strange-looking man entering the bank.
   (= A man entered the bank.)
   Kim noticed a strange-looking man when entering the bank. (= Kim entered the bank.)

   Last week Rod met an old friend looking for a job.
   (= The friend was looking for a job.)
   Last week Rod met an old friend while looking for a job.
   (= Rod was looking for a job.)

Participles which correspond to an **adverbial clause of time** do **not** usually **begin with a conjunction**. But we have to use a conjunction when the main clause has an object *(a strange-looking man, an old friend)*, if we want to avoid ambiguity: The participle clause begins with *when* or *while* when the subject of the main clause *(Kim, Rod)* is also the subject of the participle.

▶ Subject in participle constructions: 162

b If given the chance, Katie will make a first-class doctor.
   If Katie is given the chance, …

   Though badly hurt, the motorcyclist managed to phone for an ambulance.
   Though the motorcyclist was badly hurt, …

Participles can also **replace other adverbial clauses**, e.g. conditional clauses or adverbial clauses of contrast. To avoid ambiguity, we must begin the clause with a conjunction. Some frequently used conjunctions are: *although/though*, *as if*, *if* or *unless*.

▶ Adverbial clauses: 267-272
▶ Conditional clauses: 251-257

> **Note**
> Since escaping from prison, the thief has not been seen.
> Since his escape from prison, … (preposition)
> Since he escaped from prison, … (conjunction)

After, *before* and *since* can all be either a preposition or a conjunction. It is therefore not possible to say definitely whether the *-ing* form (here: *escaping*) is a gerund or a participle.

To avoid ambiguity: begin with a conjunction

162 The subject in participle constructions

a 1 **Being bored** with school, Jerry decided to leave.
      Da Jerry sich in der Schule langweilte, entschied er …

   2 **His sister being bored** with school, Jerry advised her to leave.
      Da sich seine Schwester in der Schule langweilte, riet ihr Jerry, …

   3 **Having finished** their talks, the delegates went home.
      Nachdem die Delegierten ihre Gespräche beendet hatten, gingen sie nach Hause.

   4 **The conference having finished**, the delegates went home.
      Nachdem die Konferenz beendet war, gingen die Delegierten nach Hause.

In examples 1 and 3, the participle construction and the main clause have the **same subject** (*Jerry, the delegates*). The subject appears only in the main clause.

In each of the examples 2 and 4, the participle construction has its **own subject** (*his sister, the conference*). This subject is different from the subject of the main clause (*Jerry, the delegates*).

▶ Finite and non-finite forms of the verb: 118c
▶ Subject in infinitive and gerund constructions: 127, 149

b **With mobile phones sold** world-wide, there's hardly anybody without one.
   Da Mobiltelefone in der ganzen Welt verkauft werden, …

   No wonder everything went wrong **with Nina doing** the organizing.
   …, da Nina alles organisiert hat.

   Sally left the room **with her head held** high.
   Sally verließ das Zimmer erhobenen Hauptes.

Participle constructions with their own subject often have **with at the beginning**, especially when they describe accompanying circumstances.
This structure is used not only in writing but also in spoken English.

c **The club having closed**, the guests went home.
   Nachdem der Klub geschlossen worden war, gingen die Gäste heim.

   The procession marched down the street, **the crowds waving**.
   Während die Prozession sich die Straße hinunterbewegte, winkten die Zuschauer.

Participle constructions which have their own subject but do **not have with** are only used in written English. They are always separated from the main clause by a comma.

163 Fixed phrases with participles

Generally speaking, German cars are reliable.
Allgemein gesagt/Im Allgemeinen sind deutsche Autos …
Strictly speaking, this word is a participle, not an adjective.
Genau genommen, ist dieses Wort …
Talking of holidays, Tim flew to Rio last week.
Da wir gerade von Urlaub sprechen, Tim ist …

Some participles are also used in **fixed phrases**. These expressions do not relate to the following subject; rather they show the speaker's viewpoint, or they are a comment on what is said.

Phrasal and prepositional verbs

164 Introduction
165-166 Phrasal verbs
167 Prepositional verbs

164 Introduction

a 1 I had to take the bus – my car's **broken down** again.
      Ich musste den Bus nehmen – mein Auto ist schon wieder kaputt.
   2 That jacket's nice. Don't **give** it **away**.
      Die Jacke ist schön. Gib sie nicht weg!
   3 You must come. I'm **counting on** you.
      Du musst kommen. Ich zähle auf dich.
   4 Do you **believe in** astrology?
      Glaubst du an Astrologie?

Many English verbs can combine with certain particles, i.e. adverbs or prepositions (*down, on, in*). Those **verbs** which combine **with an adverb** (examples 1 and 2) are called **phrasal verbs**. Verbs which combine **with a preposition** (examples 3 and 4) are called **prepositional verbs**. This distinction is important for word order.

> **Note**
> How can we **get out of** this mess?
> The minister **handed** the document **over to** his secretary.

Some verbs can combine with both an adverb and a preposition.

b 1 We **looked up** the word in a dictionary.
   2 We **looked** the word **up** in a dictionary.
   3 We **looked at** the title.

When we use a phrasal verb, we usually **stress** the adverb (examples 1 and 2: *up*). But when we use a prepositional verb, we usually stress the verb and not the preposition (example 3: *looked*).

c The youth club meeting **has been put off** until next Saturday.
   … wurde … verschoben.

   Families with many children **are** often **stared at**.
   … werden oft angestarrt.

Some phrasal and prepositional verbs which can have an object can also be used in the **passive**.

▶ Adverbs: 205
▶ Forms and functions of prepositions: 246
▶ Passive: 113

'Sister, I can't believe you hacked into the Vatican system.'

Phrasal verbs

165 Meaning

a Did you get your history test back?
Hast du deinen Geschichtstest zurückbekommen?

There were no chairs, so we couldn't sit down.
…, also konnten wir uns nicht hinsetzen.

I'm going to throw these old posters away.
Ich werde diese alten Poster wegwerfen.

The **meaning** of a phrasal verb is sometimes clear from the meaning of its **parts**.

Sarah hung up before I had finished talking.
Sarah legte auf, bevor ich ausgeredet hatte.

Don't believe him. All his stories are made up.
Glaub ihm nicht! All seine Geschichten sind erfunden.

Pete's hair gel really turns me off.
Petes Haargel stößt mich wirklich ab.

However, phrasal verbs often have an **idiomatic meaning** which is different from the basic meanings of the verb and adverb. If this meaning cannot be understood from the context, you will have to use a dictionary.

b He was blowing up the balloons. (= *aufblasen*)
The story was blown up. (= *aufbauschen*)
Terrorists have tried to blow up the television tower. (= *sprengen*)

Phrasal verbs often have **more than one meaning**.

c Will you be in next week?
Bist du nächste Woche zu Hause?

Big earrings are in at the moment.
Große Ohrringe sind zurzeit Mode.

What's on at the cinema?
Was läuft denn im Kino?

We can also combine **be** with an adverb to form a phrasal verb. It has more than one meaning.

166 Use

a 1 Suddenly Charlie came in.
Plötzlich kam Charlie herein.

2 He took his shoes off and turned the TV on.
Er zog sich seine Schuhe aus und machte den Fernseher an.

3 He took off his shoes and turned on the TV.
Er zog sich seine Schuhe aus und machte den Fernseher an.

Some phrasal verbs are intransitive (example 1), i.e. they have no object. Others are transitive (examples 2 and 3). If the **object** is a **noun** (e.g. *shoes, TV*), it can come before the adverb (example 2) or after it (example 3).

b I tried on the boots, but I took them off when I saw the price.
Ich habe die Stiefel anprobiert, aber sie ausgezogen, als ich den Preis sah.

If the **object** is a **pronoun** (e.g. *them*), it must come before the adverb.

c I left out the three most difficult questions in the maths test.
Ich habe im Mathetest die drei schwierigsten Fragen ausgelassen.

The teacher tore up what she had written.
Die Lehrerin zerriss, was sie geschrieben hatte.

If the **object** is **very long** (e.g. *the three most difficult questions*), it usually comes after the adverb.

The verb | 115 | **Phrasal and prepositional verbs**

d 1 a Did they catch the pickpocket, or did he get away?
       Haben sie den Taschendieb gefasst oder ist er geflohen?
    b The bank robber escaped in a stolen vehicle.
       Der Bankräuber floh in einem gestohlenen Auto.

   2 a Go on reading until I tell you to stop.
       Lies weiter, bis ich dir sage, dass du aufhören sollst.
    b The team continued working on the project.
       Das Team arbeitete an dem Projekt weiter.

We often use phrasal verbs in **informal English** (examples 1 a and 2 a). In formal written English, other verbs are often preferred (examples 1 b and 2 b).

167 Prepositional verbs

a 1 The police are looking into the matter.
      Die Polizei untersucht den Fall.
   2 John asked for a new sheet of paper.
      John bat um ein neues Blatt Papier.
   3 Jeff was looking at her.
      Jeff sah sie an.

The **meaning** of a prepositional verb is clear from the meaning of its **parts** (e.g. *look into, ask for*). A prepositional verb in an active sentence always has an **object**. The object comes immediately after the preposition (e.g. *into the matter*). Even when the object is especially long (example 2: *a new sheet of paper*) or when it is a pronoun (example 3: *her*), it still follows the preposition.

b What were you laughing about?
   (We were laughing about the film.)

   Where do you come from?
   Woher kommst du?

   Which bus are you waiting for?
   Auf welchen Bus wartest du?

   Who did you speak to?
   but: (in formal English)
   To whom did you speak?

We cannot leave the preposition out of a **question about the object**. The preposition is almost always at the end of the sentence, separated from the question word (= *what, where, which, who*).

▶ Word order: 5 e, 9
▶ Questions with question words: 4

c Don't spend all your pocket money on sweets.
   Gib nicht dein ganzes Taschengeld für Süßigkeiten aus.

   Industry has spent a large amount of money on anti-pollution measures in the last few years.
   Die Industrie hat in den letzten Jahren eine Menge Geld für Umweltschutzmaßnahmen ausgegeben.

Prepositional verbs are used in both **informal** and **formal English**.

> **Note**
>
> 1 We've thought the problem through and found an answer. (adverb)
>   *Wir haben das Problem durchdacht ….*
> 2 The editor worked through the manuscript, then discussed it with the author. (preposition)
>   *Der Redakteur arbeitete das Manuskript durch, …*

Some particles can be used both as **adverbs** and as **prepositions** (e.g. *along, down, in, on, over, through* and *up*). When a particle is used as a preposition, it must come before the object (example 2: *worked through the manuscript*).

The noun

168-180

168 Kinds of nouns	177 Uncountable nouns
169 The gender of nouns	178 Common determiners with countable and uncountable nouns
170-174 Countable nouns	
175 Plural nouns	179-180 The possessive form and the *of*-phrase
176 Collective nouns	

168 Kinds of nouns

woman, John, dog, tree, table, water, love, democracy

Nouns refer to people, animals, plants, things, materials, feelings, ideas, etc.

It is important to distinguish between these kinds of nouns:

a   man, family, country, city, day, optimist

- **Common nouns** refer to people or things in general.

Mr Clark, the Blacks, Australia, New York, Monday

- **Proper nouns** (names) refer e.g. to a specific person or thing. Proper nouns in English begin with a capital letter, as in German.

b   a girl – two girls
a car – three cars
a question – a lot of questions

- **Countable nouns** refer to things we can count.

money, water, music, optimism
information, health

- **Uncountable nouns** refer to things we cannot count.

The optimist

169 The gender of nouns

a
the man	the woman	the house
der Mann	die Frau	das Haus

The man said he would ask his wife.
The woman woke up. She opened her eyes.
The house is new. It looks nice with its blue door.

In contrast to German – where the article shows the gender of a noun – English nouns **do not have grammatical gender**.

In the choice of pronoun and possessive determiner we distinguish between people and things:

- For **people** we use the pronouns *he/him* or *she/her* and the determiners *his* or *her*.

- For **things** we use the pronoun *it* and the determiner *its*.

▶ Personal pronouns: 227-229
▶ Pronouns for animals: 228b
▶ Forms of the article: 181 a/b

b
Where's your friend? – He's upstairs with his brother.
　　… Freund? – Er …　　　… seinem …

Was that your new neighbour? Do you like her?
　　　… Nachbarin?　　　… sie?

Mrs Taylor is our new French teacher.
　　　… Französischlehrerin.

'I spent the evening at a friend's, Mum.'

In contrast to German, most nouns referring to people can be used for **both males and females**. Whether a male or female person is meant will often be clear from the context (e.g. from the use of a pronoun or a name). Here are some examples of nouns referring to people:

assistant	Assistent/in, Verkäufer/in
author	Autor/in
colleague	Kollege/in
tennis coach	Tennistrainer/in
cousin	Cousin/e
doctor	Arzt/Ärztin
driver	Fahrer/in
foreigner	Ausländer/in
friend	Freund/in
neighbour	Nachbar/in
pupil	Schüler/in
reader	Leser/in
singer	Sänger/in
student	Student/in, Schüler/in
teacher	Lehrer/in
tourist	Tourist/in
visitor	Besucher/in
writer	Schriftsteller/in

Notes

1 Have you ever asked your partner whether he or she likes your hairstyle?
　… er oder sie …?

2 If anybody wants to see me, tell them I'm not at home.
　… jemand …　　　… ihm …
Somebody has forgotten their umbrella.
Jemand …　　　… seinen …

When talking about a person of unknown sex, there is an increasing tendency in formal English to use the phrase *he or she/his or her/him or her*.

When we use the pronouns *everyone/everybody, anyone/anybody, someone/somebody*, etc., we avoid *he/him* and *she/her* so as not to refer specifically only to men or only to women. Instead we use *they/them/their*.

▶ *Somebody, anybody*, etc. + *they/them/their*: 225 a

The noun | **118** | **The gender of nouns**

c

male	female	
boyfriend	**girl**friend	Sometimes it may be necessary to **make it clear whether we mean a male or a female**. To do this we use:
male model	**female** model	
male secretary	**female** secretary	• an extra word to show which sex we mean
husband	wife	
man	woman	• different words
monk	nun	
waiter	waitr**ess**	• the ending -*ess* for a female (used only rarely
actor	actr**ess**	as it is felt to be discriminating).
lion	lion**ess**	
prince	princ**ess**	

d

Jane's a stewardess with British Airways.
Jane's a flight attendant with British Airways.
    … *Flugbegleiterin* …

We chose Marie Barnes as our spokeswoman.
We chose Marie Barnes as our spokesperson.
    … *zu unserer Sprecherin.*

Nowadays a **word covering both sexes** is often preferred, especially with words for jobs. Such words include:

flight attendant	Flugbegleiter/in
spokesperson	Sprecher/in
headteacher	Schulleiter/in
police officer	Polizist/in
fire fighter	Feuerwehrmann/-frau
chairperson	Vorsitzende(r)
ambulance staff	Sanitäter

170 Countable nouns

a boy – three boys
a chair – ten chairs
this house – these houses
a mistake – some mistakes

Nouns like *boy*, *chair*, *house* and *mistake* can be counted. They are therefore called **countable nouns**. They can be either **singular** or **plural**, and they can combine with the indefinite article, with numbers and with other determiners.

▶ Uncountable nouns: 177
▶ Common determiners: 178

171 Regular plurals

a **Form:**

singular	plural
hat	hats
tree	trees
bus	buses
bush	bushes
watch	watches
box	boxes

We normally form the plural of a noun **by adding -s** to the singular.

If a noun ends with the letters -s, -ss, -sh, -ch or -x (a sibilant sound), then we **add -es**.

b **Spelling rules:**

singular	plural
family	families
party	parties
day	days
boy	boys
knife	knives
half	halves
leaf	leaves
life	lives
shelf	shelves
thief	thieves
wife	wives
but:	
belief	beliefs
proof	proofs
roof	roofs
kilo	kilos
photo	photos
disco	discos
potato	potatoes
tomato	tomatoes
buffalo	buffalos/buffaloes
mosquito	mosquitos/mosquitoes
tornado	tornados/tornadoes
torpedo	torpedos/torpedoes

If a noun ends in a **consonant** + **y**, then we write **-ies** in the plural.

If a noun ends in a **vowel** + **y**, then we write **-ys** in the plural.

Most nouns ending in **-f** or **-fe** have a plural with **-ves** [-vz].

Most nouns ending in **-o** have a plural with **-os**.

Some nouns ending in **-o** have a plural with **-oes**.

Some nouns ending in **-o** can have a plural **either** with **-os** or with **-oes**, with **-os** becoming more common.

Countable nouns

c **The pronunciation of the plural -s:**

singular	plural		
bag [-g] van [-n] boy [-ɔɪ]	bags vans boys	} [-z]	If a noun ends with a **voiced** sound, we say [-z].
map [-p] ticket [-t] roof [-f]	maps tickets roofs	} [-s]	If a noun ends with one of the **voiceless** sounds [-p], [-t], [-k], [-f] or [-θ], we say [-s].
bus [-s] nose [-z] watch [-tʃ]	buses noses watches	} [-ɪz]	After the **sibilant** sounds [-s], [-z], [-ʃ], [-tʃ] or [-dʒ], the -es ending is pronounced [-ɪz].

house [-s]   houses [-zɪz]   Be careful with the pronunciation of the words
mouth [-θ]   mouths [-ðz]   **houses** and **mouths**.

▶ Pronunciation of the verb ending -s: 64 c

172 *Irregular plurals*

a

singular		plural	
child	[tʃaɪld]	children	['tʃɪldrən]
man	[mæn]	men	[men]
woman	['wʊmən]	women	['wɪmɪn]
foot	[fʊt]	feet	[fiːt]
tooth	[tuːθ]	teeth	[tiːθ]
mouse	[maʊs]	mice	[maɪs]
penny	['penɪ]	pence	[pens]

A number of nouns have a special **plural form without -s**.

b
fish   fish
sheep   sheep
aircraft   aircraft
hovercraft   hovercraft
spacecraft   spacecraft
crossroads   crossroads
series   series
species   species
means   means

A few nouns have **the same form** in the **singular** and in the **plural**.

> **Note**
>
> We caught two fish yesterday.
>   … zwei Fische …
> **but:**
> He's an expert on the fishes of the Caribbean coral reefs.
>   … für Fischarten …

When *fish* means a species of fish, the plural can have -es.

Note

fashion show**s**, grown-up**s**, travel agent**s**, take-off**s**	With compound nouns, the plural *-s* usually comes at the end of the compound.
mother**s**-to-be, passer**s**-by, runner**s**-up, son**s**-in-law	There are some exceptions to this rule, however. It is therefore advisable to use a dictionary to find the correct plural form.

173 Nationality words

The Americans have more public holidays than **the English**.
The Japanese love travelling.

There are different ways of forming the plural of **nationality words**:

a single person	several people	nationality in general	
an American	many Americans	(the) Americans	• A number of nationality words have a **plural with -s**.
a German	many Germans	(the) Germans	
an English**man**	many English**men**	the English	• Nationality words which are compounds with *-man* or *-woman* have an **irregular plural** with *-men* or *-women*.
a French**woman**	many French**women**	the French	
a Japan**ese** [-iːz]	many Japanese	the Japanese	• Nationality words ending in *-ese* or *-ss* have the **same singular** and **plural form**.
a Swi**ss**	many Swiss	the Swiss	

174 Foreign plurals

With words borrowed **from other languages** (especially from Latin or Greek), the best thing is to use a dictionary to find the correct plural form.

singular	plural	
analys**is** [-ɪs]	analys**es** [-iːz]	• In English some of these words have **kept their original plural form**.
bacteri**um** [-əm]	bacteri**a** [-ɪə]	
bas**is** [-ɪs]	bas**es** [-iːz]	
cris**is** [-ɪs]	cris**es** [-iːz]	
criteri**on** [-ən]	criteri**a** [-ɪə]	
nucl**eus** [-ɪəs]	nucl**ei** [-ɪaɪ]	
radi**us** [-ɪəs]	radi**i** [-ɪaɪ]	
stimul**us** [-əs]	stimul**i** [-aɪ]	
area	area**s**	• Others have **-(e)s in the plural**.
chorus	chorus**es**	
demon	demon**s**	
cact**us** [-əs]	cact**i**/cact**uses** [-aɪ/-əsɪz]	• A third group can either have the **original plural ending** or the **plural with -(e)s**.
formul**a** [-ə]	formul**ae**/formul**as** [-iː/-əz]	
ind**ex** [-eks]	indi**ces**/ind**exes** [-ɪsiːz/-əksɪz]	
medi**um** [-ɪəm]	medi**a**/medi**ums** [-ɪə/-ɪəmz]	
stadi**um** [-ɪəm]	stadi**a**/stadi**ums** [-ɪə/-ɪəmz]	

175 Plural nouns

a

My sister has bought some new glasses.
Meine Schwester hat sich eine neue Brille gekauft.

These are my pyjamas, not yours.
Das ist mein Schlafanzug, nicht deiner.

I've packed a pair of shorts and two pairs of long trousers.
Ich habe eine Shorts und zwei lange Hosen eingepackt.

Pair nouns refer to things which consist of two identical parts. They include:

trousers, pants (AE)	(lange) Hose(n)
shorts	kurze Hose(n), Shorts
leggings	Leggings
tights	Strumpfhose
overalls (BE)	Overall, Arbeitsanzug
jeans	Jeans
pyjamas	Schlafanzug
swimming trunks	Badehose
glasses	Brille
goggles	Schutzbrille
headphones	Kopfhörer
pliers	Kombizange
scissors ['sɪzəz]	Schere
binoculars [bɪˈnɒkjələz]	Fernglas

Pair nouns are used **only in the plural**. They **cannot be used with a/an or with numbers**. The context tells us whether one item is meant or several.

If we want to give the exact number, we have to use **a/one pair of** or **two/three/... pairs of**.

b

Clothes are quite cheap in the USA.
Kleidung ist in den USA ziemlich billig.

Good looks are sometimes an advantage.
Gutes Aussehen ist manchmal von Vorteil.

These stairs lead to the attic.
Diese Treppe führt zum Dachboden.

My wages are always paid on Fridays.
Mein Lohn wird immer freitags gezahlt.

In English there are nouns which have **no singular**. The determiners, verbs and pronouns which combine with these nouns are **plural** – in contrast to German. Such nouns include:

belongings	Besitz, Habe
clothes	Kleidung, Kleider
congratulations	Glückwunsch/-wünsche
earnings	Verdienst
looks	Aussehen
manners	Benehmen
remains	Rest(e)
stairs	Treppe(nstufen)
surroundings	Umgebung
thanks	Dank
wages	(Arbeits-)Lohn

▶ Common determiners: 178

Note

Another five years is needed to finish the project.
A whole three hours was lost waiting for the plane.
30% of his income goes to the tax department.

When we use an expression of quantity, the number + noun (e.g. *five years*) is usually seen as a whole. The determiner and verb are therefore singular.

176 Collective nouns

a Class 2c is/are difficult to teach.
   Klasse 2c ist schwer zu unterrichten.

   Has the band finished playing?
   Hat die Band aufgehört zu spielen?

   The band are putting away their instruments.
   Die Band räumt ihre Instrumente weg.

Collective nouns refer to a **group of people**. After a collective noun in the singular, the verb and following pronoun can be either in the singular or the plural. If we are thinking of the **group as a whole**, we use the **singular**. If we are thinking of the **individual members** of the group, we use the **plural** form of the verb, pronoun or determiner. (But in American English the singular is normally used.)
Collective nouns include:

army	Armee
audience	Publikum, Zuhörer/innen
band	Band, Kapelle
the BBC	die BBC
class	Klasse
club	Klub, Verein
committee	Ausschuss, Komitee
couple	Paar
crew	Mannschaft, Besatzung
crowd	(Menschen-)Menge
enemy	Feind
family	Familie
government	Regierung
group	Gruppe
jury	Jury, die Geschworenen
majority	Mehrheit
management	Management, (Geschäfts-)Leitung
minority	Minderheit
opposition	Opposition
party	Partei
press	Presse(leute)
public	Öffentlichkeit
staff	Kollegium, Personal
team	Team, Mannschaft

'… so it is very important that you remember **not** to allow yourselves to be intimidated* by the opposition, **whoever** they are …'

intimidate einschüchtern

b There were only a few people in the bank.
   Es waren nur ein paar Leute in der Bank.

   The police have set up a road-block.
   Die Polizei hat eine Straßensperre errichtet.

   The cattle are hungry.
   Das Vieh hat Hunger.

The following collective nouns are **always plural**:

people	(die) Leute
the police	die Polizei(beamten)
cattle	Vieh, Rinder

Note

The Navajo are a peace-loving people.
        … ein friedliebendes Volk.
The peoples of Africa speak many different languages.
Die Völker Afrikas …

People can also mean a community or a nation (German: *Volk*). When it has this meaning, we can use it as a countable noun with a singular form *people* and a regular plural with *-s*.

177 Uncountable nouns

a plastic, coffee, water, paper, land, sugar, music

Nouns like *plastic*, *water*, *coffee* and *paper* cannot be counted. They are therefore called **uncountable nouns**. They have **no plural** and do **not** combine **with a/an or** with **numbers** (e.g. *one*, *two*, *three*, …).

b a piece of plastic
a cup of coffee
some drops of water
a piece of paper

If we want to express a **particular quantity** (i.e. make an uncountable noun countable), we have to use phrases like **a piece/bit/packet/slice/cup of, some drops of** or **several items of** before the noun.

▶ Countable nouns: 170

Notes

1

countable	uncountable
today's papers *die Zeitungen von heute* important papers *wichtige Papiere/Dokumente*	toilet paper *Toilettenpapier*
some hairs on your pullover *einige Haare (= Einzelhaare) …*	Your hair looks nice. *Deine Haare (= deine Frisur) …*
my favourite sports *meine Lieblingssportarten*	Are you fond of sport? *Treibst du gern Sport?*

Some nouns can be either countable or uncountable, often with different meanings. In such cases you should use a dictionary.

2 Two coffees, please.
Could I have a beer, please?

Words for types of drink are often used as countable nouns, e.g. when ordering drinks in a café or restaurant.

c

In contrast to German, the following nouns are **uncountable**, i.e. they have no plural and the **determiners**, **verbs** and **pronouns** they combine with are **singular**:

Sarah's advice was very helpful.
Sarahs Rat war/Sarahs Ratschläge waren sehr hilfreich.

New evidence has been found by the police.
Es sind neue Beweise von der Polizei gefunden worden.

I like your new furniture. Where did you buy it?
Ich mag deine neuen Möbel. Wo hast du sie gekauft?

Three exercises? That's too much homework.
… Das sind zu viele Hausaufgaben.

Where did you get this information?
Wo hast du diese Information/en her?

advice	Rat, Ratschläge
damage	Schaden, Schäden
equipment	Ausrüstung, Geräte
evidence	Beweis(e)
furniture	Möbel
homework	Hausaufgabe(n)
housework	Hausarbeit(en)
information	Information(en)
knowledge	Wissen, Kenntnis(se)
progress	Fortschritt(e)
shopping	Einkauf, Einkäufe

That's a useful bit of information.
Das ist eine nützliche Information.

Two new pieces of evidence were presented to the court.
Zwei neue Beweise wurden dem Gericht vorgelegt.

If we want to make an uncountable noun countable, we say **a/two/ … piece(s) of**. In informal English we can also use **a/two/ … bit(s) of**.

▶ Common determiners: 178

The noun | **125** | **Common determiners**

d

No news is good news.
Keine Nachrichten sind gute Nachrichten.

I think politics is interesting.
Ich finde, Politik ist interessant.

The United States/USA consists of 50 states.
Die Vereinigten Staaten/USA bestehen aus 50 Staaten.

In spite of their **plural form** with -s, the following nouns are **singular**:

aerobics	Aerobic
athletics	Leichtathletik
billiards	Billiard
economics	(Volks-)Wirtschaft
mathematics	Mathematik
maths (BE), math (AE)	Mathe
measles	Masern
news	Nachricht(en)
physics	Physik
politics	Politik
the United States/USA	die Vereinigten Staaten/USA

Uncountable nouns:
— no plural
— no 'a/an'
— no numbers

178 *Common determiners with countable and uncountable nouns*

determiner	countable noun		uncountable noun
	singular	plural	
the	the cup	the cups	the tea
a/an	a cup	—	—
one/two/three/…	one cup	two/three/… cups	—
my/your/…	my/your/… cup	my/your/… cups	my/your/… tea
this/that	this/that cup	—	this/that tea
these/those	—	these/those cups	—
some/any	any cup	some/any cups	some/any tea
a lot of	—	a lot of cups	a lot of tea
many/few	—	many/few cups	—
much/little	—	—	much/little tea
all	—	all the cups	all the tea
no	no cup	no cups	no tea

The possessive form and the of-phrase

179 The possessive form

a **Form:**

Mrs Dean's [-z] husband my aunt's [-s] car James's [-ɪz] sister	We add **'s** to a noun in the **singular**.
our neighbours' [-z] dog the students' [-s] room the Evanses' [-ɪz] house	We add an **apostrophe** (') to a **plural form with -(e)s**.
the children's [-z] mother the men's [-z] voices	We add **'s** to an **irregular plural form**.

▶ Pronunciation of the plural -s: 171 c

the runner's trainer

the runners' trainer

> **Notes**
>
> **1** Ms Richards's [-zɪz] school/Ms Richards' school
> Mr Philips's wife/Mr Philips' wife
>
> When a name ends in -s, we can just add an apostrophe (') instead of 's.
>
> **2** Jane and Peter's parents
> *Janes und Peters Eltern*
>
> When nouns are linked by *and*, we usually put the 's only after the last noun.
>
> **3** someone's umbrella
> everybody's darling
>
> There is a possessive form of *everyone/everybody, anyone/anybody, someone/somebody*, etc.

b **Use:**

This is my sister's CD collection.
  ... die CD-Sammlung meiner Schwester/von meiner Schwester.

Is that your parents' idea?
  ... die Idee deiner Eltern/von deinen Eltern?

Which is your friends' house?
  ... das Haus deiner Freunde?

We use the **possessive form** with **people** and often also with **animals**. We use it to show who someone or something belongs to. In English the possessive form (e.g. *my sister's*) always comes **before** the word it relates to (e.g. *CD collection*).

c Is there a chemist's (shop) near here?
   … *ein Apotheker/eine Apotheke* …?

   We went to a party at the Baxters' (house).
   … *bei den Baxters.*

   You should go to the doctor's.
   … *zum Arzt* …

When we talk about certain **places** such as shops or the homes of people we know, we use a possessive form on its own. The following noun (e.g. *shop*, *house*, etc.) is understood but is normally left out.

d The car over there is my sister's (car).
   Das Auto da drüben gehört meiner Schwester.

   Whose stupid idea is that? – It's my parents' (idea).
   … – *Die meiner Eltern.*

We sometimes **leave out** the **noun** after a possessive form to avoid repetition.

e Last month's sales figures were excellent.
   Die Verkaufszahlen des letzten Monats …

   Have you read yesterday's newspaper?
   … *die Zeitung von gestern/die gestrige Zeitung* …?

   It's a three days' journey by car. It's better to fly.
   … *eine dreitägige Reise/eine Reise von drei Tagen.* …

Certain **phrases of time** can be used in the possessive form before a noun. Some examples are *last month*, *next week*, *yesterday*, *today*, *tomorrow*, *three days*, *an hour* and *twenty minutes*.

180 The *of*-phrase

a Do you like the colour of our new bikes?
   … *die Farbe unserer neuen Räder/von unseren neuen Rädern?*

   We missed the beginning of the film.
   … *den Anfang des Films/vom Film.*

   The doors of the hotel rooms were open, so we looked in.
   Die Türen der Hotelzimmer/von den Hotelzimmern standen offen, …

We use the **of-phrase** for **things**. It expresses the idea that something belongs to or is part of something else.

> **Note**
>
> Britain's economy/the economy of Britain
> New York's skyscrapers/the skyscrapers of New York
> the party's decision/the decision of the party
> the firm's furniture/the furniture of the firm
> the government's policy/the policy of the government

We can often use the possessive form instead of the *of*-phrase for things. We can do this with things which have an obvious connection to people, e.g. with countries, cities and institutions.

b They're the children of our friends from Glasgow.
   Sie sind die Kinder unserer Freunde aus Glasgow.

   She's the daughter of the woman who runs the hotel in Victoria Street.
   Sie ist die Tochter der Frau, die das Hotel in der Victoria Street führt.

We use the *of*-phrase **for people** when the noun is modified by a phrase or a subordinate clause.

c	five litres of paint *fünf Liter Farbe* a piece of cake *ein Stück Kuchen* half a pound of salt *ein halbes Pfund Salz* two kilos of sugar *zwei Kilo Zucker* five bottles of milk *fünf Flaschen Milch*	We use the *of*-phrase in **expressions of amount or quantity**. ▶ *A pair of*: 175a ▶ Uncountable nouns: 177b/c
d	a postcard of Belfast *eine Postkarte von Belfast* a member of our team *ein Mitglied unseres Teams* a kind of puzzle *eine Art Puzzle* the city of New York *die Stadt New York* the month of May *der Monat Mai* the role of the teacher *die Rolle des Lehrers* the miners of Wales *die walisischen Bergarbeiter* the works of Shakespeare *die Werke Shakespeares* a picture of the Pope *ein Bild des Papstes* a tour of London *ein Rundgang durch London*	We use the *of*-phrase in certain other **contexts**.

> **Note**
>
> She is a friend of Susan's. (= She is one of Susan's friends.)
> *Sie ist eine Freundin von Susan.*
> **but:**
> She is Susan's friend.
> *Sie ist Susans Freundin.*

We use the possessive form in an *of*-phrase after a noun which has the indefinite article, a number or another kind of determiner.

▶ Possessive pronouns: 231d

Possessive form mostly for people
'of'-phrase mostly for things

The article

181-195

181 Forms and pronunciation
182-188 The definite article
189-195 The indefinite article

In English, as in German, there are two articles: the **definite** and the **indefinite article**.

181 Forms and pronunciation

a | the man | the woman | the animal | The **definite article** is *the*.
  | *der Mann* | *die Frau* | *das Tier* |

the [ðə] table
the [ðə] blue coat
the [ðə] farm

- When it comes before a word beginning with a **consonant**, the definite article is pronounced [ðə].

the [ði] egg
the [ði] invitation
the [ði] old bike

- When it comes before a word beginning with a **vowel**, the definite article is pronounced [ði].

b | a man | a woman | an animal | The **indefinite article** is *a* or *an*.
  | *ein Mann* | *eine Frau* | *ein Tier* |

a table
a blue coat
a farm

- The indefinite article *a* comes before a word beginning with a **consonant** and is pronounced [ə].

an egg
an invitation
an old bike

- The indefinite article *an* comes before a word beginning with a **vowel** and is pronounced [ən].

c a/the European country [ə/ðə ˌjʊərə'piːən]
   a/the university [ə/ðə ˌjuːnɪ'vɜːsətɪ]
   a/the one-pound coin [ə/ðə wʌn paʊnd 'kɔɪn]

Whether we pronounce the article [ðə] or [ði] or whether we use *a* or *an* depends on the **initial sound of the following word** and not on the spelling.

 a/the uniform [ə/ðə 'juːnɪfɔːm] – an/the umbrella [ən/ði ʌm'brelə]
a/the hotel [ə/ðə həʊ'tel] – an/the hour [ən/ði 'aʊə]

 Note

She is the [ðiː] computer expert in our school.
Sie ist in unserer Schule die (die = herausragende) Computerexpertin.

That's a [eɪ] possibility, but it isn't the only one.
That's one possibility, but it isn't the only one.
Das ist eine Möglichkeit (eine = eine von vielen), …

If we want to stress the definite article *the*, we pronounce it [ðiː], even before a consonant.

If we want to stress the indefinite article *a* or *an*, we pronounce it [eɪ] or [æn]. But mostly we use *one*.

The definite article

182 Use

The man over there is David's English teacher.
Der *Mann dort drüben ist Davids Englischlehrer.*

We live in the house at the end of the road.
Wir leben in dem Haus am Ende der Straße.

As in German, the **definite article** is used when we want to **specify** a person, a thing or an idea and distinguish it from other ones. But there are some important differences in usage between the two languages.

183 The *with abstract nouns, material nouns and nouns in the plural*

a

A noun can be **without the definite article** when it is **used in a very general sense**, i.e. when we do not specify which one we mean. This is especially so with:

How did life begin?
 … *das Leben …?*
Life in New York is exciting.
Das Leben in New York …
Children often respect nature more than adults.
 … *die Natur …*

- **abstract nouns** (e.g. *life, death, nature, history, society*)

Bread tastes best fresh from the oven.
Brot …
Water makes up nearly two-thirds of our weight.
Wasser …

- **nouns for substances or materials** (e.g. *bread, water, glass*)

People talk.
Die Leute …
Petrol prices have gone up again.
Die Benzinpreise …

- **nouns in the plural**.

How did human life begin?
 … *das menschliche Leben/menschliches Leben …?*

Nouns used in this general sense can be without an article even when they are preceded by an adjective.

b We know little about the life of Shakespeare.
 … *das Leben Shakespeares.*

The bread we bought from the supermarket wasn't fresh.
Das Brot, das wir im Supermarkt gekauft haben, …

The people in our street are nice.
Die Leute in unserer Straße …

As in German, a noun **has a definite article** when it is **made more concrete** or when we **specify** which we mean, e.g. by means of an *of*-phrase (*of Shakespeare*) or a relative clause (*we bought from the supermarket*). The examples are not about life, bread and people in general but about the particular life of Shakespeare, the particular bread from the supermarket and the particular people in our street.

No 'the' with nouns used in a very general sense

The article | **131** | **The definite article**

184 The with church, school, prison, etc.

a My parents go to church every Sunday.
  … in die Kirche.
Most pupils don't go to school on Saturday.
  … zur Schule.
The thief went to prison for two years.
  … ins Gefängnis.

Some nouns are used **without the definite article** when it is the **purpose of the building** that is in our mind. They are church, school, prison, university, college, class, court and hospital:

go to church (to attend service)
be at school (to attend class)
go to prison (to serve a sentence)

'So do I, Gary, so do I.'

> **Note**
> Kate studies at the university.
> After the accident the driver was taken to the hospital.

In American English university and hospital are normally used with the definite article.

▶ American English: 290-298

b There's a concert in the church next week.
  … in der Kirche.
Go up to the school and turn left.
  … bis zur Schule …
Tom went to the prison to visit his friend.
  … zum Gefängnis …

We use church, school, prison, university, college, class, court and hospital **with the definite article** when we are thinking of the **building** rather than its purpose:

the church (a particular church)
the school (a particular school building)
the prison (a particular prison)

185 The with names

a Lake Constance is very popular with tourists.
Der Bodensee …

I live in Station Road.
  … in der Bahnhofstraße.

near Lake Erie

on Mount Everest

in London Road, in Central Park, around Piccadilly Circus, on London Bridge

in Rockefeller Center, to Buckingham Palace, from Victoria Station

little Joe, poor Mary, modern Britain

Most proper names in English are **without the definite article**. This is especially so – in contrast to German – in the case of:

• lakes

• most names of mountains

• most names of streets, parks, squares and bridges

• many buildings

• proper nouns preceded by an adjective.

The article | **132** | **The definite article**

b The Grants invited their new neighbours for lunch.
   Die Grants ...

   The Pacific Ocean covers over a third of the earth's surface.
   Der Pazifische Ozean ...

   the Connors, the Highlands, the Alps

   the Thames, the Atlantic

   the British Museum, the Globe Theatre, the Odeon (Cinema), the Hilton (Hotel)

   the House of Commons, the Tower of London

We use a **definite article** with:

- proper nouns in the plural
- rivers and seas
- the names of most museums, theatres, cinemas and hotels
- phrases with *of*.

> **Note**
>
> England, France, Italy, Switzerland, Turkey, Ukraine
> the USA, the UK, the Netherlands, the Czech Republic, the Bahamas

Some names of countries are without the definite article, but with others we use *the*. (no rule)

186 The *with phrases of time*

a

   in April, since March
   im April, seit März

   on Monday, next Tuesday (evening)
   am Montag, am nächsten Dienstag(abend)
   but: at the weekend
              am Wochenende

   at night, by day, at midday
   nachts, tagsüber, mittags
   but: during the day, in the morning
              während des Tages, am Morgen

   at Christmas, over Easter
   (zu) Weihnachten, über Ostern

   during breakfast, after lunch
   während des Frühstücks, nach dem Mittagessen

The following phrases of time are usually **without the definite article**:

- months
- days of the week

- some parts of the day (But we use *the* with parts of the day after *during* or *in*.)

- holidays
- meals.

b The July of 1996 was very wet.
   Der Juli 1996 ...

   Do you remember the Sunday before the storm?
   ... an den Sonntag vor dem Sturm?

We use the **definite article** with a phrase of time when we **specify** e.g. which July or which Sunday we mean.

> **Note**
>
> in winter/in the winter
> in summer/in the summer
>
> I like the fall best.

Seasons of the year (*spring, summer, autumn* and *winter*) can be used with or without the article.

In American English *the* is always used with *fall* (= *autumn*).

The article **133** **The definite article**

187 All, both, double, half, most of, twice + the

all the time
die ganze Zeit

both (the) cars
beide Autos/die beiden Autos

half the cake
der halbe Kuchen

double the size
die doppelte Größe

most (of the) boys
die meisten Jungen

twice the amount
die doppelte/zweifache Menge

The **definite article** comes **after all, both, double, half, most of** and **twice**.
In German the article comes before *ganz*, *beide*, etc.

▶ *All, both*: 221, 222a

Notes

1 Most girls wear jeans for school.
Die meisten Mädchen …
Most of the girls at the party were wearing jeans.
Die meisten Mädchen …

Most is without the definite article when the noun has a general sense. We use the definite article when we are talking about a specific group.

2 Which of you has made most/the most mistakes?
… die meisten Fehler …

When *most* has a superlative meaning, it can be with or without the definite article.

188 Fixed phrases with and without the

Bob has played the trumpet since he was six.
Bob spielt Trompete …

What's on TV?
Was gibts im Fernsehen?

Fixed phrases **with the definite article** are:

it is the custom	es ist Brauch
it is the fashion	es ist Mode, Brauch
with the exception of	mit Ausnahme von
at the expense of	auf Kosten von
play the piano/trumpet/…	Klavier/Trompete/… spielen
listen to the radio	Radio hören

Fixed phrases **without the definite article** are:

on condition that	unter der Bedingung, dass
at work	bei der Arbeit
at first sight	auf den ersten Blick
by car/bus/…	mit dem Auto/Bus/…
(be) on TV	im Fernsehen (sein)
come into/out of fashion	in Mode/aus der Mode kommen
go to bed	ins Bett gehen
in bed	im Bett
live in town	in der Stadt leben

'I've told you before not to phone me at work.'

The indefinite article

189 *Use*

Yesterday I met a girl on the bus.
       … *ein Mädchen* …

We'll have to buy a new car.
       … *ein neues Auto* …

That's a good idea.
       … *eine gute Idee.*

We use the **indefinite article a/an** to talk about one person, thing or idea but without **specifying** which one. There are some differences between English and German.

190 *A/An before jobs, nationalities, etc.*

My sister wants to become an astronaut.
       … *möchte Astronautin werden.*
Winston Churchill was an Englishman.
       … *war Engländer.*
I'm a member of our local tennis club.
Ich bin Mitglied …

Gwen has been a non-smoker for 20 years.
Gwen ist seit 20 Jahren Nichtraucherin.

If we want to say that someone is in a certain **job**, has a certain **nationality** or belongs to some other **group,** then we have to use the **indefinite article**.

 Winston Churchill was English.

We often use an **adjective** (without *a/an*) to express nationality.

191 *A/An after as and without*

You can use this dish as an ashtray.
       … *als Aschenbecher* …
Don't go out without a coat.
       … *ohne Mantel* …
You can't get to our house without a car.
       … *ohne Auto* …

The **indefinite article** comes **after as** (= *als*) and **without** (= *ohne*) + a countable noun in the singular.

▶ Countable nouns: 170

192 *A/An meaning per*

We sell about 90 TV sets a month.
       … *pro/im Monat.*
We get maths homework three times a week.
       … *pro/in der Woche.*
Slow down. The speed limit is thirty miles an hour.
       … *in der Stunde.*

Potatoes are 95 pence a kilo.
       … *pro/das Kilo.*

The **indefinite article** means the same as *per*.

- before a **phrase of time**, often in expressions of frequency or speed,

- before an **expression of amount or quantity**, especially when talking about prices.

The article | **135** | **The indefinite article**

193 A/An or one

I've won a thousand pounds in the lottery, one thousand and twenty-five, in fact.

Ron bought a CD. He bought one CD, Emma bought three.

A/an and **one** both mean the same as German **ein** or **eine**. *One* emphasizes the exact number.

194 Half, quite, rather, such, what + a/an

a half an hour   such a fool
   eine halbe Stunde   ein solcher/so ein Dummkopf

   quite a good film   rather a nice girl/a rather nice girl
   ein recht guter Film   ein ziemlich nettes Mädchen

The **indefinite article** comes **after half, quite** and **such** and often after **rather**. Note the different word order in German.

b What a lovely day!
   Was für ein schöner Tag!

   What a big dog!
   Was für ein großer Hund!

The **indefinite article** comes **after what** in exclamations with a countable noun in the singular.

▶ Exclamations: 14

⚠ Was für ein schreckliches Wetter!
   not: What a terrible weather!
   but: What terrible weather!

The **indefinite article** does **not** come before an uncountable noun.

195 Fixed phrases with a/an

I'm in a hurry, so I can't stay long.
Ich bin in Eile, also kann ich nicht lange bleiben.

If you've got a temperature, you ought to stay at home.
Wenn du Fieber hast, solltest du zu Hause bleiben.

Fixed phrases **with a/an**:

be in a hurry	in Eile sein
come to an end	zu Ende gehen
have (got) a headache/ a cold/a temperature	Kopfschmerzen/ Schnupfen/Fieber haben
have a wash	sich waschen
have/take a shower	(sich) duschen
have/take a bath	baden
have/take a holiday	Urlaub machen
make a noise	Lärm machen
take a seat	Platz nehmen
as a rule	in der Regel
for a change	zur Abwechslung
for a long time	lange Zeit
for a time	eine Zeit lang
in a loud voice	mit lauter Stimme
it is a pity/what a pity	es ist schade/ wie schade
without a break	ohne Unterbrechung

'Yes, it is true! I've finally persuaded Derek to take a holiday.'

The adjective

196-202

The adjective

196 Use
197-200 Comparison
201 *One/Ones* after adjectives
202 The adjective used as a noun

196 Use

a Mr Fox is an important man.
Do you like my new watch?
My French isn't very good.
Our homework wasn't difficult.

Adjectives describe the **qualities** and **characteristics** of people, things, ideas, etc.

b

	adjective	noun
We've got a	blue	van.
Have you seen these	funny	photos?
That was an	interesting	idea.

An adjective can be **attributive**, i.e. it can come **before a noun**.

	verb	adjective
Our van	is	blue.
These photos	look	funny.
Your idea	sounded	interesting.

An adjective can also be **predicative**. This means that it can come **after certain verbs**. These are linking verbs like *appear, be, become, feel, get, grow, look, remain, seem, sound, stay* and *taste*.

▶ Linking verbs: 18
▶ Adverbs or adjectives after certain verbs: 209

⚠ The plan looks good at first sight.
Der Plan sieht gut aus …

***look* + adjective**: describing a quality

She looked angrily at her partner.
Sie sah ihren Partner zornig an.

***look* + adverb**: describing how something happens

c Are you afraid of snakes?
Fürchtest du dich … ?

Tony has to stay indoors because he's ill.
…, weil er krank ist.

Some adjectives can **only** be used **predicatively**. They include: *afraid, alive, alone, asleep, glad, pleased, sorry, ill* (= *krank*), *upset* and *well/fine* (= *gesund*).

⚠ *der verängstigte Mann*
not: the ~~afraid~~ man
but: the frightened man

das schlafende Kind
not: the ~~asleep~~ child
but: the sleeping child

Adjectives used only predicatively cannot be attributive. Before a noun we have to use **adjectives with similar meanings**, e.g. *frightened, living* or *sleeping* instead of *afraid, alive* or *asleep*.

The adjective **137** **Comparison**

d   Mike is my elder brother.
Mike ist mein älterer Bruder.
That can't be the main reason.
Das kann nicht der Hauptgrund sein.

Some adjectives can **only** be used **attributively**. They include: *chief* (= *Haupt-*), *elder/eldest* (= *älterer/ältester*), *former* (= *früherer*), *main* (= *Haupt-*), *sole* (= *einziger*) and *utter* (= *vollkommener*).

Notes

1 Let's go somewhere quiet.
Lass uns irgendwohin gehen, wo es ruhig ist.

An adjective comes after a compound with *every*, *some*, *any* or *no*.

2 He's a good swimmer.
Er ist ein guter Schwimmer.
He is so good a swimmer that he wins competitions.
Er ist ein so guter Schwimmer, …

An adjective usually comes after the indefinite article *a/an*. But in this structure with *as*, *how*, *so* and *too*, it comes before *a/an*.

He is such a good swimmer that he wins competitions.
Er ist so ein guter Schwimmer, …

In informal English we use a different structure, e.g. *such a*.

Comparison

197 Regular comparison

We can compare people and things by using the comparative and superlative forms of adjectives. These are forms like *bigger* (= *größer*) and *biggest* (= *größte*). In English there are **two kinds of comparison**: one with *-er/-est* and one with *more/most*. Which forms are used with a particular adjective depends primarily on its length.

a

	comparative	superlative	
small	small**er** [-ə]	small**est** [-ɪst]	We usually use **-er/-est** with:
klein	*kleiner*	*kleinste/am kleinsten*	• **one-syllable** adjectives
loud	loud**er**	loud**est**	
silly	sill**ier**	sill**iest**	• **two-syllable** adjectives **ending in -y**.
angry	angr**ier**	angr**iest**	

Spelling and pronunciation rules:

| fat | fa**tt**er | fa**tt**est | When a single consonant (*-p*, *-b*, *-t*, *-d*, *-g*, *-m*, *-n*) at the end of a word follows a single vowel letter, we **double** the **consonant**. |
| thin | thi**nn**er | thi**nn**est | |

but:

fast	fas**t**er	fas**t**est	We do **not double** the consonant when it follows
clean	clea**n**er	clea**n**est	• another consonant
			• two vowel letters.

| nic**e** | nic**e**r | nic**e**st | We leave out a **silent -e** at the end of a word. |
| larg**e** | larg**e**r | larg**e**st | |

| sill**y** | sill**i**er | sill**i**est | **-y** changes to **-i-**. |
| eas**y** | eas**i**er | eas**i**est | |

| long [-ŋ] | long**er** [-ŋgə] | long**est** [-ŋgɪst] | After [ŋ] we say an **extra** [g]. |
| young [-ŋ] | young**er** [-ŋgə] | young**est** [-ŋgɪst] | |

The adjective | **138** | **Comparison**

b

	comparative	superlative	
famous	more famous	most famous	We use **more/most** with:
berühmt	*berühmter*	*berühmteste/ am berühmtesten*	• most **two-syllable** adjectives **not ending in -y**.
expensive	more expensive	most expensive	• all adjectives with **more than two syllables**.
difficult	more difficult	most difficult	

> **Note**
>
> | real | more real | most real | We use *more/most* with the adjectives *real, right* and |
> |---|---|---|---|
> | bored | more bored | most bored | *wrong* and with one-syllable adjectives ending in *-ed*. |

c

Some adjectives form the comparative and superlative **either** with *-er/-est* or with *more/ most*. They include:

	comparative	superlative	
sure	surer/ more sure	surest/ most sure	• the one-syllable adjectives *clear, free, keen, safe, sure, true* and *wise*
common	commoner/ more common	commonest/ most common	• the two-syllable adjectives *clever, common, likely, pleasant, polite, simple, stupid* and *subtle*
good-looking	better-looking/ more good-looking	best-looking/ most good-looking	• some compound adjectives, e.g. *good-looking, well-known*.

▶ Irregular comparison: 198

Comparison of adjectives:

1 with '-er/-est': — one-syllable adjectives
  — two-syllable adjectives ending in '-y'

2 with 'more/most': — two-syllable adjectives not ending in '-y'
  — adjectives with more than two syllables

broker *Börsenmakler*

The adjective — Comparison

198 Irregular comparison

	comparative	superlative
good	better	best
bad	worse [wɜːs]	worst [wɜːst]
far	farther/further	farthest/furthest

The adjectives *good*, *bad* and *far* have **irregular comparative** and **superlative forms**.

▶ Comparison with quantifiers: 219 f

Note

	comparative	superlative
little	smaller	smallest

James has a little flat in Soho. But my flat's even smaller.

The adjective *little* (= *klein*) does not have a comparative or superlative form. We use the forms *smaller* and *smallest*.

▶ (a) little: 219 d/e

199 Adjectives with two forms of comparison

a

	comparative	superlative
far	farther/further	farthest/furthest
–	further	–
near	nearer	nearest
–	–	next
late	later	latest
–	–	last

The adjectives *far*, *near* and *late* have **two different sets of comparative and superlative forms**, each with a different meaning.

b 1 Is the bank farther/further than the supermarket?
    2 Jack's house is the farthest/furthest from here.
    3 Are there any further questions?

Farther/further (= *weiter*) and **farthest/furthest** (= *am weitesten*) are used for physical distance (examples 1 and 2). If we mean German *weiter* in the sense of *zusätzlich* or *noch*, we can only use *further* (example 3).

The nearest bus stop is in Bond Street.
We must get off at the next stop.

Nearest means physically the closest, and **next** means the following one in a sequence (in place or time).

the latest news; Madonna's latest album; the latest trend; …
my last word on the subject; arrive at the last minute; the last time I saw you; …

Be careful not to confuse **latest** (= *the most recent, the newest in a sequence*) and **last** (= *the final one in a sequence*).

Note

Leeds and Arsenal lead the Premier League on 35 points. The latter play at Spurs tomorrow evening.

The latter (the opposite of *the former*) means the same as the German *Letzterer*.

Have you got an older/elder sister?
My oldest/eldest sister lives in Frankfurt.

Elder and *eldest* (= *älter* and *älteste*) are used only with members of a family. They are always attributive. We can use *older* and *oldest* instead of *elder* and *eldest*.

200 Sentences with comparisons

a Lynn is taller than [ðən] Ranjit.
   ... größer als ...
   Lynn is the tallest.
   ... die größte.
   Julie is as tall as Ranjit.
   ... (genau)so groß wie ...
   Ranjit is not as/so tall as Lynn.
   ... nicht so groß wie ...
   Julie often wears less fashionable clothes than Lynn.
   ... weniger modische Kleidung als ...

There are different ways of expressing a **comparison**.

Lynn   Ranjit   Julie

 größer als
   not: taller as
   but: taller than

b 1 a Bob isn't as old as me.
     b Bob isn't as old as I am.
        ... wie ich.
   2 a Lucy was faster than him.
     b Lucy was faster than he was.
        ... als er.

In a comparison we normally use the **object form of the personal pronoun**: me, him, her, us and them (examples 1a and 2a). The subject form of the personal pronoun + verb can also be used (examples 1b and 2b).

▶ Subject and object form of the personal pronoun: 227a

c There were fewer people in the disco than we expected.
   In der Disko waren weniger Leute, als wir erwartet hatten.

   It's better to solve the problem than to ignore it.
   Es ist besser, das Problem zu lösen, als es zu ignorieren.

We can also express a comparison by means of a **subordinate clause** (e.g. than we expected) or an **infinitive construction** (e.g. than to ignore it).

d Your English is getting better and better.
   ... immer besser.
   The film got more and more exciting.
   ... immer aufregender.

When two comparatives are linked by and, this expresses a **gradual increase**: in German immer besser, immer aufregender.

e The bigger the car, the more expensive it is usually.
   Je größer ...,   desto/umso teurer ...

   The older Kelly gets, the sillier she becomes.
   Je älter ...,   desto/umso alberner ...

The German **je – desto** or **je – umso** is equivalent to the English **the – the**.

▶ Comparison of adverbs: 213

201 One/Ones after adjectives

Louise has got a big dog and a small one.
                         ... einen kleinen.
Keith has got three brothers – a younger one and two older ones.
... – einen jüngeren und zwei ältere.

Instead of repeating an already mentioned (countable) noun after an adjective, we use **one/ones**.
There is no equivalent word in German for one/ones.

▶ Prop-word one/ones: 239

202 The adjective used as a noun

a Our class collected money for the blind (= blind people).
   … die Blinden/Blinde ….

   The disabled have to fight for their rights.
   Die Behinderten/Behinderte …

   The government has devised new measures to help the unemployed.
   … (den) Arbeitslosen …

In contrast to German, only a few English **adjectives** can be used **as nouns**. These adjectives each refer to a group of people with something in common. The *blind* means blind people **in general**, all blind people. These adjectives come **after the**. They **cannot have a plural -s**, but we use them with a **verb in the plural**. Such adjectives include:

the blind	die Blinden
the dead	die Toten
the deaf	die Gehörlosen
the disabled	die Behinderten
the gifted	die Hochbegabten
the homeless	die Obdachlosen
the hungry	die Hungernden
the lonely	die Einsamen
the old	die Alten
the poor	die Armen
the rich	die Reichen
the sick	die Kranken
the strong	die Starken
the unemployed	die Arbeitslosen
the weak	die Schwachen
the young	die Jungen, die junge Generation

b I helped the two blind men across the street.
   … den beiden Blinden/den beiden blinden Männern …

   The sick woman was taken to hospital.
   Die Kranke/Die kranke Frau …

   Several unemployed people were arguing with their local MP.
   Mehrere Arbeitslose/arbeitslose Leute …

When we talk about **one individual person** or about a group of **several individual people**, in English the adjective must be followed by a noun such as *girl(s), boy(s), woman/women, man/men, person(s)* or *people*.

c Discrimination against blacks (= black people) is still common.
   The Conservatives lost the elections.

Adjectives such as **black, white, native, Catholic, Protestant** and **Conservative** have become 'real nouns' and so have a plural form with -s.

d You must learn to take the good with the bad.
   … das Gute mit dem Schlechten …

   The good thing about school is that you can meet your friends there.
   Das Gute …

   The bad thing about school is that you have to learn a lot of unnecessary things.
   Das Schlimme …

The + adjective does not always refer to a group of people. It can have a **general, abstract meaning**.

When we talk about something **specific**, we have to use *thing*.

The adverb

203-216

203 Adjectives and adverbs in contrast
204 Kinds of adverbs
205-208 Forms
209 Adverbs or adjectives after certain verbs
210-213 Comparison
214-215 Position
216 English verbal expressions for German adverbs

203 Adjectives and adverbs in contrast

a **Adjective:**

Mrs Blair is a careful driver.
    … eine vorsichtige Fahrerin.

He was nervous before the English test.
Er war nervös …

An **adjective** tells us what someone or something is like. It modifies a **noun** (e.g. *driver*) or a **pronoun** (e.g. *he*).

b **Adverb:**

Mrs Blair drives carefully, especially at night.
    … fährt vorsichtig …

Dave is extremely nervous before tests.
    … äußerst nervös.

The school band played very well.
    … sehr gut.

We had quite a lot of rain last week.
    … ziemlich viel …

Pete was late. Fortunately, the bus was late too.
    … Glücklicherweise war der Bus auch zu spät.

An **adverb** can modify

• a **verb**

• an **adjective**

• another **adverb**

• a **quantifier**

• or a **whole sentence**.

'Don't be alarmed*, folks. … He's completely harmless unless something startles* him.'

alarmed beunruhigt
startle erschrecken

204 Kinds of adverbs

Adverbs can be divided into a number of different types, according to how we **use** them:

Speak *clearly* and *slowly* at the interview.
My stomach's aching *terribly*.

- **Adverbs of manner** tell us how something happens. They often modify a verb.

Do you like it *here*?
Why didn't you go *there*?

- **Adverbs of place** refer to a place or a direction.

The next train leaves very *soon*.
What's the date *today*?

- **Adverbs of time** refer to a point of time or a period of time.

I *often* visit museums.
I *usually* go to karate class after school.

- **Adverbs of frequency** tell us how often something happens.

David Lodge's new novel is *very* good.
Kim did *rather* badly in the maths test.

- **Adverbs of degree** can strengthen the meaning of other words (e.g. *very good*), or they can weaken it (e.g. *rather badly*).

My dad gets up early *even* at weekends.
I *only* got here five minutes ago.

- **Focusing adverbs** relate to a word or phrase.

Unfortunately, our best player was injured.
I like your new sweatshirt. – Oh, *really*?

- **Sentence adverbs** modify a whole sentence.

I want to say two things. *Firstly*, behave yourselves.
And *secondly*, I hope you'll have a great time.

- **Linking adverbs** join sentences together.

Sharon loved parties. After what Ian had said to her, *however*, she didn't feel like going to this party.

Note

We felt *kind of* sorry for him.
Er tat uns irgendwie Leid.
I *sort of* thought you wouldn't come back.
Eigentlich dachte ich, du würdest nicht zurückkommen.

In informal English *kind of* or *sort of* can mean the same as German *irgendwie* or *eigentlich*.

205 Forms

We can also group adverbs according to their **form**:

nervously, usually, happily, simply, …

- adverbs which are **formed from adjectives** (by adding *-ly*)
  ▶ 206

fast, hard, early, late, long, daily, …

- adverbs which have the **same form as adjectives**
  ▶ 207

always, often, now, then, still, sometimes, soon, today, there, up, down, perhaps, …

- '**natural**' adverbs, i.e. adverbs not formed from adjectives,

in the evening, next week, two days ago, in the street, near Miami, to the shop, at 10.25, every Tuesday …

- **adverbial phrases**.

206 The formation of adverbs from adjectives

a

adjective	adverb
slow	slowly
clever	cleverly
surprising	surprisingly

To form an adverb from an adjective, we **add -ly** to the adjective.

b

adjective	adverb
angry	angrily
happy	happily
exception:	
shy	shyly

There are some **special points** to note:

- When an adjective ends with *-y*, we replace *-y* with *-i-*.

probable	probably
terrible	terribly

- When an adjective ends with a consonant + *-le*, we replace **-le** with **-ly**.

fantastic	fantastically
basic	basically
exception:	
public	publicly

- When an adjective ends with **-ic**, we add **-ally**.

dull	dully
full	fully

- To the adjectives *full* and *dull*, we just add **-y**.

whole	wholly
due	duly
true	truly

- From the adjectives *whole*, *due* and *true* we form the adverbs **wholly**, **duly** and **truly**.

friendly	in a friendly way
silly	in a silly manner

- When an adjective ends in **-ly** (e.g. *friendly, lively, lovely, silly, ugly*), we use an adverbial phrase with **in a(n) … way/manner**.

good	well

- *Good* corresponds to the adverb **well**.

⚠️ Jane is well again.
Jane ist wieder gesund.

Well can **also** be an **adjective** meaning *healthy*.

Notes

1 Please, don't talk so loud/loudly.
Debbie eats quick/quickly.

In informal English, the *-ly* ending can be left off some adverbs. They include *cheaply, loudly, quickly, slowly* and *tightly*.

2 It just worked out good/well, didn't it?
Our new teacher is a real/really nice woman.

In informal American English, *good* is often used as an adverb instead of *well*. *Real* is also often used instead of *really* when it relates to an adjective.

207 Adverbs with the form of adjectives

adjective	adverb
I like the early morning.	We left the party early.
Bob is a fast runner.	Don't drive so fast.
Sandra was late again.	Sandra always arrives late.
Jump over! The wall's low enough.	The plane flew really low.

Some adverbs have the **same form as** the equivalent **adjectives**. They include:

close	dicht, nahe
daily	täglich
deep	tief
early	früh
fair	fair, gerecht
far	weit
fast	schnell
free	frei; kostenlos
hard	hart; schwer
high	hoch
late	spät
long	lang(e)
low	niedrig
right	richtig
wide	weit, breit
wrong	falsch

'Have you been waiting here long?'

Patent Office Patentamt

208 Adverbs with two forms

Some adverbs have **two forms**, one without the *-ly* ending and one with *-ly*. These two forms have different meanings.

adverb without -ly	adverb with -ly
Play fair or don't play at all. … fair …	It was fairly late when the Masons arrived. … ziemlich …
Children under two fly free on all airlines. … frei/kostenlos …	Dogs can run around freely in the park. … frei/ungehindert …
We had to work hard for the exams. … hart/schwer …	I can hardly believe Leo's story. … kaum …
Jump as high as you can. … hoch …	That was a highly amusing film. … höchst/sehr …
Jake woke up late. … spät …	Kate has been doing better at school lately. … in letzter Zeit …
I like watching TV most of all. … am meisten.	We mostly stay at home at the weekend. … meistens …
Don't go too near. … nahe (heran) …	Miss White nearly had an accident. … fast/beinahe …
Laura is a pretty clever girl. … ziemlich …	The little girls were dressed very prettily for Ann's wedding. … hübsch …
I'll try to do it right this time. … richtig …	The workers rightly refused to work longer. … zu Recht …
You've written the number down wrong. … falsch …	He was wrongly accused of theft. … zu Unrecht …

The adverb 146 Adverbs or adjectives after certain verbs

209 Adverbs or adjectives after certain verbs

a You seem tired. (= You are tired.)
Du scheinst müde zu sein.
Emma looks excited. (= Emma is excited.)
Emma sieht aufgeregt aus.
Everybody felt relaxed. (= Everybody was relaxed.)
Jeder fühlte sich entspannt.

After a verb which expresses a **state** or a **quality**, we **use an adjective**, not an adverb. Such verbs can be replaced with *be*.

The weather is getting better.
Das Wetter wird besser.
Internet shopping is becoming more and more popular.
Das Einkaufen im Internet wird immer beliebter.

We also **use an adjective**, not an adverb, after verbs which express a **change of state**. Such verbs mean the same as the German *werden*.

b

We can use either an adverb or an adjective after the verbs *feel, look, smell, sound* and *taste*.

It was so dark that we had to feel our way carefully along the wall.
…, dass wir uns vorsichtig an der Wand entlang tasten mussten.

We **use an adverb** when we talk about an **action**.

Ben felt ill after the test.
Ben fühlte sich nach dem Test schlecht.

We **use an adjective** when we talk about a **state** or a **quality**.

▶ State verbs: 70
▶ Activity verbs: 69

210 Comparison

Sorry, I couldn't come earlier.
Es tut mir Leid, ich konnte nicht früher kommen.
The Hilton is the most conveniently situated hotel.
Das Hilton ist das am günstigsten gelegene Hotel.

In English the **comparative forms** of adverbs are used only occasionally; the **superlative forms** are not often used at all.

211 Regular comparison

a

	comparative	superlative
fast	faster [-ə]	fastest [-ɪst]
hard	harder	hardest
early	earlier	earliest

We form the **comparative and superlative** of adverbs in the same way as we do with adjectives.

One-syllable adverbs and *early* form the comparative and superlative with **-er/-est**.

b

| strongly | more strongly | most strongly |
| nervously | more nervously | most nervously |

Adverbs ending with **-ly** form the comparative and superlative with **more/most**.

▶ Comparison of adjectives: 197

Note

	comparative	superlative
cheaply/cheap	more cheaply/cheaper	most cheaply/cheapest
loudly/loud	more loudly/louder	most loudly/loudest

Adverbs such as *cheaply, loudly, quickly,* etc., which can be used informally without *-ly*, have two different sets of comparative and superlative forms.

The adverb 147 **Comparison**

212 Irregular comparison

	comparative	superlative
well	better	best
badly	worse [wɜːs]	worst [wɜːst]
far	farther/further	farthest/furthest
much	more	most
(a) little	less	least

The adverbs *well*, *badly*, *far*, *much* and *(a) little* have **irregular comparative and superlative forms**.

▶ Irregular comparison of adjectives: 198

'I'm learning how to relax, doctor – but I want to relax better and faster! I WANT TO BE ON THE CUTTING EDGE* OF RELAXATION!'

on the cutting edge of sth.   an vorderster Front von etw.

213 Sentences with comparisons

a   Mum drives just as badly as Dad, in my opinion.
      … (genau)so schlecht wie …
   Tim doesn't take life as seriously as Ben.
            … nicht so ernst wie …
   Serena plays tennis more aggressively than her sister.
               … aggressiver als …
   Of the four girls, Vanessa dresses (the) most attractively.
            … am schönsten/hübschesten/besten …

As with an adjective, there are different ways of expressing a **comparison** with an adverb.

b   1 a My brother plays chess as well as me.
   b My brother plays chess as well as I do.
                  … wie ich.
   2 a The dog can jump higher than us.
   b The dog can jump higher than we can.
                  … als wir.

In comparisons we normally use the **object form of the personal pronoun**: *me*, *him*, *her*, *us* and *them* (examples 1a and 2a).
We can also use the subject form of the personal pronoun + verb (examples 1b and 2b).

▶ Subject and object form of the personal pronoun: 227 a

c   The carousel went faster and faster.
         … immer schneller.
   Peter is behaving more and more strangely these days.
         … immer seltsamer.

When two comparatives are linked by *and*, this expresses a **gradual increase**: in German *immer schneller*, *immer seltsamer*.

d   The more quietly she spoke, the more carefully we listened.
   Je leiser …, desto/umso aufmerksamer …
   The sooner you come the better.
   Je eher …,   desto/umso besser.

The German *je – desto* or *je – umso* is equivalent to the English *the – the*.

▶ Comparison of adjectives: 200

Position

> **214** *Summary*

Adverbs can come in **various places** in the sentence. There are basically three positions:

front-position		mid-position		end-position
adverb	subject (+ auxiliary)	adverb	main verb (+ object)	adverb

a **Front-position:**

adverb	subject			
Suddenly	the car	stopped.		The adverb comes **before the subject**.

b **Mid-position:**

subject	adverb	main verb		
The sun	always	rises	in the east.	The adverb comes **between the subject and the main verb**.

subject	be	adverb		
Christopher	is	often	nervous before a test.	The adverb comes **after a form of *be***.

subject	auxiliary	adverb		
You	can	always	ask me.	If there is an auxiliary verb, the adverb comes **after the (first) auxiliary**.
The money	has	never	been found.	
Tom	doesn't	usually	come late.	

c **End-position:**

	main verb	object	adverb	
I	shouted		angrily.	The adverb comes **after the main verb (+ object)**.
Tina	opened	the door	quietly.	

Mein Bruder putzt nie sein Zimmer.
not: My brother cleans never his room.
but: My brother never cleans his room.

Meine Cousine spricht gut Französisch.
not: My cousin speaks well French.
but: My cousin speaks French well.

In English the adverb does **not** come **between the main verb and the (direct) object**.

215 The position of the various types of adverbs

a Front-position:

Unfortunately, it turned rather cold.
Luckily, we had our anoraks with us.

I don't like Latin. In fact, I hate it.
… Finally, I would like to say …

These adverbs usually go in front-position:

- **sentence adverbs** such as *maybe, perhaps, of course, hopefully, (un)fortunately, luckily* and *obviously*, which express the speaker's attitude to the content of the sentence,

- **linking adverbs** such as *at first, then, in fact, finally* and *however*.

b Mid-position:

We soon found Jill's house.
Uncle Jack has just phoned.

We always go to the disco on Saturdays.
There are often adverts for part-time jobs in the local newspaper.

These adverbs usually go in mid-position:

- some (short) adverbs of **indefinite time** such as *soon, now, just, still, ever* and *already*

- adverbs of **indefinite frequency** such as *always, often, usually, sometimes, rarely* and *never*.

c End-position:

Helen draws and paints beautifully.
The guide answered the questions politely.

John and Pat have gone to live abroad.
I'm meeting my boyfriend at the station.

Craig sold his motorbike yesterday.
We moved here from Dover two years ago.

I've been to San Francisco twice.
Our theatre group meets every Friday.

These adverbs usually go in end-position:

- adverbs of **manner** such as *beautifully, carefully, politely, quickly, quietly* and *well*

- adverbs of **place** such as *here, there, abroad, everywhere, in/to London* and *at the station*

- adverbs of **definite time** such as *yesterday, on May 1st, in 1989* and *two years ago*

- adverbs of **definite frequency** such as *once, twice* and *daily* and **phrases of frequency** such as *several times, every Friday* and *most evenings*.

> **Note**
>
> 1 The guide answered the questions politely.
> 2 The guide politely answered the questions.

Adverbs of manner usually go in end-position. But they can go in mid-position if they do not need to be especially emphasized. The word *politely* in example 2 (mid-position) has less weight than it does in example 1 (end-position).

d More than one adverb in end-position:

	manner	place	time
Jason is flying		to New York	tomorrow.
Gina acted	strangely	at the party	last night.

If there is more than one adverb in end-position in a sentence, the word order is usually **manner – place – time**.

e The position of adverbs of degree:

Your new camera looks very expensive.
The biology homework was too difficult.
Todd really believes he'll be famous one day.

Adverbs of degree usually come directly before the word they relate to. These adverbs include *very, hardly, just, nearly, quite, rather, really* and *too* (= *zu*).

f   **The position of focusing adverbs:**

I'm only having a cup of tea.
Nicola loves cycling – she even cycles in the rain.
We decided on a holiday only at the last moment.
Even taxi drivers have difficulty in finding the place.

Focusing adverbs such as *also, even, only, mainly* and *mostly* go in mid-position or directly before the word they emphasize.

g   **Changes to the usual order:**

We usually spend Easter at home. Sometimes we go to my aunt's.

I didn't feel very well yesterday. But today I'm fine.

Where did you see Matthew? – I saw him yesterday at the club.

If an adverb does **not** come **in the usual position** in a sentence, this is often because it needs special emphasis or because it is used to link two sentences in a text.

> **Note**
>
> Are you going to Steve's party? – Definitely.
>   … – Bestimmt.
> A speed limit ought to be imposed here. – Exactly.
>   … – Richtig/Genau.
> I've never smoked in my life. – Honestly?
>   … – Ehrlich?

We can also use an adverb as a one-word statement or question, especially in spoken English.

216 *English verbal expressions for German adverbs*

Kelly likes skiing, and she also enjoys snowboarding.
Kelly läuft gern Ski und sie fährt auch gern Snowboard.

Roger prefers cycling to walking.
Roger fährt lieber Rad, als dass er läuft.

Sheila hates walking.
Sheila geht sehr ungern/überhaupt nicht gern zu Fuß.

Laura keeps falling for the wrong guys.
Laura verliebt sich immer in die falschen Typen.

Go on reading, please.
Lies bitte weiter!

Liz used to collect telephone cards.
Liz hat früher Telefonkarten gesammelt.

I hope to see you before you go on holiday.
Hoffentlich sehe ich Sie noch, ehe Sie in Urlaub fahren.

Where's Sandra? – At home, I suppose. She seems to have left early.
Wo ist Sandra? – Vermutlich zu Hause. Sie ist anscheinend schon früh gegangen.

Did Ranjit happen to be at the concert?
War Ranjit zufällig im Konzert?

A German adverb often corresponds to a **verbal expression** in English.

'Arlen keeps bragging* about running 26 miles. What he fails* to tell people is that it took him eight months to do it.'

brag angeben
fail (hier) versäumen

Quantifiers

217-225

217 Introduction
218 *Some* and *any*
219 *A lot of/Lots of*, *much*, *many*, *(a) little* and *(a) few*
220 *Every*, *each* and *any*
221 *All*
222 *Both*, *either* and *neither*
223 *No* and *none*
224-225 Compounds with *some*, *any*, *every* and *no*

217 Introduction

a Some teenagers were waiting for the bus.
There aren't any free seats.
We made lots of new friends on holiday.
Two members of the group were late.

Some, any, lots of, etc. are **quantifiers**.
Cardinal numbers (e.g. *one, two, three,* etc.) are also quantifiers.

b

	countable noun singular	countable noun plural	uncountable noun
some		some boys	some water
any	any boy	any boys	any water
a lot of/lots of		a lot of/lots of boys	a lot of/lots of water
much			much water
many		many boys	
(a) little			(a) little water
(a) few		(a) few boys	
every	every boy		
each	each boy		
all		all boys	all water
both		both boys	
either	either boy		
neither	neither boy		
no	no boy	no boys	no water

When we put a quantifier before a noun, we use it as a **determiner**. The table shows the possible uses of quantifiers with countable and uncountable nouns. Further information can be found in the sections below on the individual quantifiers.

'Haven't you brought any vegetables with it?'

c 1 I need some money. Can you lend me some?
2 We have two video recorders. Both are broken at the moment.
3 I've only eaten a few of these biscuits – they're full of calories.

When we use a quantifier without a noun (examples 1 and 2), we use it as a **pronoun**. A quantifier can also come before an *of*-phrase (example 3).

 I've read every book on that shelf.
There were no guests in the restaurant.

Every and ***no*** are **always** used **with a noun** and cannot come before an *of*-phrase.

None of the tourists gave the guide a tip.

None cannot be used with a noun. It can only come before an *of*-phrase.

d There's somebody at the door.
I can't see anyone behind the counter.
Everything is so tidy. What a surprise!
The kids have nowhere to go in the evening.

Some, *any*, *every* and *no* can form **compounds** with *-body*, *-one*, *-thing* and *-where*.

▶ Compounds with *some*, *any*, *every* and *no*: 224

218 Some *and* any

a I need some new clothes.
    … einige/ein paar …
We haven't had any rain here for two weeks.
    … keinen Regen …

Some and *any* often express an **indefinite amount** or **number**.

Note

Are there some [səm] apples left?
    … einige/ein paar Äpfel …?
Some [sʌm] schools have their own Web sites.
Einige (aber nicht alle) Schulen …

When *some* is unstressed, we pronounce it [səm].

When we want to emphasize *some*, we pronounce it [sʌm].

b There's some butter in the fridge.
    … (etwas) Butter …
There are some onions too.
    … (einige/ein paar) Zwiebeln.
Is there any milk left? – Well, I can't see any.
… noch (etwas) Milch …?   *… keine …*
And we haven't got any tomatoes.
    … keine Tomaten.

We use **some** and **any**:
- with **uncountable nouns** like *butter*, *milk*, *sugar*, *time*, *music*, etc.
- with **nouns in the plural**.

Note that *some* and *any* (in questions) often have no German equivalents.

c I'll get some money from my savings account.
    … (etwas) Geld …
Dave is helping some friends.
    … (einigen/ein paar) Freunden.

We use **some** mainly in **positive statements**.

We didn't have any free time.
    … keine Freizeit.
Are there any buses after midnight?
    … Busse?

We use **any** mainly in **negative statements** and in **questions**.

▶ *Every*, *each* and *any*: 220 b

Notes

1 If you need some/any small change for the machine, I've got a pocket full.

In a subordinate clause with *if*, we can use either *some* or *any*.

2 Our teacher never gives us any hints before a test.
There are hardly any clean cups in the cupboard.

In a positive statement *any* is used after words with a negative or restrictive meaning, e.g. *never* or *hardly*.

Quantifiers 153 *A lot of/Lots of, much, many, (a) little and (a) few*

d   Could you give me some help?
(= Please give me some help.)

Would you like some sandwiches?
(= Have some sandwiches.)

Did you get some computer magazines?
(= I expect you got some computer magazines.)

Some (not *any*) is used in **offers** and **requests**.
Some is also used in **questions** which expect the answer '**yes**'.

> **Notes**
>
> **1** Some official is supposed to be opening the new building.
>   *Irgendein Beamter …*
>
> **2** There were some hundred people on board the ferry.
>   *… ungefähr hundert Menschen …*

Some before a countable noun in the singular can mean an unknown person or thing.

Some before a number means *about*, in German: *ungefähr* or *etwa*.

e   You can choose any book you like.
    … jedes (= jedes beliebige) Buch …

Any in a **positive statement** means the same as German *jeder* (= *jeder beliebige …*).

▶ Compounds with *some* and *any*: 224 a/b
▶ *Somebody, anybody*, etc. + *they/them/their*: 225 a

'some' mainly in positive statements
'any' mainly in negative statements and in questions

219   A lot of/Lots of, much, many, (a) little *and* (a) few

a   We've got a lot of/lots of time before the train leaves.
    … viel Zeit …
We need a lot of/lots of bananas.
    … viele Bananen.

There's a lot/lots to do.
    … viel …

We use **a lot of** or **lots of** (= *viel, viele*)
• with **uncountable nouns** like *butter, sugar, time, music*, etc.
• with **nouns in the plural**.
Lots of is used mainly in informal English.

When there is no noun or pronoun, we leave out *of*.

b   Move up, please. We haven't got much room.
    … nicht viel Platz.
How much money do we need? – Not much.
Wie viel Geld …? – Nicht viel.

There weren't many mistakes in your test.
    … nicht viele Fehler …
How many Metallica CDs have you got? – Not very many.
Wie viele Metallica-CDs …? – Nicht sehr viele.

We use **much** (= *viel*) only with **uncountable nouns**.

We use **many** (= *viele*) only with **nouns in the plural**.

c | I haven't got much time to spare.
How many stars can you count? | We use **much** and **many** mainly in **negative statements** and in **questions**.

We get a lot of rain here.
Lots of fans were queuing for the concert. | In a **positive statement** *a lot of* or **lots of** is more usual.

There are too many people in the swimming-pool.
There was so much traffic that we were late. | After *too, so, as, very* and *how* we always use *much* or *many*.

> **Note**
>
> The project cost a great deal of money.
> There's no rush. We've got masses of time.

There are other expressions that we can use instead of *a lot of/lots of, much* and *many*. They are *a large number of, a great deal of* and *a large/huge amount of*. In informal English we also use *masses of, heaps of, tons of, miles of* and *millions of*.

d | Could I have a little sugar?
    … ein wenig/ein bisschen/etwas Zucker …? | We use **a little** (= *ein wenig, ein bisschen, etwas*) only with **uncountable nouns**.

We had lots of food, but I only ate a little.
    … ein wenig/ein bisschen …

The teacher asked us a few questions.
    … ein paar/einige Fragen … | We use **a few** (= *ein paar, einige*) only with **nouns in the plural**.

> **Notes**
>
> **1** A handful of people were arrested.
> You've got a bit of oil on your shirt.
>
> **2** There were less cars on the road than last Sunday.

Other expressions for *a little* and *a few* are *several, a handful of, a small amount of* and *a bit of* (informal).

Less (= *weniger*) is the comparative form of *a little*. In informal English we can use it with countable nouns in the plural, although in more formal contexts it is used only with uncountable nouns.

e | There was little time for discussion.
Few fans can afford the best seats. | **Little** and **few** (without *a*) expressing a small quantity are **rather formal**.

There was only a little/not much cake left.
Only a few/Not many of my friends helped me. | In informal English we normally use *only a little/only a few* or *not much/not many*.

f		comparative	superlative
much } many } a lot of }	more	most
(a) little	less	least
(a) few	fewer	fewest

Much, many, a lot of and *(a) little* have **irregular comparative and superlative forms**.

(A) few has regular comparative and superlative forms.

'much' and 'a little' + uncountable nouns
'many' and 'a few' + nouns in the plural

220 Every, each *and* any

a Every/Each child had to take three tests.
Jedes Kind …

Every child enjoys watching cartoons.
Jedes Kind (= Alle Kinder im Allgemeinen) …

Each runner has her own number.
Jede Läuferin (= Jede einzelne Läuferin) …

Every and *each* both mean *all*. They are used like the German *jeder*. They are often interchangeable. But remember:
- We use **every** to mean *all* in a very **general sense**.
- We use **each** when we are thinking of **all the individual people or things**. There is usually a definite number of them.

 There are ten runners and each has her own number.
Each of the runners has her own number.

We can **only** use **each** (and not *every*) **on its own** or **before an *of*-phrase**.

> **Note**
>
> The doctor had to look at the patient every 30 minutes.
> Almost every student had a good test result.
> Practically every applicant had excellent qualifications.

In combination with numbers and with words like *almost*, *nearly* and *practically* we use *every* (and not *each*).

b All the buses that pass our house go to the station. So you can take any bus.
… jeden (= jeden beliebigen/irgendeinen) Bus …

Think of a number. Choose any number between one and fifty.
… irgendeine Zahl …

We use **any** to mean 'it doesn't matter which'. The equivalent in German is **jeder beliebige …** or **irgendein …**

 We aren't doing anything this week. You can come any day.
… an jedem beliebigen Tag …

I take the dog out every day.
… jeden Tag …

Any day means *Monday* **or** *Tuesday* **or** *Wednesday*, etc.

Every day means *Monday* **and** *Tuesday* **and** *Wednesday*, etc.

▶ *Some* and *any*: 218
▶ Compounds with *any* and *every*: 224 a-c
▶ *Somebody, anybody*, etc. + *they/them/their*: 225

'every …' = *'jeder, alle'* …
'each …' = *'jeder einzelne'* …
'any …' = *'jeder beliebige'* …

221 All

a **All trees** need sunlight.
Alle Bäume …

All of us love parties. / **We all** love parties.
Wir alle …

We've spent **all our money**.
… unser ganzes Geld/all unser Geld …

Not **all water** is suitable for drinking.
Nicht alles Wasser …

Lara was ill. She had to stay in bed **all day**.
… den ganzen Tag …

b Last October **all the trees in the park** still had leaves.
… alle Bäume im Park …
What are **all these people** doing here?
… alle diese Leute …?
Jenny has drunk **all the cola**.
… die ganze Cola …

All + **noun in the plural** means the same as the German *alle* …

All + **singular noun** means the same as the German *ganzer* … or *all* …
Some expressions with *all* are:
all day	den ganzen Tag
all morning	den ganzen Morgen
all week	die ganze Woche
all the time	die ganze Zeit

If we talk about something **definite** (e.g. *the trees in the park*, not trees in general), then **all** must be followed by the **definite article** *the* or by some other determiner (e.g. *this, these, my*, etc.). *The* is used in the same way as it would be used without *all*.

'I hacked into the school's computer and changed all my grades. Then the school hacked into my computer and deleted* all my games!'

delete zerstören

 Alle waren glücklich.
not: ~~All were~~ happy.
but: **Everybody** was happy.

Alles war in Ordnung.
not: ~~All~~ was OK.
but: **Everything** was OK.

The German *alle* and *alles* are usually equivalent to English **everybody** and **everything** and not *all*.

Notes

1 **All our guests** were late. /
All of our guests were late.
All of them were late.

2 The guests have **all** arrived now.

Before a determiner + noun *all* and *all of* are equally possible. In American English *all of* is more usual. Before a personal pronoun (e.g. *them*) we must use *all of*.

All can go in mid-position, like an adverb.

▶ Mid-position of adverbs: 214 b

222 Both, either *and* neither

a Both children play the piano. /
Both (of) the children play the piano.
Beide Kinder/Die beiden Kinder …

Both of us like 'The Simpsons'. /
We both like 'The Simpsons'.
Wir beide …

Kate has got two brothers. Both live in New York.
… Beide…

Both means **the one and the other**. It is equivalent to the German *beide*.

 Ich kenne die beiden Männer.
not: I know the both men.
but: I know both (of) the men.

In contrast to German, **both** comes before the definite article or other determiner.

b Either team could win. They are equally good.
Jedes Team (= Das eine oder das andere Team) …

Look carefully. Have you seen either of these men before?
… einen dieser (beiden) Männer …

Both these jackets cost under a hundred pounds. You can have either for your birthday.
… eine (von beiden) …

Either [ˈaɪðə] means **the one or the other**. It is equivalent to the German *jeder* or *einer von zweien*.

> **Note**
>
> The shops on either side of the street are expensive. /
> The shops on both sides of the street are expensive.

There are some contexts where we can use *both* or *either*.

c Neither of the two boys spoke Italian.
Keiner der zwei Jungen/Keiner von beiden Jungen …
– Did either of the two boys speak French?
– No, neither (of them).
   …, keiner von beiden.

Neither girl knew what to do next.
Keines der beiden Mädchen …

Neither [ˈnaɪðə] means **not the one and not the other**. It is equivalent to the German *keiner von zweien*.

> **Note**
>
> The committee found neither of the two candidates acceptable.
> I watched both the videos, but I didn't like either of them.

In informal English we often use *not … either* instead of *neither*.

Quantifiers 158 *No* and *none*

223 No *and* none

a The children had no money to buy a present.
   ... kein Geld ...

There is no bank in our village.
   ... keine Bank ...

There are no tourists here in winter.
   ... keine Touristen ...

No means **not any** and is the equivalent of the German *kein*. It comes **before a noun**.

b There are no buses after midnight.
(= There aren't any buses after midnight.)

No has a **stronger** negative meaning than *not any*. This is also true for compounds with *no*.

▶ Compounds with *no*: 224 d
▶ *Somebody, anybody*, etc. + *they/them/their*: 225 a

c None of my friends wanted to stay.
   Keiner meiner Freunde/Keiner von meinen Freunden ...

We can't have tea – there's none (= no tea) left.
   ... es gibt keinen mehr.

None [nʌn] means **not a single one** and is the equivalent of the German *keiner*. We use it before an *of*-phrase or when we do not want to repeat a noun.

 keiner meiner Brüder
not: no of my brothers
but: none of my brothers

224 Compounds with some, any, every and no

We can form **compounds** with *some, any, every* and *no*.

a There's somebody/someone at the door.
    … jemand …
  I want something to eat.
    … etwas …
  Shandy must be somewhere in the garden.
    … irgendwo …
  I didn't know anybody/anyone at the barbecue.
    … niemanden …
  We haven't heard anything about the accident.
    … nichts …
  Can you see my glasses anywhere?
    … irgendwo …

The compounds with **some** and **any** are:

somebody/someone	jemand
something	etwas
somewhere	irgendwo(hin)
anybody/anyone	(irgend)jemand
anything	(irgend)etwas
anywhere	irgendwo(hin)
not … anybody/anyone	niemand, keiner
not … anything	nichts
not … anywhere	nirgends, nirgendwo(hin)

The rules about *some* and *any* apply also to compounds with *some* and *any*.

b Anybody can tell you where the station is.
  Jeder (Beliebige) …

  I'm very hungry – I'll eat anything.
    … *alles (egal was)*.

We can form the following compounds from **any** meaning *jeder beliebige* …:

anybody/anyone	jeder Beliebige
anything	alles
anywhere	überall(hin)

c Everybody relaxed after the long journey.
  Jeder/Alle …

  Did you really look everywhere?
    … *überall* …?

The compounds with **every** are:

everybody/everyone	jeder, alle
everything	alles
everywhere	überall(hin)

d Nobody/No one came to visit me.
  Niemand/Keiner …
  I've had nothing to eat since breakfast.
    … *nichts* …
  These poor people have nowhere to live.
    … *nirgendwo* …

The compounds with **no** are:

nobody/no one	niemand, keiner
nothing [ˈnʌθɪŋ]	nichts
nowhere	nirgends, nirgendwo(hin)

225 Somebody, anybody, *etc.* + they/them/their

a Someone has parked their (= his or her) car behind mine.

  Do you know anybody who has been on an exchange to Paris? When did you see them (= him or her) last?

  Everybody said where they (= he or she) came from.

  Nobody wants to help, do they (= he or she)?

After *someone, anybody*, etc., the **verb is in the singular**. But **personal pronouns** and **possessive determiners** and **pronouns** relating to *someone*, etc. are often **plural**: **they, them** and **their**. This avoids having to say whether we are talking about males or females.

b Every/Each child had their (= his or her) own present.

In informal English, after **every** and **each** we often use **their** instead of *his or her*.

Pronouns

226-239 Pronouns

226 Introduction	235-236 The emphasizing pronoun
227-229 The personal pronoun	237-238 The demonstrative determiner and the demonstrative pronoun
230-231 The possessive determiner and the possessive pronoun	239 The prop-word *one*
232-234 The reflexive pronoun	

226 Introduction

She and *I* went to the same school.
These aren't my CDs, *they* are *yours*.
I hurt *myself* with a hammer.

She, *I*, *they*, *yours* and *myself* are **pronouns**.

▶ Relative pronouns: 258 a
▶ Quantifiers used as pronouns: 217 c
▶ *Who*, *whose*, *which* and *what* used as question words: 241 b

The personal pronoun

227 Forms

a

		subject form		object form	
singular		I	ich	me	mir, mich
		you	du; Sie	you	dir, dich; Ihnen, Sie
		he	er	him	ihm, ihn
		she	sie	her	ihr, sie
		it	es; er; sie	it	ihm, es; ihm, ihn; ihr, sie
plural		we	wir	us	uns
		you	ihr; Sie	you	euch; Ihnen, Sie
		they	sie	them	ihnen, sie

Personal pronouns in English have two forms: the **subject form** and the **object form**.

> **Note**
>
> Can *you all* come over here?
> I've got a job for *you two*.
> Do *you guys* want to come with us or not?
> What are *you lot* doing here?

We can add a word to make clear that *you* refers to more than one person.

b   Please *phone me* or *send me* a postcard.
           … *mich* …   … *mir* …
Well, we're going – *with you* or *without you*.
           … – *mit dir oder ohne dich.*

We use the object form of a personal pronoun after a verb or after a preposition. In contrast to German, there is **only one object form** in English.

Pronouns 161 **The personal pronoun**

Ask Jody. She's my friend. You can always ask her.
Frag Jody. Sie ist meine Freundin. Du kannst sie immer fragen.

Where are the boys? – They're here. I've seen them.
Wo sind die Jungen? – Sie sind hier. Ich habe sie gesehen.

Are you Mrs Barber? Here's a letter for you.
Sind Sie Mrs Barber? Hier ist ein Brief für Sie.

Is that your new bag? It's fantastic.
Ist das deine neue Tasche? Sie ist fantastisch.

Note the various English equivalents of the **German sie/Sie**.

c Who plays table tennis? – Me.
                   … – I do.
                   … – *Ich.*

Tim's sister is as tall as him.
           … as he is.
           … *wie er.*

Don't panic. It's only us.
           … *Wir sinds nur.*

In **short answers** (without a verb), in **comparisons** and after a form of **be**, we often use the **object form** (e.g. *me, him, us*). We can also use the subject form + verb (e.g. *I do, he is*).

▶ Short answers: 8c
▶ Comparisons: 200b, 213b

228 Some uses of it

a Don't sit on that chair. It's wet.
          … *den Stuhl. Er …*
I've got an idea, but you won't like it.
     … eine Idee, …   … sie …
What happened to the window? – It's broken.
              … dem Fenster …? – Es …

We use *it* when we talk about **things** and **ideas**. In German *er, sie* or *es* is used, depending on the (grammatical) gender.

b Sally has got a new cat. It's sweet.
I saw the horse. It was standing by the gate.

This is my dog. He's called Shep.
I've got a cat. She's very fat.

We use *it* for **animals** with which we have no personal connection.

If we have a personal connection to an animal (e.g. a pet), we use *he* or *she*.

c There's someone at the door. It might be your brother.
                   … *Es könnte dein Bruder sein.*
Who is that? – It's Mike. / It's Tom and Sally.
           … *– Es ist Mike. / Es sind Tom und Sally.*

We use *it* + **a form of *be*** when we 'identify' someone, i.e. when we say who the person is. In German we use *es*.

There's someone at the door. He's got green hair.
                … *Er hat grüne Haare.*
Who is Mrs Benson? – She's our new teacher.
           … *– Sie ist unsere neue Lehrerin.*

In all other cases we use *he* or *she* for a person.

▶ There is/are = *es ist/sind, es gibt*: 52

229   The German *man*

a   You can't have everything.
Man kann nicht alles haben.

One should look after oneself.
Man sollte sich um sich selbst kümmern.

We can use **you** and **one** when we talk about people in general. The speaker is included. *One* is formal.

b   They speak a strange dialect in this area.
Man spricht einen seltsamen Dialekt in dieser Gegend.

They're going to build a new leisure centre.
Man hat vor/Sie haben vor, ein neues Freizeitzentrum zu bauen.

They has a less general meaning than *you* and *one* and refers to specific groups, e.g. *the people in this area* or *the authorities*.

They say (= People say) that the new headmaster is going to bring in a lot of changes.
Man sagt (= Die Leute sagen), dass der neue Direktor eine Menge von Veränderungen bewirken wird.

A common expression is **they say** (= *people say*).

c   Nothing could be done.
Man konnte nichts machen.

A German sentence with *man* sometimes corresponds to a **passive sentence** in English.

▶ Prop-word *one*: 239

The possessive determiner and the possessive pronoun

230   Forms

	possessive determiner		possessive pronoun	
singular	my	mein	mine	meiner
	your	dein; Ihr	yours	deiner; Ihrer
	his	sein	his	seiner
	her	ihr	hers	ihrer
	its	sein, ihr	—	—
plural	our	unser	ours	unserer
	your	euer; Ihr	yours	eurer; Ihrer
	their	ihr	theirs	ihrer

Is that your car, Mrs Ashton?
Ist das Ihr Auto, Mrs Ashton?

Susan is 14 and her brother is nine.
Susan ist 14 und ihr Bruder ist neun.

The Carters haven't paid for their new house yet.
Die Carters haben ihr neues Haus noch nicht bezahlt.

Note the various English equivalents of the **German ihr/Ihr**.

Look at that cat. What's the matter with its foot?
It's nice to have a pet.

its = *sein, ihr*
it's = *it is*

Pronouns | **163** | **The possessive determiner and the possessive pronoun**

231 Use

a

possessive determiner	possessive pronoun
Is this your pen, Rita?	No, Sue, it's yours.
… dein Füller, …?	… deiner.
Trish has done her work.	Lisa hasn't done hers.
… ihre Arbeit …	… ihre …
We're looking for our dog.	Whose is this? – It's ours.
… unseren Hund.	… unserer.

The **possessive determiners** *my*, *your*, *his*, *her*, etc. always come **before a noun** and are therefore also called possessive adjectives.
The **possessive pronouns** *mine*, *yours*, *his*, *hers*, etc. are used **on their own**, i.e. without a noun. We use them to avoid repeating a noun we have already mentioned.

b I saw it with my own eyes.
　　　　　… mit meinen eigenen Augen …
Most students bring their own sandwiches.
　　　　　　　　… ihr eigenes Brot …

My, *your*, *his*, *her*, etc. can be **emphasized** by the use of **own**.

⚠ *Ich hätte so gern eine eigene Wohnung.*
not: I'd love to have an own flat.
but: I'd love to have a flat of my own.

Er hat keine eigenen Ideen.
not: He's got no own ideas.
but: He's got no ideas of his own.

When *own* comes in the same phrase as the indefinite article, *no*, a number or other determiners, then *my own*, *your own*, *his own*, etc. must come in an **of-phrase** after the noun.

c I've broken my right leg.
Ich habe mir das rechte Bein gebrochen.
Take off your shoes, please.
Zieh bitte die Schuhe aus!
Several people lost their lives in the explosion.
Mehrere Menschen verloren bei der Explosion ihr Leben.
The news of their deaths was broadcast immediately.
Die Nachricht von ihrem Tod wurde sofort verbreitet.

In contrast to German, English uses a **possessive determiner** (*my*, *your*, *his*, *her*, etc.) with **parts of the body**, **items of clothing** and with certain other nouns such as *life*, *mind* and *death*. These nouns are usually plural when we are talking about more than one person.

d Lynn has always been a friend of mine.
　　　　　(= … one of my friends.)
　　　　　　… eine Freundin von mir …

Mr Walker is a neighbour of ours.
　　　(= … one of our neighbours.)
　　　　　… ein Nachbar von uns.

The **possessive pronouns** *mine*, *yours*, *his*, etc. can be used **in an of-phrase**, e.g. when we talk about one among a number of friends or neighbours.

⚠ *Das ist eine gute Idee von dir.*
not: That's a good idea of you.
but: That's a good idea of yours.

▶ *Of*-phrase: 180

'My, your, his, her, …' before a noun
'Mine, yours, his, hers, …' on their own

The reflexive pronoun

232 Forms

singular	(I)	myself	mir, mich
	(you)	yourself	dir, dich; sich
	(he)	himself	sich
	(she)	herself	sich
	(it)	itself	sich
	(one)	oneself	sich
plural	(we)	ourselves	uns
	(you)	yourselves	euch; sich
	(they)	themselves	sich

The **stress** is on the second syllable of a reflexive pronoun: *myself* [-'-], *yourself* [-'-], etc.

The **plural** pronouns end with *-selves* [-selvz].

233 Use

a I cut myself with a breadknife.
Ich habe mich mit einem Brotmesser geschnitten.

Jane is teaching herself Italian.
Jane bringt sich Italienisch bei.

My grandparents can look after themselves.
Meine Großeltern können sich selbst versorgen.

A reflexive pronoun (e.g. *myself, herself, themselves*) **refers to the subject** of the sentence (e.g. *I, Jane, my grandparents*). The word *reflexive* means 'looking back'. The pronoun refers to the same person (or thing) as the subject.

Some common expressions are:
Enjoy yourself/	Viel Spaß! Amüsier dich/
yourselves.	Amüsiert euch gut!
Help yourself/	Greif zu! Bedien dich! /
yourselves.	Bedienen Sie sich!
I did it by myself.	*Ich habe es allein gemacht.*

Notes

1 Everybody was happy except me/myself.
  ... *außer mir.*

2 My boyfriend and I/myself were late.
  ... *ich ...*

After *as, than, like, but* (= *außer*) and *except*, we can use either a personal pronoun or a reflexive pronoun.

Sometimes *myself* is used instead of *I*.

⚠ **Compare:**
Jim hurt himself. (reflexive pronoun)
Jim hat sich (selbst) verletzt.

Jim hurt him. (personal pronoun)
Jim hat ihn verletzt.

Note the difference between a **reflexive pronoun** and a **personal pronoun**.

Pronouns **165** **The reflexive pronoun**

b

I wish I could afford that red sweatshirt.
Ich wünschte, ich könnte mir das rote Sweatshirt leisten.

We complained about the food.
Wir beschwerten uns über das Essen.

Turn off the TV and concentrate on your work.
Mach den Fernseher aus und konzentriere dich auf deine Arbeit!

I can't imagine living in the country.
Ich kann mir nicht vorstellen, auf dem Land zu leben.

Don't move.
Beweg dich nicht!

The article refers to the novel.
Der Artikel bezieht sich auf den Roman.

Do you remember our last trip to Mexico?
Erinnerst du dich an unsere letzte Reise nach Mexiko?

I wonder why Margo hasn't phoned.
Ich frage mich, warum Margo nicht angerufen hat.

There are many reflexive verbs in German whose **English** equivalents are **not reflexive**. They include:

afford	sich leisten
apologize	sich entschuldigen
argue	sich streiten
change	sich (ver)ändern
complain	sich beschweren
concentrate on	sich konzentrieren auf
feel	sich fühlen
hide	sich verstecken
hurry (up)	sich beeilen
imagine	sich (etw.) vorstellen
lie down	sich hinlegen
look forward to	sich freuen auf
meet	sich treffen
move	sich bewegen
open	sich öffnen
refer to	sich beziehen auf
relax	sich entspannen
rely on	sich verlassen auf
remember	sich erinnern, sich merken
rest	sich ausruhen
sit down	sich (hin)setzen
turn round	sich umdrehen
wonder	sich fragen
worry	sich Sorgen machen

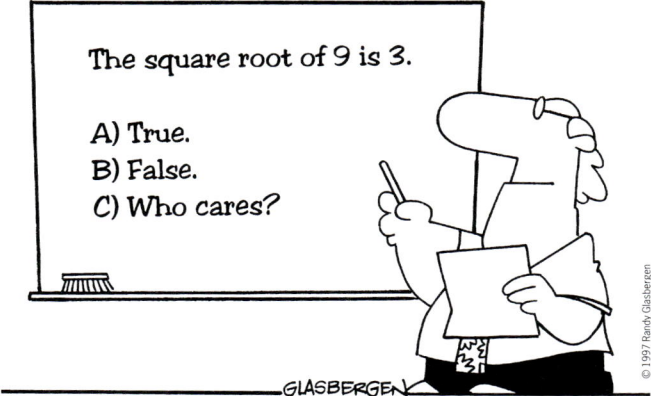

Many students actually look forward to Mr Atwadder's math tests.

square root Quadratwurzel

 I can't remember where I put the key.
Ich kann mich nicht erinnern, …

Remind me to buy some new drum sticks.
Erinnere mich daran, …

Remember means *sich (= sich selbst) erinnern*.

Remind means *jemanden (= jemand anderes) erinnern*.

Pronouns | **166** | **The emphasizing pronoun**

234 Each other/One another

Bob and Liz help each other with their homework.
Bob und Liz helfen sich (= sich gegenseitig, einander) bei den Hausaufgaben.

Do you send each other/one another Christmas cards?
Schickt ihr euch (= euch gegenseitig, einander) Weihnachtskarten?

We use **each other/one another** to express a **two-way relationship** between two or more people.

The girls are laughing at themselves. | The girls are laughing at each other.

⚠ *Amy und Dave gaben sich gegenseitig die Schuld, den Streit angefangen zu haben.*
not: Amy and Dave blamed ~~themselves~~ for starting the quarrel.
but: Amy and Dave blamed each other for starting the quarrel.

'myself, yourself, …': looking back to the subject
'each other/one another …': a two-way relationship

The emphasizing pronoun

235 Forms

myself, yourself, himself, …

Emphasizing pronouns have the **same form as the reflexive pronouns**.

236 Use

We spoke to the President himself.
Wir haben mit dem Präsidenten selbst gesprochen.

I myself saw the accident.
Ich habe den Unfall selbst/selber gesehen.

I saw the accident myself.
We can't help you. We're strangers here ourselves.

An emphasizing pronoun lays **special emphasis** on a **noun** (e.g. *the President*) or a **pronoun** (e.g. *I*). It usually comes **after** the word it emphasizes. The pronoun is always stressed.
The German equivalent of an emphasizing pronoun is *selbst* or *selber*.
If we lay **emphasis** on the **subject**, the emphasizing pronoun can also come at the **end of the sentence**.

⚠
emphasizing
I saw the accident myself.
I saw the accident.

reflexive
I hurt myself.

Unlike the reflexive pronoun, the **emphasizing pronoun** can be **left out**.

The demonstrative determiner and the demonstrative pronoun

237 *Forms*

singular	plural
this [ðɪs]	these [ðiːz]
that [ðæt]	those [ðəʊz]

238 *Use*

a

This car is expensive. But those cars are cheaper.
Dieses Auto (hier) ...   ... jene Autos /die Autos dort ...

This is a Japanese car. Those are German cars.
Dies ist ...   Das (dort) sind ...
What's this/that? – It's a new computer game.
   ... das? – ...

This, that, these and those can be used in different ways:
- as **demonstrative determiners**, i.e. together with a noun,
- or as **demonstrative pronouns**, i.e. on their own.

b

'I like these coloured shirts (here).'
Coloured shirts are very popular this summer.

This and **these** generally refer to something **near** the speaker (in space or time).

'What about those pullovers (over there)?'
Lucy wore one of them at that disco last week.

That and **those** refer to something **further away** from the speaker (in space or time).

Some common expressions are:
Is that Valerie? (BE)	Ist dort/Spreche ich mit
Is this Valerie? (AE)	Valerie? (on the telephone)
this morning	heute Morgen
these days	heutzutage
in those days	damals, zu jener Zeit
that's why	deshalb, darum

c   This/That is a nice photo.

This and **that** are often **interchangeable**.

Pronouns | **168** | **The prop-word** *one*

d I haven't done any revision. That's what's worrying me.
      … Das ist es, was mich beunruhigt.

Tell me this. Who's going to do all the work?
Sag mir Folgendes. …

We can use **this** or (more often) **that** to refer to something **just said**.

We use **this** to refer to something we are **going to say**.

⚠ Who's this/that? – It's Peter and Sally.
What are these/those? – They're computer disks.

A question which contains *this, that, these* or *those* is normally **answered** in a sentence beginning with ***it*** or ***they***.

'this, that' + singular
'these, those' + plural

internal (hier) innerbetrieblich

239 *The prop-word* one

a This video shop isn't as good as the one in our street.
Diese Videothek ist nicht so gut wie die in unserer Straße.

These T-shirts are nice. What about a green one?
– Oh, I like the blue ones best.
… Wie wäre es mit einem grünen? – Oh, ich mag die blauen am liebsten.

One (plural: *ones*) is called the **prop-word**. We use it to avoid repeating a (countable) noun (e.g. *video shop, T-shirts*) that we have already mentioned.

 That's my car – the one with the red doors.
                       … – das mit den roten Türen.
Which pen do you want? – The blue one.
                       … – Den blauen.

In contrast to German, we **cannot** use the **definite article** or an **adjective on its own**.

b The green shirt is the most expensive (one).
LPs have been around for a long time. The first (ones) were made in 1948.

I think this poster is nicer than that (one).
There were five dogs, each (one) had its own food bowl.

We have all these colours. Which (one) would you like?

We can **leave out** *one/ones* after
• a superlative adjective
• an ordinal number

• a demonstrative determiner
• *each, any, another, either* or *neither*

• *which*.

Question words

240-245

240 Introduction
241 Summary
242 Who
243 Who and which
244 What and which
245 Fixed phrases with question words

240 Introduction

Who are those people over there?
When does our plane leave?
Can you let me use the phone first?

We can form a question either with a **question word** like *who* or *when* or without a question word.

241 Summary

a Who saw the boxing match last night? – Me.
Who did you see at the party? – All my friends.

Who (= *wer, wem, wen*) asks about people.

Whose mobile phone is this? – It's Lucy's.
Whose band won the competition? – Nick's.

Whose (= *wessen*) asks about possession or belonging (Whose is …? = Wem gehört …?).

What did you eat? – A pizza.
What are you doing? – I'm writing an e-mail.

What (= *was, was für*) asks about things or about actions and events, etc.

Which bus goes to the town centre? – Number two.
Which doctor did you see? – Dr Brown.

Which (= *welcher*) asks about things or people.

When did you phone? – Shortly after ten.

When (= *wann*) asks about a point of time or a period of time.

Where's Robert? – In the garage.
Where are you going? – To the supermarket.

Where (= *wo, wohin*) asks about place or direction.

Why can't you come? – I'm too busy.

Why (= *warum, weshalb*) asks about the reason for something.

How did you sleep? – Very well, thank you.
How tall are you? – One metre eighty-five.

How (= *wie*) asks about manner or extent.

▶ Word order in questions: 5, 6

⚠ Who's (= Who is) there? – The postman.
Wer ist …? – …
Whose parents can't come? – Mine.
Wessen…? – …

Who's (= *wer ist*) should not be confused with **whose** (= *wessen*).

> **Note**
>
> What pupil would do a thing like this?
>
> We can also use *what* + noun to ask about people.

b What did you read?   What book did you read?
Which did you like best?   Which film did you like best?
Whose is this CD?   Whose CD is this?

Who did you see?

What, **which** and **whose** can be used **on their own** (as pronouns), or they can be determiners (**before a noun**).

Who is used **on its own**, i.e. without a noun.

Question words | **170** | *Who, who* and *which*

242 Who

a 1 **Who** phoned you last night? – **Nicole** did.
(= **Nicole** phoned me.)
Wer …? – …

2 **Who** did you phone last night? – Nicole.
(= I phoned **Nicole**.)
Wen …? – …

Who can ask about the **subject** (example 1) or about the **object** (example 2) of a sentence.

Earl hates his answerphone*.

anyhow (hier) schon
answerphone Anrufbeantworter

b **Who** could we ask? – We could ask **Mrs Larson**.
Wen …? – …

Whom could we consult on this question? – We could consult **Mrs Larson**.
Wen …? – …

In **questions about the object**, we can sometimes use **whom** (= *wem, wen*) instead of *who*. *Whom* is used in formal English.

c **Who** did you **buy** this **for**?
Für wen …?

For whom were these goods purchased?
Für wen wurden diese Waren erworben?

When a **preposition** relates to **who**, the preposition usually comes immediately after the verb.

But when the **preposition** relates to **whom**, then the preposition usually comes before the question word.

243 Who *and* which

a **Who** scored the goal? – **Louise** did.
Wer …? – …

Who did you tell about the burglary? – **Helen**.
Wem …? – …

Who did you meet at the party? – **Carla**.
Wen …? – …

To ask about **people**, we normally use **who** (= *wer, wem, wen*).

b

Which girl scored the goal? – Louise did.
Welches Mädchen …? – …

Which of the girls scored the goal? – Louise.
Welches von den Mädchen …? – …

We also use **which** in questions about **people**, but only:

- before a noun

- before an *of*-phrase.

▶ *Who* and *which* in relative clauses: 260, 261, 265 b/c, 266

⚠ *Wer von euch …?*
not: ~~Who~~ of you …?
but: **Which** of you …?

Question words | **171** | **What and which**

244 What *and* which

a What are your favourite colours?
   Was/Welche …?

   What shampoo do you use?
   Was für ein/Welches Shampoo …?

We normally use **what** when we ask about **things** which are among an **unlimited** number.

b Which colour would you like? Red, blue or green?
   Welche Farbe/Was für eine Farbe …? …

   Which way do we go at the crossroads?
   Welchen Weg…?

   Which do you prefer? Cola or orange juice?
   Was…? …

We normally use **which** when we ask about **things** which are among a **limited** number.

c What bus are we going to take?
   or:
   Which bus are we going to take?

   What newspaper do you read?
   or:
   Which newspaper do you read?

What and **which** are sometimes **interchangeable**.

 Which of these colours would you like?

Before an **of-phrase** we can **only** use **which**.

'what' with an unlimited choice of answers
'which' with a limited choice of answers

'What's my favourite book?
How about Death of a Salesman?'*

annual jährlich
Death of a Salesman 'Tod eines Handlungsreisenden'.
                       Drama von Arthur Miller

245 Fixed phrases with question words

Question words are frequently used in **fixed phrases**:

What time is it?	Wie viel Uhr/Wie spät ist es?
What size are you?	Wie groß bist du/sind Sie? / Welche Größe hast du/haben Sie?
What colour is the car/…?	Welche Farbe hat das Auto/…?
What do you call …?	Wie heißt …?
What's the weather like?	Wie ist das Wetter?
What's the matter?	Was ist los?
What's that for?	Wofür ist das?
What did you do that for?	Warum hast du/haben Sie das (denn) gemacht?
What's that to you?	Was geht dich/Sie das an?
What about/How about a cup of tea/…?	Wie wäre es mit einer Tasse Tee/…?
Why not ask Sam/…?	Warum fragst du/fragen Sie nicht Sam/…?
Why not come with us?	Warum kommst du/kommen Sie nicht mit uns mit?
How are you? – Fine, thank you.	Wie geht es dir/Ihnen? – …
How do you do? – How do you do? (formell)	Freut mich (, Sie kennen zu lernen). – Ganz meinerseits. / Angenehm.
How so? / How's that? / How come?	Wieso? / Wie kommt das? / Wieso das?
How are things at school/…?	Wie läuft es in der Schule/…?
How do you know?	Woher weißt du/wissen Sie das?
How much is the shirt/…?	Wie viel kostet das Hemd/…?

'Lunch on Tuesday? I won't be free. How about Thursday week*?'

Thursday week Donnerstag in einer Woche

 Was für ein hübsches Geschenk!
not: ~~What for~~ a nice present.
but: What a nice present.

Prepositions

246-250

246 Forms and functions
247 Meanings
248 Frequent prepositions of place and direction
249 Phrases of time with *at*, *in* and *on*
250 Fixed phrases with prepositions

246 Forms and functions

a   Dan told his father about the match.
    According to the forecast, it'll rain tomorrow.
    The bus in front of us stopped suddenly.

    The first telephone was made in the USA.
    We arrived on Sunday.
    Because of the snow all the trains were late.

A **preposition** can consist of a single word or of more than one word.

Prepositions express different kinds of meanings:
- **place**
- **time**
- **other** meanings, e.g. reason.

b   in Scotland   in Schottland   (spatial)
    in 1999   (im Jahr) 1999   (temporal)
    rich in oil   reich an Öl   (figurative)

We can often use a **preposition** in **different ways**, and prepositions often have both literal and figurative meanings.

   Compare:
   Can you see Nicole in the picture?
                ... auf dem Bild ...?
   I think I should put you in the picture.
                ... ins Bild setzen.
   (= explain the situation)

c   Sue went to France.
    There was someone in front of me.
    Check the tyres before going on a long journey.

A preposition usually comes **before**
- a **noun**
- a **pronoun**
- an **-ing form**.

d   Who are you looking for?
    I wonder what Sarah is interested in.
    The girl I was travelling with spoke Italian.
    Mr Carter needs someone to talk to.
    Last week our flat was broken into.

A preposition comes at the **end** of
- a **question** with *who*, *what*, *where*, etc.
- an **indirect question**
- a **relative clause**
- an **infinitive construction**
- a **passive sentence**.

e   Did you believe in ghosts as a child?
    I'm not really interested in punk rock.
    What's the difference between a present participle and a gerund?

A preposition can also combine **with the previous word**:
- **verb** + preposition (prepositional verb)
- **adjective** + preposition
- **noun** + preposition.

▶ Prepositional verbs: 164, 167

247 Meanings

The following list gives the **most frequent meanings** of the prepositions. Other meanings can be found in a dictionary.

about

Can you give me that book about flowers?	… über Blumen …
I'm phoning about the party.	… wegen der Party …
We walked about the town for a couple of hours.	… in der Stadt herum.
concerned about	besorgt um
enthusiastic about	begeistert von
hear about	von/über … hören

above

We were flying above the clouds.	… über den/oberhalb der Wolken.
Jeff's marks in maths are above average.	… über dem Durchschnitt.
A general is above a major in the army.	… über einem Major …

⚠ above – over (= über)

I've stuck two posters above/over my bed.

Dave jumped over the wall and ran away.

Children over twelve pay full price on all airlines.

It's cold today, only two degrees above zero.

Above and **over** can often be used **interchangeably**.
But when we describe motion, we can only use *over*.
We use *over* with numbers or when we talk about someone's age or about a period of time.
We use *above* with measurements.

▶ over: 247

according to

Everything went according to our plan.	… nach/gemäß unserem Plan.
According to the test results, the project should be a success.	Den Testergebnissen zufolge …

across

The man walked across the street to the other side.	… über die Straße …
Two girls sat across the table from Ian.	… Ian gegenüber am Tisch.

after

We went swimming after breakfast.	… nach dem Frühstück …
Don't bang the door after you when you leave!	… hinter dir …
The policewoman ran after the thief.	… hinter dem Dieb her.
C comes after B in the alphabet.	… nach B … (in a sequence)

against

A boy was kicking a football against the wall.	… an/gegen die Mauer.
The majority were against my suggestion.	… gegen meinen Vorschlag.
You ought to protect the plants against frost.	… vor Frost …
German salaries are high (as) against those of other EU countries.	… gegenüber denen anderer EU-Länder.

ahead of

You'll see the castle directly ahead of you.
As many other historical figures, Galilei was punished because he was ahead of his time.

… vor dir …
… seiner Zeit voraus …

along

A boat was going along the canal.

… den Kanal entlang.

among

I feel happier among friends.
Dover is among Britain's oldest ports.

… unter/zusammen mit Freunden.
… zählt zu den ältesten Hafenstädten …

 ## among – between (= *zwischen, unter*)

I found this book among some old papers in the attic.

Among relates to a **group** of people or things.

Peter sat between Mary and Kathy.
There isn't much cake, so divide it between the three of you.

Between relates to **two** people or things. But it can also refer to several people or things if we are thinking of each individual person or each individual thing.

▶ between: 247

apart from

Apart from his nose, Mr Penn is quite good-looking.

Abgesehen von seiner Nase …

around

We sat around the table.
The tourists walked around the lake.

… um den Tisch (herum).
… um den See (herum).

at

The bus stopped at the church.
My aunt works at a bank.
Frank is at Bob's (house).
Fred got up at eight o'clock.
She looked at me but I didn't react.
Dave can shoot a hole in a Cola can at 50 metres.
    at breakfast
    at home
    at a party
    at … miles an hour
    at night
    at school
    at the baker's
    at the moment
    clever at
    good at

… an der Kirche …
… bei/in einer Bank.
… bei Bob.
… um acht Uhr …
… mich an/zu mir her, …
… aus 50 Metern Entfernung …
    beim Frühstück
    zu Hause
    auf einer Party
    mit … Meilen pro Stunde
    nachts, bei Nacht
    in der Schule
    beim Bäcker
    im Augenblick
    geschickt bei/in
    gut in

because of

Bob stayed at home because of the storm.

… wegen des Sturms …

Prepositions 176 **Meanings**

before

I don't go to bed before eleven.
B comes before C in the alphabet.

… vor elf …
… vor C … (in a sequence)

 ## before – in front of *(= vor)*

Don't park your motorbike in front of the neighbours' house.
I usually get up before my sister.
The prince knelt before the throne.

In front of expresses **place**; **before** expresses **time** or sequence.

In formal English, **before** can also express place.

▶ in front of: 247

behind

We've got a little garden behind our house.

… hinter unserem Haus.

below

Please do not write below this line.

… unter diese/unterhalb (von) dieser Zeile …

beside

When I'm doing my homework, I put my mobile on the table beside me.

… neben mich …

 ## beside – besides

I was sitting beside Sharon on the sofa.
I haven't got a real friend besides (= except) you.

Beside (= *next to*) expresses place (German: **neben**); **besides** (= *except*) means the same as German **außer**.

besides

There are many rivers in England besides the Thames.

… außer/neben der Themse.

between

A van was parked between the two cars.
I'm usually free between ten and twelve.
Tim and Jane will settle their quarrel between them. Don't interfere.

… zwischen den beiden Autos …
… zwischen zehn und zwölf.
… unter sich …

▶ among: 247

beyond

Innsbruck lies just beyond the mountains on the right.
That's far beyond your abilities.

… jenseits der Berge …
… über deine Fähigkeiten hinaus.

by

I wouldn't like a house by a river.
The thief was arrested by the police.
The town was destroyed by an earthquake.
Is the house heated by gas or by oil?
Sally goes to school by bus.
Can you repair the camera by tomorrow?
The army attacked the camp by night.
Officials are paid by the month.

… (nahe) bei einem Fluss.
… von der Polizei …
… durch ein Erdbeben …
… mit Gas oder Öl …
… mit dem Bus …
… bis morgen …
… während der Nacht.
… pro Monat/monatlich …

close to
Helen waited close to the escalator. … dicht/nahe bei der Rolltreppe.

despite
John swam out too far, despite warnings from his friends. … trotz der Warnungen …

down
Stones rolled down the hill. … den Hügel hinunter/hinab …

due to
The flight was cancelled due to bad weather. … aufgrund/wegen des schlechten Wetters …

during
I often work during the holidays. … während der Ferien.

> ⚠ **During** is a **preposition** and comes before a noun:
> … während der Ferien.
> **While** is a **conjunction** and introduces a subordinate clause:
> …, während ich im Urlaub war.

I met Jane during the holidays.

I met Jane while I was on holiday.

except (for)
The restaurant is open every day except (for) Monday. … außer Montag.

for
Are all these presents for me? … für mich?
We went out for a meal. … zum Essen …
Is this the bus for Glasgow? … nach Glasgow?
Munich is famous for its beer, among other things. … für sein Bier …
What did you get for your birthday? … zu deinem Geburtstag …
I've had this computer for five years. … seit fünf Jahren.
   for joy/fear   aus Freude/Angst
   for pleasure   zum Vergnügen
   for her abilities   wegen ihrer Fähigkeiten

▶ since: 247

from
The flight from London to Berlin was late. … von London nach Berlin …
Has the train from Liverpool arrived? … aus Liverpool …
We're open from nine till six. … von neun bis sechs …
This watch is a present from my parents. … von meinen Eltern.
Steel is made from iron. … aus Eisen …
What conclusions were drawn from the data? … aus den Daten …

from – of *(= von)*

a postcard from New York	*eine Postkarte aus New York*
a postcard of New York	*eine Postkarte von New York* (= with a picture of New York)
	▶ of: 247

in

We saw three lions in a cage.	*… in einem Käfig.*
Which is the biggest city in the world?	*… auf der Welt?*
Bill Morgan left school in 1994.	*… (im Jahr) 1994.*
She jumped in her car and raced off round the corner.	*… in ihr Auto …*
Please, wait here, I'll be back in a minute.	*… in einer Minute/sofort …*
It's an old building, but it's in good repair.	*… in gutem Zustand.*
Barlow is an expert in the field of Indian art.	*… auf dem Gebiet indianischer Kunst.*
Today one in three marriages breaks up.	*… jede dritte Ehe …*
The instructions were given in French.	*… auf Französisch …*
in the country	*auf dem Land*
in town	*in der Stadt*
in the picture	*auf dem Bild/im Bilde*
in the sky	*am Himmel*
in the street (AE: on the street)	*auf der Straße*

in favour of

Are you in favour of commercial TV?	*… für kommerzielles Fernsehen?*

in front of

We couldn't park in front of the hotel.	*… vor dem Hotel …*
	▶ before: 247

inside (AE: inside of)

Are we allowed to take photos inside the museum?	*… im Museum/innerhalb des Museums …*

in spite of

Tim went to work in spite of his headache.	*… trotz seiner Kopfschmerzen …*

instead of

We sometimes drink coffee instead of tea.	*… (an)statt/anstelle von Tee.*

into

Let's go into the house.	*… ins Haus (hinein) …*
Translate the passage into German.	*… ins Deutsche.*

like

I've always wanted a garden like yours.	*… wie deinen.*
You're behaving like children.	*… wie Kinder.*

near

There was a lake near the youth hostel.	*… nahe/bei der Jugendherberge.*
Ashton is a village near Chester.	*… in der Nähe von Chester.*

next to

We live next to the Smiths.	… neben den Smiths.
Next to skiing her favourite sport was skating.	Nach Skifahren …

of

Can you repair the handle of the umbrella?	… den Griff des Schirms …
Our new friends are of Italian descent.	… italienischer Abstammung.
He told us of his travels.	… von seinen Reisen.
The ring was made of gold.	… aus Gold …
Harlem is north of Central Park.	… nördlich des Central Park.
Mrs Lee died of a serious illness.	… an einer schweren Krankheit …
one of my friends	einer meiner Freunde
a kilo of tomatoes	ein Kilo Tomaten
the works of Shakespeare	die Werke Shakespeares
a picture of the Queen	ein Bild der Königin

▶ from: 247

off

The books fell off the shelf.	… vom Regal herunter.
The cat jumped off the garage roof.	… vom Garagendach.

on

Don't sit on the floor.	… auf dem/den Boden.
Who wrote these words on the board?	… an die Tafel …
Look at the picture on page 13.	… auf Seite 13 …
I like lying on the beach.	… am Strand …
London lies on the Thames.	… an der Themse.
Maureen's flat is on the fifth floor.	… in der fünften Etage/im fünften Stock.
We met on the bus/on the train/on the plane to Paris.	… im Bus/im Zug/im Flugzeug …
The meeting was held on Wednesday.	… am Mittwoch …
Did you see the programme on jazz?	… über Jazz …
They lived on bread and water.	… von Wasser und Brot.
on earth	auf der Erde
on foot	zu Fuß
on the left/right (hand side)	links/rechts, auf der linken/rechten Seite
on the phone	am Telefon
on the radio/on TV	im Radio/im Fernsehen
questions on the text	Fragen zum Text

onto

The cat jumped onto the roof.	… auf das Dach.
Everybody cheered when the team ran onto the field.	… auf das Feld …

on top of

Put this CD on top of the others.	… (oben) auf die anderen.
Tom has a good salary and on top of that a company car.	… und noch dazu einen Firmenwagen.

opposite

The bank is opposite the supermarket.	… gegenüber dem/vom Supermarkt.

out of

Mr Black was looking out of the window.	… aus dem Fenster.
My wife is out of town this week.	… nicht in der Stadt.
He did it out of pity.	… aus Mitleid …
20 out of 240 passengers died.	20 von 240 Passagieren …

outside

The class waited outside the museum.	… draußen vor dem Museum.
It's a small village just outside Chester.	… außerhalb von Chester.

'Nobody calls me stupid. Meet me outside the saloon when the big hand* and the little hand are on the 12.'

hand Zeiger

over

Put a cover over the budgie's cage at night.	… über den Vogelkäfig.
There were thick clouds over the airport.	… über dem Flughafen.
They looked over the wall.	… über die Mauer.
My father is over two metres tall.	… über/mehr als zwei Meter …

▶ above: 247

owing to

Owing to heavy rain, the parade was cancelled.	Wegen/Infolge des starken Regens …

past

Walk past the church and then turn right.	… an der Kirche vorbei …
It was five minutes past nine.	… nach neun.
Tom learnt nothing for the history test, so he hardly got past the first question.	… über die erste Frage hinaus.

per

The holiday costs £350 per person per week.	… pro Person die Woche.

round (BE)

The earth moves round the sun.	… um die Sonne (herum).

since

I've known Jane since 1997.	… seit 1997.

 ## since – for *(= seit)*

We've been here since two o'clock.	**since** + point of time
We've been here for two hours.	**for** + period of time

▶ for: 247
▶ Use of *since* and *for* with the present perfect: 84

through

The thief got in through one of the windows.	… durch eines der Fenster …
Through hard work you can reach almost any goal.	Durch harte Arbeit …

throughout

There were strikes throughout the country.	… überall im Land …
It rained throughout the night.	… während der Nacht/die Nacht hindurch …

till/until

The shops are open till/until six.	… bis sechs …
Liz won't be here till/until tomorrow.	… erst morgen/nicht vor morgen …

to

We're going to Spain for our holidays.	… nach Spanien.
Kevin was taken to hospital after his accident.	… ins Krankenhaus …
Mrs Cook drove us to the station.	… zum Bahnhof.
I've never been to Italy before.	… in Italien …
Reg wrote a card to his friend.	… an seinen Freund …
The dog has chewed my shoe to pieces.	… in Stücke …
It's five minutes to nine.	… vor neun.
The key to the door was gone.	… für die/zu der Tür …
Have you got a solution to the problem?	… für das Problem?
a visit to	ein Besuch bei
the answer to	die Antwort auf
welcome to	willkommen in

towards (BE)/toward (AE)

We walked towards the town.	… auf die Stadt zu/in Richtung Stadt …
Please phone me towards the end of the week.	… gegen Ende der Woche …
Our teachers are very friendly towards us.	… zu uns/uns gegenüber.
An important step toward political unity has already been taken.	… zu einer politischen Einheit …

under

The children hid under the bed.	… unter dem Bett …
Do oil pipelines go under the sea?	… unter dem Meer?
It took us under an hour to get there.	… unter einer/weniger als eine Stunde …
Would Britain be better off under the Tories?	… unter den Tories …

unlike

Unlike her brother, Sue was quite ambitious.	*Im Gegensatz zu ihrem Bruder …*
Van Gogh's last paintings are unlike his earlier works.	*… anders als seine früheren Werke.*

up

The old man went up the stairs slowly.	*… die Treppe hinauf.*

up to

Lynn watches TV up to four hours a day.	*… bis zu vier Stunden …*
The woman came up to me and asked the time.	*… auf mich zu …*

via

Bill travelled to Chicago via New York.	*… über New York …*

with

Jock cut the branch with a knife.	*… mit einem Messer …*
We've got a house with a garden.	*… mit Garten.*
Tom lives with his parents.	*… bei seinen Eltern.*
Simon has a good relationship with his boss.	*… zu seinem Chef.*
The injured girl cried with pain.	*… vor Schmerzen …*
angry with	*zornig über*
pleased with	*zufrieden mit*
be fed up with	*es satt haben mit*

within

The girl returned within an hour.	*… innerhalb (von) einer Stunde …*
Some secrets should be kept within the family, don't you think?	*… in/innerhalb der Familie …*

without

The explorers spent two days in the jungle without food.	*… ohne Nahrung …*
He left without saying goodbye.	*…, ohne sich zu verabschieden.*

248 Frequent prepositions of place and direction

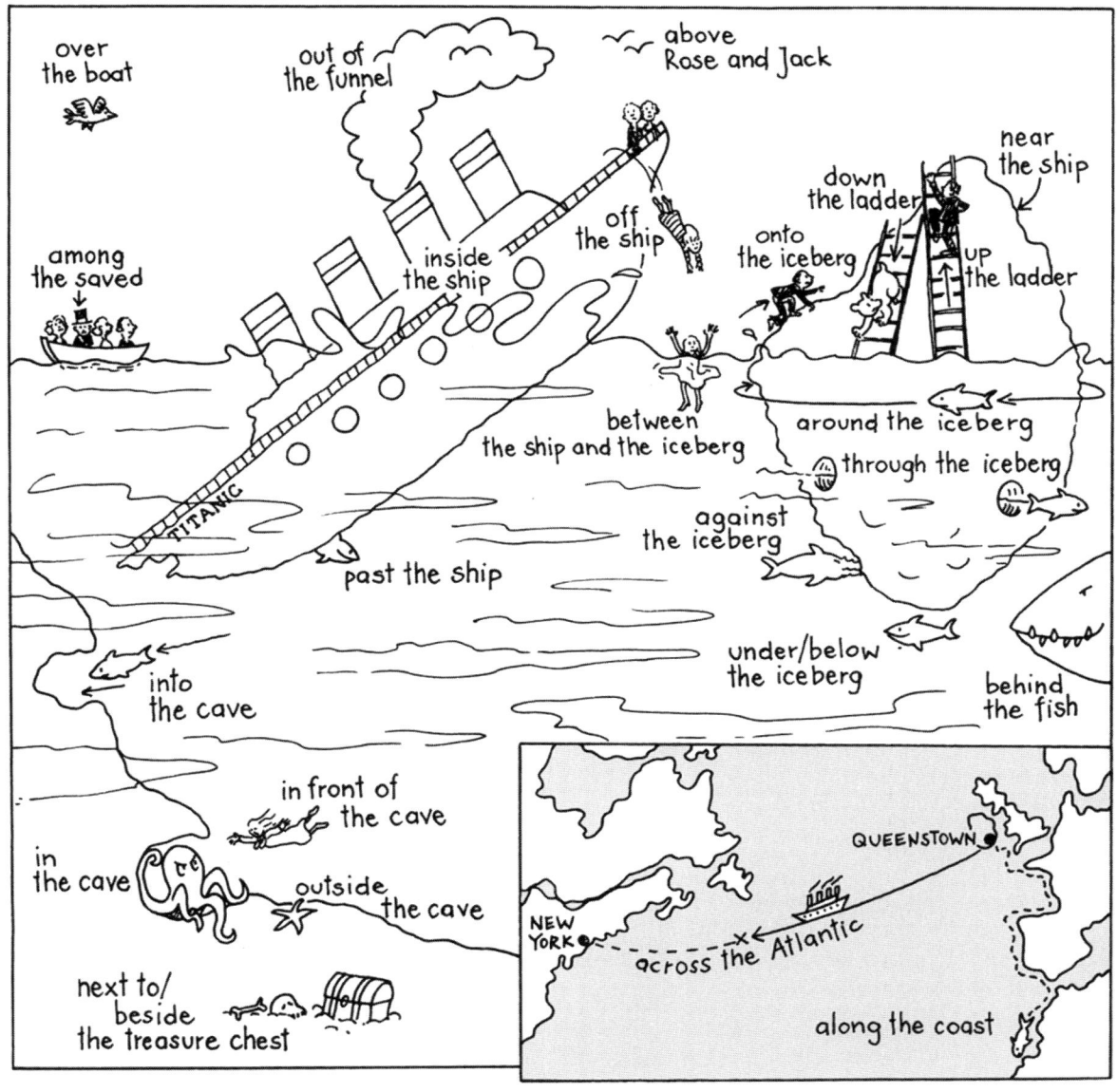

funnel Schornstein
cave Höhle
treasure chest Schatzkiste

Prepositions | **Phrases of time with *at*, *in* and *on***

249 Phrases of time with at, in and on

a

	We use **at**
School starts at eight o'clock. … um acht Uhr.	• with the time of day
I'll see you at lunchtime. … zur Mittagszeit/mittags.	• with meal times
What are you doing at Christmas? … an/zu Weihnachten?	• with holiday times such as Christmas, Easter, etc.
I visited my aunt at (AE: on) the weekend. … am Wochenende … At night most people are asleep. In der Nacht/Nachts … I'm very busy at the moment. … im Moment/zurzeit. Elvis Presley died at the age of 42. … im Alter von 42 Jahren/mit 42 …	• in some fixed expressions.

b

	We use **in**
My birthday is in April. … im April. We always go to France in (the) summer. … im Sommer. It didn't rain much in 1992. … (im Jahr) 1992 …	• with longer periods of time
I can't work well in the morning. … am Morgen/morgens … I work best in the evening. … am Abend/abends …	• with unspecific times of day (exception: *at night*).

c

	We use **on**
The next meeting will be on Tuesday afternoon. … am Dienstagnachmittag. It was on a cold morning last winter. … an einem kalten Morgen …	• when we say which part of which day
Let's meet on Wednesday. … am Mittwoch … My birthday is on April 2nd. … am 2. April.	• with days and dates.

⚠️ We met last Monday.
… (am) letzten Montag …
I phoned my girlfriend every evening.
… an jedem Abend/jeden Abend …

We do **not** use **at, in** or **on** before phrases of time with *last, next, this* or *every*.

'I forgot to make a back-up copy of my brain, so everything I learned last semester was lost.'

250 Fixed phrases with prepositions

The following list contains some frequent **phrases** with prepositions.

be about to do sth.	im Begriff sein, etwas zu tun
How/What about …?	Wie wäre es mit …?
above all	vor allem
after all	schließlich, immerhin
at last	endlich
at first	zuerst, zunächst
at least	mindestens, wenigstens
(not) at all	überhaupt (nicht)
at the age of	im Alter von
be behind time	Verspätung haben
be behind sb./sth.	hinter jd./etwas zurück sein
be beside oneself with joy/anger/…	außer sich sein vor Freude/Zorn/…
for a change	zur Abwechslung
for a long time	lange Zeit
for example	zum Beispiel
for heaven's sake	um Himmels willen
for sale	zu verkaufen, zum Verkauf
for sure	sicherlich, gewiss
What's for lunch?	Was gibt es zum Mittagessen?
What did you do that for?	Warum/Wozu hast du das getan?
for all that	trotz allem
for this reason	aus diesem Grund
in case	für den Fall, dass
have in common	gemeinsam haben
in fact	tatsächlich
in general	im Allgemeinen
in particular	besonders
in the end	schließlich
in the long run	auf Dauer
in those days	damals
in a hurry	in Eile
in my opinion	meiner Meinung nach
in principle	im Prinzip
in your own words	mit eigenen Worten
in a loud voice	mit lauter Stimme
in different ways	auf verschiedene Weise
I'm really into computers.	Ich bin Computerfan.
on his/her own	allein
on the other hand	andererseits
on holiday	im Urlaub
be onto sb.	jd. auf der Spur sein
over and above that	darüber hinaus
to my surprise	zu meiner Überraschung

Complex sentences | **Conditional sentences**

251-280 Complex sentences

A **complex sentence** is formed when we combine a main clause with a subordinate clause. The most important kinds of subordinate clause are:

If you hurry, you'll catch the bus.
Most people who move house suffer some degree of stress.
We arrived at the cinema after the film had started.

▶ Main clauses and subordinate clauses: 15, 16

- ***if*-clauses** in conditional sentences ▶ 251-257
- **relative clauses** ▶ 258-266
- **adverbial clauses**. ▶ 257-272

251-257 Conditional sentences

251 Introduction
252 Conditional sentence I
253 Conditional sentence II
254 Conditional sentence III
255 Mixed types
256 Omission of *if* + inversion
257 Shortened clauses

251 Introduction

a If Pam calls, I'll give her her CDs back.
Wenn Pam vorbeikommt, gebe ich ihr ihre CDs zurück.

Jessie would phone if she wasn't so busy.
Jessie würde anrufen, wenn sie nicht so viel zu tun hätte.

A conditional sentence consists of a **subordinate clause with *if*** and a **main clause**.
The *if*-clause expresses a **condition**. The main clause expresses the **consequence**, what happens if the condition is fulfilled.

b
if-clause	main clause
If Pat calls this afternoon, *Wenn/Falls Pat heute Nachmittag anruft,*	I'll ask her to supper. *werde ich sie fragen, ob sie mit mir zu Abend essen möchte.*
If you have done your work, *Wenn/Falls du deine Arbeit getan hast,*	you can go to the disco. *kannst du in die Disko gehen.*
If I earned more, *Wenn ich mehr Geld verdiente/verdienen würde,*	I could go out more. *könnte ich mehr ausgehen.*
If you had phoned me last night, *Wenn du mich letzte Nacht angerufen hättest,*	I would have given you Andy's new number. *hätte ich dir Andys Nummer gegeben.*

There are two kinds of conditions:

- **real** or **open conditions**: The condition is **fulfilled** or **can be fulfilled**. We see it as **possible** that the condition will be fulfilled. (Conditional sentence I) ▶ 252

- **unreal conditions**: The condition **cannot be fulfilled** or will **very probably not be fulfilled**. It is only **theoretically possible** that it will be fulfilled. (Conditional sentence II) ▶ 253

  The condition relates to the past. It **can no longer be fulfilled**. (Conditional sentence III) ▶ 254

The choice of **verb forms** depends on the **kind of conditional sentence** we are using.

	main clause	if-clause	
c	We'll stay at home	if it rains this afternoon.	The **if-clause** can also come **after the main clause**. In this case we do not usually use a comma in English.

d You can't use the computer unless you know the password.
…, außer wenn du das Password kennst.
Take some sandwiches in case there's nothing to eat on the train.
…, für den Fall, dass es im Zug nichts zu essen geben sollte.
You can borrow my notes as long as you don't lose them.
…, solange/sofern du sie nicht verlierst.
Supposing you win, what will you do with the prize money?
Angenommen, du gewinnst, …

The subordinate clause is usually introduced by *if* (= wenn/falls). We can also use the **conjunctions** *unless* (= wenn nicht, außer wenn), *in case* (= falls; wenn; für den Fall, dass), *as long as* (= solange, sofern), *suppose/ supposing* (= angenommen).

 If I'm in London next week, I'll visit you.
Wenn/Falls ich nächste Woche in London sein sollte, …

When I'm in London next week, I'll visit you.
Wenn/Sobald ich nächste Woche in London bin, …

If (= wenn, falls) introduces a subordinate **conditional clause**.

When (= wenn, sobald) introduces a subordinate **clause of time**.

252 Conditional sentence I

	if-clause	main clause	
a	1 If you book your flight early, Wenn du deinen Flug früh buchst, (It is possible that you will book your flight early.)	you'll get it cheaper. bekommst du ihn billiger.	A conditional sentence of type I refers to the **future** or the **present**. In the **if-clause**, we normally use the **simple present**, and in the **main clause** we use the **will-future** or a **modal auxiliary** + **infinitive**. When we use the simple present in the *if*-clause, we express a real or open condition: we see it as **possible** that the condition will be fulfilled (examples 1 and 2). Or we can refer to **something that we already know is true** (example 3).
	2 If Vicky needs advice, Wenn Vicky einen Rat braucht, (It is possible that Vicky needs advice.)	she should talk to her teacher. sollte sie mit ihrer Lehrerin sprechen.	
	3 If Pat is English, Wenn Pat Engländerin ist, (Pat is English).	you can ask her what 'plc' means. kannst du sie fragen, was „plc" bedeutet.	
	if-clause: **simple present**	**main clause:** **will-future** or **modal auxiliary + infinitive**	

Complex sentences | **188** | **Conditional sentences**

b | *if*-clause | main clause
| If it rains heavily, | the river overflows.
| *Wenn es stark regnet,* | *tritt der Fluss über die Ufer.*
| If you eat too much, | you get fat.
| *Wenn du zu viel isst,* | *wirst du dick.*
| If/When I take a deep breath, | I get a pain right here.
| *Wenn ich tief einatme,* | *tut es mir hier weh.*

If we want to express the idea that in the **same circumstances** the same thing **always happens**, we use the **simple present** in both the ***if*-clause** and the **main clause**. Here *if* means the same as *whenever* (= *jedes Mal wenn, immer wenn*). We could use *when* instead of *if* in these sentences.

c | *if*-clause | main clause
| If it's raining, | we'll have to take the bus.
| If Kate has missed the bus, | she won't be here on time.
| If Bob has been driving all day, | he'll be very tired.
| If you can't speak English, | you won't get the job.
| If Ed should sell his car, | he'll let you know.
| If you wear those funny trousers, | everybody is going to laugh at you.
| If Simon comes at eight, | we'll be watching the match on TV.
| If I work hard enough, | I'll have finished by tomorrow.
| If the train is late, | take a taxi.

The verb form in the *if*-clause depends on the **situation** that we are describing. A conditional sentence of this type behaves like many other complex sentences: we can use **different combinations of verb forms**.

▶ Tenses of the full verbs: 72, 73
▶ Short forms of the auxiliaries: 58, 59

'Remember son, if at first you don't succeed*, make it look like someone else's fault, then sue* them.'

succeed Erfolg haben
sue verklagen

Notes

1 I used to live over a pizzeria. If friends came round, I just fetched a couple of pizzas.
… *Wenn mich Freunde besuchten, holte ich einfach ein paar Pizzas.*

If you became suspicious, why didn't you tell the police?
Wenn du Verdacht geschöpft hast, warum hast du der Polizei nichts gesagt?

An open condition in the past is expressed by means of a past tense form.

2

If Mike will take me to the station, I won't need a taxi.
Wenn Mike bereit ist, mich zum Bahnhof zu bringen, …

If you will give me your name, I'll get your details from the computer.
Wenn Sie mir bitte Ihren Namen nennen würden, …

If the camcorder won't work, we'll have to take it back to the shop.
Wenn der Camcorder nicht funktionieren will, …

Will and *won't* are not normally used in the *if*-clause. But we can use them to express:

• a wish or a polite request

• a refusal.

Conditional sentence I:
Open condition → *What is …, if …?*

253 Conditional sentence II

a

if-clause	main clause
1 If I found £100, Wenn ich 100 Pfund fände/finden würde, (It is unlikely that I will find £100.)	I would take (= I'd take) it to the police. würde ich sie zur Polizei bringen.
2 If I got more pocket money, Wenn ich mehr Taschengeld bekäme/bekommen würde, (It is unlikely that I will get more pocket money.)	I could buy a computer. könnte ich einen Computer kaufen.
3 If my parents were ten years younger, Wenn meine Eltern zehn Jahre jünger wären, (The parents are not ten years younger.)	they might travel round the world. würden sie vielleicht eine Weltreise machen.

Although a conditional sentence of type II has a verb in the simple past, it refers to the **future** or the **present**.
We think it is **improbable** (examples 1 and 2) that the condition will be fulfilled (unreal condition), but we imagine the consequence if the condition was fulfilled. Or we can talk about a condition that **cannot be fulfilled** (example 3) because it is unreal.

if-clause: **main clause:**
simple past   **would/could/might + infinitive**

▶ Short forms of the auxiliaries: 58, 59

⚠ *Wenn du ein Schloss besitzen würdest, …*
not: If you ~~would own~~ a castle, …
but: If you owned a castle, …

Don't use **would** in the *if*-clause.

▶ Cf. however note p. 190

⚠ If we had a house, I would have more room for my pets.
    … hätten,   hätte …

If Mary was at home, she would be much happier.
    … wäre,   wäre …

Note the various equivalents of the **German hätte** and **wäre** in the *if*-clause and the main clause.

b

if-clause	main clause
If Jeff passes his driving test tomorrow,	I'll be pleased.
If Pete passed his driving test tomorrow,	I'd be pleased.

Compare conditional sentences I and II:

- **Conditional sentence I:**
  The speaker thinks it is **possible** or **probable** that Jeff will pass his driving test.
- **Conditional sentence II:**
  The speaker thinks it is **improbable** or perhaps even **impossible** that Pete will pass.

Complex sentences | 190 | **Conditional sentences**

 If I/he/she was in London, …
(= If I/he/she were in London, …)
Wenn ich/er/sie in London wäre, …

If I were you, I would take the job.
Wenn ich du wäre, würde ich die Stelle annehmen.

In conditional sentence II we sometimes use **were instead of was** in the *if*-clause. But this happens only in formal English, except for the very common expression *if I were you …*

'Stockbroking* is a good career. Yes, if I were you, I'd marry a stockbroker!'

stockbroking Wertpapierhandel

c	*if*-clause	main clause
	If you **were telling** the truth,	you'd look me straight in the eye.
	Wenn du die Wahrheit sagtest/sagen würdest,	*würdest du mir in die Augen sehen.*
	If Nick **could come** with us,	the evening would be more fun.
	Wenn Nick mitkommen könnte,	*hätten wir am Abend mehr Spaß.*

In the **if-clause** we can use not only the simple past but also **other past tense forms**, e.g. the past progressive or *could* + infinitive.

▌ *Note*

I'd be grateful **if** you **would return** the form as soon as possible.
Ich wäre Ihnen dankbar, wenn Sie das Formular so schnell wie möglich zurückschicken würden.

We do not normally use *would* in the *if*-clause. But we can do so to express a polite request.

Conditional sentence II:
Unreal condition → What would … be, if …?

Complex sentences | **191** | **Conditional sentences**

254 Conditional sentence III

if-clause	main clause
If the weather had been better,	we would have gone to Brighton.
Wenn das Wetter besser gewesen wäre,	wären wir nach Brighton gefahren.
(In reality the weather was bad.)	
If Peter had told me about his problems,	I could have helped him.
Wenn Peter mir von seinen Problemen erzählt hätte,	hätte ich ihm helfen können.
(Peter did not tell anything about his problems.)	
If we had shouted louder,	you might have heard us.
Wenn wir lauter gerufen hätten,	hättet ihr uns vielleicht gehört.
(We didn't shout loud.)	

if-clause:
past perfect

main clause:
would/could/might + have + past participle

A conditional sentence of type III refers to the **past**.
We imagine a past situation which **in reality did not happen** because the condition was **not fulfilled** (unreal condition). We know that the condition is impossible, but we imagine the consequence.

⚠ If I'd stayed, I'd have met Tim.
(= If I had stayed, I would have met Tim.)

If you'd been here, you'd have enjoyed yourself.
(= If you had been here, you would have enjoyed yourself.)

The **short form 'd** stands for different long forms in the if-clause and the main clause.

▶ Short forms of the auxiliaries: 58 b/c, 59

⚠ If Carol had been at the party, I would have stayed longer.
    … gewesen wäre,   wäre … geblieben.

If Sue had helped me last week, I would have helped her today.
    … geholfen hätte,   hätte … geholfen.

Note the various equivalents of the **German hätte** and **wäre** in the if-clause and the main clause.

Conditional sentence III:
Unreal condition → What would … have been, if …?

255 Mixed types

if-clause	main clause
If you knew Jane better,	you wouldn't have invited her to the party.
Wenn du Jane besser kennen würdest,	*hättest du sie nicht zu der Party eingeladen.*
If Mike was more like his brother,	he would have paid you the money back earlier.
Wenn Mike seinem Bruder ähnlicher wäre,	*hätte er dir das Geld früher zurückgezahlt.*
If I had had the chance,	I would now be a successful doctor.
Wenn ich die Gelegenheit gehabt hätte,	*wäre ich jetzt eine erfolgreiche Ärztin.*
If Dave hadn't borrowed my bike,	I wouldn't be sitting here at home.
Wenn Dave sich nicht mein Fahrrad ausgeliehen hätte,	*säße ich nicht hier zu Hause.*
If the train left at two,	it won't get in until four at the earliest.
Wenn der Zug um zwei abgefahren ist,	*wird er nicht vor vier Uhr ankommen.*
If Sarah knew the address,	she didn't tell me.
Auch wenn Sarah die Adresse kannte,	*sie hat sie mir nicht gesagt.*
If you stand here,	you might see the stage better.
Wenn du dich hier hinstellst,	*siehst du die Bühne vielleicht besser.*
If I could have saved you a seat,	I would have done.
Wenn ich dir einen Sitz hätte reservieren können,	*hätte ich es getan.*

As in German, there can be **mixed types** of conditional sentences in English, depending on the context. Verb forms from different types of conditional sentence can occur in the same sentence if the sense demands it.

'You realise, of course, that if you showed the same enthusiasm for lectures as the other students, I could have had the day off*!'

have the day off den Tag frei haben

256 Omission of if + inversion

if-clause	main clause
Should anyone phone,	tell them I'll be back at one.
(= If anyone should phone,	…)
Had Tom known about your problem,	he would have lent you some money.
(= If Tom had known about your problem,	…)

In an *if*-clause with *should* or with the past perfect, **if** can be **omitted**. In such a case we have to use **inversion**, which means that *should* or *had* comes before the subject. Conditional sentences of this kind are more typical of formal English.

▶ Inversion: 10 a

257 Shortened clauses

a
if-clause	main clause
If in difficulty,	please phone the emergency number.
(= If you are in difficulty,	…)
If in doubt,	consult a lawyer before you act.
(= If you are in doubt,	…)

In formal English, the **subject + be** can sometimes be **omitted** from an *if*-clause.

b There is little if any public support for the government's tax reform plans.
(= There is little public support …, if there is any at all.)

The committee seldom if ever takes an immediate decision on an important issue.
(= The committee seldom takes an immediate decision …, if it ever takes an immediate decision …)

In formal English, **if** can be used **together with** words like **any**, **anything**, **ever** or **not** in a kind of shortened clause.

c If only I could speak fluent German.
Wenn ich doch nur fließend Deutsch sprechen könnte.

If only we hadn't wasted so much time.
Hätten wir nur nicht so viel Zeit vergeudet.

If only at the beginning of a clause expresses a wish. This wish can refer to the present, the future or the past. We do not use a main clause.

d What if we don't answer the letter?
(= What will happen if we don't answer the letter?)

What if the taxi gets stuck in the traffic?
(= What will happen if the taxi gets stuck in the traffic?)

The shortened form **what if …?** means *what will happen if …?*

Relative clauses

258-266

- 258 Introduction
- 259-264 Defining relative clauses
- 265 Non-defining relative clauses
- 266 *Which* relating to a clause

258 Introduction

a
The woman who answered the phone couldn't help me.
Die Frau, die ans Telefon ging, konnte mir nicht helfen.

Here are some photos that show my family.
Hier sind ein paar Fotos, auf denen meine Familie zu sehen ist.

The boy who delivered the newspapers has moved away.
Der Junge, der die Zeitungen austrug, ist weggezogen.

Larry Clark, who delivered the newspapers, has moved away.
Larry Clark, der die Zeitungen austrug, ist weggezogen.

A relative clause usually relates to a **word that comes before it**. It begins with a **relative pronoun**, e.g. *who* or *that*. All the relative pronouns can relate to either a singular or a plural noun.

There are two kinds of relative clause in English:
- **defining relative clauses**
  ▶ 259-264
- **non-defining relative clauses**.
  ▶ 265

b
Martin doesn't know anybody to talk to.
Martin kennt niemanden, mit dem er reden kann.

The girl wearing white jeans is the camp leader.
Das Mädchen mit den weißen Jeans ist die Campleiterin.

Infinitive and participle constructions are other structures that can relate to a previous word.

▶ *The first, the last*, etc. + *to*-infinitive: 125
▶ Noun + *to*-infinitive: 126
▶ Participles with a noun: 153c

 That's the boy who scored six goals for our school team.
Das ist der Junge, der für unsere Schulmannschaft sechs Tore geschossen hat.

(**main clause:** The boy scored six goals for our school team.
Der Junge schoss sechs Tore für unsere Schulmannschaft.)

As in all subordinate clauses, the **word order** in a relative clause is **subject – verb**, i.e. the verb comes in the same place as in a main clause.

Complex sentences | **Relative clauses**

Defining relative clauses

259 Use

a
The boy **who is talking to Mr Smart** is new here.

Don't forget the DVD **that I lent you last week**.

A **defining relative clause defines a word** (usually a noun) more closely. Without the defining relative clause it would be unclear who or what is meant (which boy or which DVD). Defining relative clauses are used in informal English as well as in formal English.

b The boy **who scored six goals** is the youngest in the team.
Der Junge, der sechs Tore geschossen hat, ist der jüngste in der Mannschaft.

In English, defining relative clauses are **not separated** from the main clause **by commas**.

260 The relative pronoun as subject

              subject
1 The man **who/that** phoned earlier is here.
    …, *der vorhin angerufen hat,* …
2 I need someone **who/that** can help me with my work.
    …, *der mir bei meiner Arbeit helfen kann.*
3 Take the videos **that/which** are on the table.
    …, *die auf dem Tisch liegen.*
4 She wants a pet **that/which** is cuddly.
    …, *das verschmust ist.*

The relative pronoun can be the **subject** of the relative clause.

If the pronoun relates to a **person**, we use **who** or (in spoken English) **that** (examples 1 and 2). *Who* is more frequent.

With **things** and **animals** we use **that** or **which** (examples 3 and 4). *Which* is more typical of formal English.

▶ *Who* and *which* as question words: 241-244

> **Note**
>
> Is that **all that** has to be done?
>   … *alles, was* …
> There's **nothing that** can help you.
>   … *nichts, was* …

After expressions of quantity such as *all*, *everything*, *nothing*, *something* or *anything*, we use *that*.

261 The relative pronoun as object

          object
1 The people **who/that** we met on holiday were nice.
    …, *die wir im Urlaub getroffen haben,* …
2 The books **that/which** I've read are all by Poe.
    …, *die ich gelesen habe,* …

The relative pronoun can be the **object** of the relative clause.

With **people**, we use **who** or **that** (example 1).

With **things** and **animals** we use **which** or (more often) **that** (example 2).

▶ Contact clauses: 264

> **Note**
>
> The police arrested a man **whom** they later identified as a car thief.
>   …, *den* …

In formal English *whom* is used instead of *who*.

Complex sentences | **196** | **Relative clauses**

262 *The relative pronoun* whose

Look, that's the boy whose brother drives him to school in a Ferrari.
…, dessen Bruder ihn mit einem Ferrari zur Schule fährt.

The first three people whose names are drawn win a free holiday.
…, deren Namen gezogen werden, …

A factory whose workers often go on strike must have serious production problems.
…, deren Arbeiter oft streiken, …

A company whose products are advertised on TV can expect to increase its profits.
…, für deren Produkte im Fernsehen Werbung gemacht wird, …

Whose (= *dessen, deren*) expresses possession or belonging. It relates mainly (but not exclusively) to **people** or **collective nouns**.
Whose is always followed by a noun (in the singular or plural).

▶ *Whose* as a question word: 241

⚠ Is that the man whose house was burgled last week?
…, in dessen Haus letzte Woche eingebrochen wurde?

The man who's waiting over there is my brother's best friend.
…, der da drüben wartet, …

Whose (= *dessen, deren*) should not be confused with the short form **who's** (= *who is*).

> **Note**
>
> He's written a book whose title I've forgotten.
> He's written a book the title of which I've forgotten.

In formal English *of which* can be used with things instead of *whose*.

263 *The relative pronoun with prepositions*

a   This is the girl who/that I told you about.
       …, von dem ich dir erzählt habe.
   (**main clause:** I told you about the girl.)

   Here's the U2 CD that/which you've been looking for.
       …, nach der du gesucht hast.
   (**main clause:** You've been looking for the U2 CD.)

A **relative pronoun** can also be the **object** of a **preposition**. In informal English the preposition comes in the same place in the defining relative clause as it would in the main clause.

> **Note**
>
> The customer for whom the goods were ordered no longer lives at that address.
> This is an issue on which I have strong views.

In formal English the preposition can come before *whom* or *which*. We cannot use *who* or *that* in this structure.

Complex clauses **197** **Relative clauses**

b That's *the house where* Julie used to live.
That's *the house in which* …

The day when Charles crashed his car was Friday, the thirteenth of March.
The day on which …

There's no *reason why* Emma shouldn't pass her driving test.

After a noun referring to a **place** (e.g. *house, shop, town*, etc.) or a **time** (e.g. *day, time, moment*, etc.), informal English prefers a relative clause with **where** or **when**. After *reason* we can use *why*.

In a defining clause:
– 'who/that' for people
– 'that/which' for things
– 'whose' = German 'dessen, deren'

264 Contact clauses

a
	object		
The girls	who	I met yesterday	are from Halle.

or:
| The girls | | I met yesterday | are from Halle. |

…, *die ich gestern getroffen habe,* …

| The bike | that | I bought last week | has been stolen. |

or:
| The bike | | I bought last week | has been stolen. |

…, *das ich letzte Woche gekauft habe,* …

When the **relative pronoun** is the **object** of a defining relative clause, we often **leave it out**. A relative clause without a relative pronoun is called a **contact clause**. Contact clauses are used in formal and informal English, both written and spoken.

b
	prepositional object		
The man	that	I was talking to	is our teacher.

or:
| The man | | I was talking to | is our teacher. |

…, *mit dem ich gesprochen habe,* …

| The bike | which | you're pointing at | is my sister's. |

or:
| The bike | | you're pointing at | is my sister's. |

…, *auf das du gerade zeigst,* …

We can also **leave out** the **relative pronoun** when it is the **object of a preposition**.

⚠️
	object	subject	
This is the boy		who	won the race.
Dies ist der Junge,		*der*	*das Rennen gewonnen hat.*

but:
| This is the boy | who | we | met at the disco. |

or:
| This is the boy | | we | met at the disco. |
| *Dies ist der Junge, den* | | *wir* | *in der Disko getroffen haben.* |

When the **relative pronoun** is the **subject** of the relative clause, we **do not leave it out**.

The relative pronoun can be left out only when it is the object of the relative clause.

Complex sentences | **198** | **Relative clauses**

265 Non-defining relative clauses

a The actor Charlie Chaplin, *who was born in England*, made most of his films in Hollywood.
Der Schauspieler Charlie Chaplin, der in England zur Welt kam, hat die meisten seiner Filme in Hollywood gedreht.

We landed at Gatwick, *which is London's second largest airport*.
Wir landeten in Gatwick, Londons zweigrößtem Flughafen.

A non-defining relative clause contains **additional information** about the word it relates to. If we left it out, the main clause on its own would still make sense.
Here are some points about non-defining relative clauses:
- They are separated from the main clause by **commas**.
- The **relative pronoun** cannot be left out.
- We do not use *that*.

b *Mother Teresa, who* was born in Skopje, spent her life caring for the sick and dying in Calcutta.

John's new *car, which* cost him all his savings, was damaged by a hit-and-run driver last week.

When the relative pronoun is the **subject** of the non-defining relative clause, we use **who** for **people** and **which** for **things**.

c *The President, whom* I had never seen before, looked older than I expected.

Mrs Baxter gave her daughter a beautiful black *dress, which* she had bought in Paris.

When the relative pronoun is the **object** of the non-defining relative clause, we use **whom** for **people** and **which** for **things**.

d Mr Grant, *with whom* our company now has little contact, used to be one of our biggest customers.

My grandfather has a valuable stamp collection, *on which* he spends a lot of time and money.

A **preposition** usually comes **before the relative pronoun** in a non-defining relative clause.

> **Note**
>
> Mrs Moore has a lot of friends, *all of whom* think she is wonderful.
> There are two possible solutions, *both of which* may be unsatisfactory.

Of whom and *of which* come after the word they relate to. This word can be a quantifier, a superlative, *first, second*, etc. or *last*.

e Agatha Christie, *whose detective novels* are world-famous, did not go to school at all.

The tourist guide pointed out the 'Wearwell' factory, *whose owners* live in Switzerland.

Whose (= *dessen, deren*) expresses possession or belonging. It relates mainly (but not exclusively) to **people** and **collective nouns**. *Whose* is always followed by a noun (in the singular or plural).

266 Which *relating to a clause*

Brian won the 100 metres, *which surprised everybody*.
..., was alle überraschte.

I get paid a bit more now, *which means* I can afford a car.
..., was bedeutet, ...

A **relative clause** can relate to **the whole** of the previous **clause**. To do this, we use the relative pronoun **which**. The relative clause is normally separated from the main clause by a comma.

Complex sentences | **Adverbial clauses**

267-272 Adverbial clauses

267 Introduction
268 Adverbial clauses of time
269 Adverbial clauses of place
270 Adverbial clauses of reason
271 Adverbial clauses of contrast
272 Adverbial clauses of purpose

267 Introduction

a **When the players came out**, everybody cheered.
Als die Spieler herauskamen, haben alle gejubelt.
She was angry **because Joseph hadn't come**.
Sie war verärgert, weil Joseph nicht gekommen war.

An adverbial clause is connected to a main clause by a **subordinating conjunction**, e.g. *when* or *because*.

b **While we were in Sydney**, we met some nice people.
Während wir in Sydney waren, haben wir ein paar nette Leute kennen gelernt.
We met some nice people **while we were in Sydney**.
Wir haben ein paar nette Leute kennen gelernt, während wir in Sydney waren.

An adverbial clause can come **before** or **after the main clause**.
If the adverbial clause comes before the main clause, there is usually a **comma** between the clauses.

c Ted refused the offer, **knowing** he was too ill to work.
(= … because he knew he was too ill to work.)
Although realizing the danger, the firemen did not hesitate to enter the building.
(= Although the firemen realized the danger, they …)

There are some other structures – used mainly in written English – which correspond to an adverbial clause:
- a **participle construction**

Please check your change **before leaving** the store.
(= … before you leave the store.)

- a **preposition + gerund construction**

We'll fax all the information **in order to save** time.
(= … so that we can save time.)

- an **infinitive construction**.

▶ Participles expressing time, reason, etc.: 157-161
▶ Preposition + gerund: 144
▶ *to*-infinitive expressing the purpose of an action: 129

d **When in London**, please look me up.
(= When you are in London, …)

Add the ending '-s' **where necessary**.
(= … where it is necessary.)

A **shortened form** of the adverbial clause can be used after the conjunctions *when*, *while*, *until*, *once*, *where* and *(al)though*.

268 Adverbial clauses of time

Liz got a job in a bank **after** she left school.
I'll phone you **as soon as** I arrive in Paris.
Once you understand the system, the machine is easy to work.
What have you been doing **since** we last met?
Whenever I see John, he's driving a different car.

Adverbial clauses of **time** are introduced by the following **conjunctions**: *after* (= nachdem), *as* (= als), *as soon as* (= sobald), *before* (= bevor), *by the time* (= bis), *once* (= sobald, wenn), *since* (= seit, seitdem), *till/until* (= bis), *when* (= wenn, wann, als), *whenever* (= wann immer; jedes Mal, wenn) and *while* (= während, solange).

Complex sentences  **Adverbial clauses**

 We'll stay here till you get back.
Wir bleiben hier, bis du zurückkommst.
The children won't be at home when we arrive.
Die Kinder werden nicht zu Hause sein, wenn wir ankommen.

Even when talking about a future action, we do **not use** a **future** form in an **adverbial clause of time**, but the simple present. Future time is expressed only in the main clause.

▶ Ways of expressing future time: 95, 97, 101, 103

269 Adverbial clauses of place

Please leave the magazine where you found it.
Tell me where I can put the bags.
There were a lot of tourists wherever we went.
Everywhere you go, someone always speaks English.

Adverbial clauses of **place** are introduced by the **conjunctions** *where (= wo, wohin), wherever (= wo/wohin auch immer)* and *everywhere (= überall wo/wohin).*

270 Adverbial clauses of reason

As Carol has been ill, we should help her.
Since we've got no money, we can't buy a new car.
Why am I leaving? I'm leaving because I'm fed up.
I fell asleep in the French lesson because I was bored.

Adverbial clauses of **reason** are introduced by the **conjunctions** *as (= da), since (= da)* and *because (= weil).* Adverbial clauses with *as* and *since* normally come before the main clause. Clauses with *because* usually come after the main clause.

 We stayed at home because it rained.
    …, weil es regnete.
We stayed at home because of the rain.
    … wegen des Regens …

Because is a **conjunction** and introduces an adverbial clause.
Because of is a **preposition** and comes before a noun.

▶ Prepositions: 247

271 Adverbial clauses of contrast

Even if you aren't interested in the discussion, please stay and listen.
Though/Although it was very late, the dockers went on working.
Peter likes going out while/whereas his wife prefers staying at home.

Adverbial clauses of **contrast** are introduced by the following **conjunctions**: *even if/even though (= auch wenn), though/although (= obwohl, obgleich)* and *while/whereas (= während).*

272 Adverbial clauses of purpose

She hid the letter so that nobody would read it.
He wore a beard and dark glasses so that his friends wouldn't recognize him.
I left the party early so (that) I could get a good night's sleep.

Adverbial clauses of **purpose** are introduced by the **conjunction** *so that (=sodass, damit).* In informal English we can use *so* instead of *so that.*

Complex sentences **201** Indirect speech

Indirect speech

273 Direct and indirect speech
274 Characteristics of indirect speech
275 Changes in pronouns
276 Changes in phrases of time and place
277 Changes in tenses
278 Changes or no changes in tenses
279 Indirect questions
280 Indirect commands, requests, advice and suggestions

273 Direct and indirect speech

Mike wants to learn to drive. He's making inquiries at a driving school. Here's part of the conversation.

Girl: 'Driving lessons are £15 an hour.'
Mike: 'Oh, I see. And how many lessons will I need?'
Girl: 'Well, that depends. Most people take about 30 lessons with an instructor. But why don't you get a provisional licence and learn with a friend or parent as well? You won't need so many lessons then. The licence costs £21 – and don't forget the *L* plates.'

Mike told his father what he had found out:
The girl told me that lessons were £15 an hour, so I asked her how many I would need.

She said people usually took about 30 lessons with an instructor.

She suggested getting a provisional licence and driving with a friend or parent.

There are different ways of reporting what someone says.

- In **direct speech** we repeat **word for word** what someone has said, written or thought. If we write down the words, we usually put them in quotation marks:
English: 'Driving lessons are £15 an hour,' said the girl.
German: „Fahrstunden kosten 15 Pfund die Stunde", sagte das Mädchen.

- In **indirect speech** (or reported speech) we **report** what someone has said, written or thought. We can keep to the exact words of the direct speech, or we can report the meaning more freely.

We can leave out unimportant expressions (e.g. *Well, that depends* in the second sentence spoken by the girl).

In direct speech we use a variety of expressions to make clear what our intention is (e.g. *But why don't you …?* to suggest getting a provisional licence). These can often be reported more briefly by means of a suitable verb (e.g. *suggest*).

Note

She stood up in a sudden impulse of terror. Escape! She must escape! Frank would save her. He would give her life, perhaps love, too. But she wanted to live. Why should she be unhappy? She had a right to happiness. Frank would take her in his arms, fold her in his arms. He would save her.
(James Joyce: 'Eveline'. *Dubliners*. Cornelsen 1989, p. 14)

The example shows a mixed form which lies between direct and indirect speech. The question is formed as in direct speech, but the pronouns and tense changes are as in indirect speech. This stylistic device is often used in modern literature and is called 'free indirect speech'. It serves to give the reader an insight into people's thoughts, their 'stream of consciousness'.

▶ Changes in pronouns: 275
▶ Changes in tenses: 277

Complex sentences | **202** | **Indirect speech**

274 Characteristics of indirect speech

a

The girl **told** Mike that she had just passed her driving test too.
She **mentioned** that the examiners were quite strict.
She **said** she had been terribly nervous before the test.

Mike **was sure** he would feel nervous too.

He **wanted to know** if the theory test was difficult.

The girl **told** him not to worry and **advised** him to start learning the 'Highway Code'.
She **asked** him to fill in the registration forms.

Indirect speech is usually introduced by a type of verb called a '**reporting verb**':

- To report a **statement** we often use *say* or *tell*. There are other verbs we can use, e.g. *add, admit, agree, answer, begin, complain, continue, mention, report, threaten* and *write*.

- To report **thoughts** and **opinions** we use e.g. *be sure, believe, know* and *think*.

- To report a **question** we use e.g. *ask, inquire, want to know* and *wonder*.
  ▶ 279

- To report a **command** we often use *tell sb.*, and we can also use *order* or *want sb. to do sth*. For a **request** we use *ask*, for **advice** we use *advise*, for a **promise** we use *promise* and for a **suggestion** we use *propose, suggest*, etc.
  ▶ 280

'I'm phoning to let you know I've faxed you to say I've sent an e-mail asking you to call me.'

Note

Ann: 'Why don't you buy a new bike, Susan?'

Ann **asked** Susan why she didn't buy a new bike.
Ann **advised** Susan to buy a new bike.
Ann **suggested** that Susan should buy a new bike.

A sentence in direct speech can often express different things depending on the stress. It can also be reported in different ways, depending on how the person reporting the sentence has understood it. The choice of reporting verb shows how the sentence is interpreted, e.g.

- as a question why
- as a piece of advice
- as a suggestion.

 Sue **said** | that she had seen a new bike in a shop.
Sue **told Ann** |

After **say** we do not usually use an object referring to a person. If we want to mention the person spoken to, we use **tell sb.**:
Sue told Ann/him/me/them/ …
Note that *tell* is always followed by an object (without *to*) referring to a person.

b Peter said (**that**) he was a member of Greenpeace.
Peter sagte, dass er Mitglied bei Greenpeace sei. /
Peter sagte, er sei Mitglied bei Greenpeace.

In English we do **not use a comma** before indirect speech. **That** is often **omitted** (especially after *say, tell sb.* and *think*). As in German, there are **no quotation marks**.

c Gemma: 'My job **is** interesting.'
   „Meine Arbeit *ist* interessant."
   ▷ Gemma said her job **was** interesting.
   *Gemma sagte, ihre Arbeit sei/wäre interessant. /
   ..., ihre Arbeit ist interessant.*

   ▷ Simon said he and his girlfriend **worked** for the same company.
   Simon sagte, er und seine Freundin arbeiteten bei derselben Firma/würden ... arbeiten.

In contrast to German, in indirect speech in English there are **no subjunctive** forms like *sei, wäre, habe* or *hätte*. Instead we usually **change the verb tense**.

In indirect speech the simple past forms *was* and *worked* refer to the present, not to the past.

⚠ Tony: 'I **don't earn** much.'
not: Tony said he ~~wouldn't earn~~ much.
but: Tony said he **didn't earn** much.
   ..., er würde nicht viel verdienen.

Tony: 'I**'ll earn** more after my training.'
▷ Tony said he **would earn** more after his training.
   ..., er würde nach seiner Schulung mehr verdienen.

Compare the different use of English **would** and German **würde**: In German, *würde* can refer to the present as well as to the future. But in English, *would* in indirect speech refers only to the future (*will* ▷ *would*). We cannot use *would* to refer to the present.

d 1 Andrew (in Glasgow) is talking to his sister Rebecca (in London) on the phone. He tells his friends what Rebecca is saying.

   Rebecca: '**I'll be** in Glasgow on Friday **next week**. Guess what, **I've bought** a new car. It **goes** like a bomb.'

   Andrew: '**Rebecca says she'll be here** on Friday next week. **She says she's bought** a new car and that it **goes** like a bomb.'

2 A week later Andrew told another friend about his sister's phone call.
   Rebecca said she would be here on Friday **this week**. **She told me she had bought** a new car that **went** like a bomb. Typical!

If we compare direct and indirect speech, we often find a number of **changes**, e.g. in

· **pronouns** (examples 1 and 2: *I* ▷ *she*)   ▶ 275
· **phrases of time** (example 2:
                next week ▷ *this week*)
· **phrases of place** (examples 1 and 2:
                Glasgow ▷ *here*).   ▶ 276

However, the **verb tenses** of the direct speech stay the same if the reporting verb in indirect speech is in the simple present (e.g. *says*) or the present perfect (e.g. *has said*): *I'll be* ▷ *she'll be* (example 1). But the tenses often change when the reporting verb is in the simple past (e.g. *said, told*; example 1):
I'll (will) be   ▷ *she would be*
I've (have) bought   ▷ *she had bought*
it goes   ▷ *it went*
                                    ▶ 277

e

(When John was 16 he decided to leave school. Soon after he started looking for a job. He wrote letters of application and asked for job interviews.)

Compare:
John **thought** he **was doing** the right thing.

He **thought/believed** he **had made** a good decision.

He **hoped/thought** he **would find** a job soon.

We can often use indirect speech even when there is **no direct speech** on which to base it, or when we do not know what the direct speech was. By the choice of a suitable tense or a suitable phrase of place or time, we can show whether the sentence refers to the time when the words were thought or spoken, or whether it refers to the time before or after the direct speech.

John was thinking about what he was doing at the time. (*Was doing* refers to what was then the present.)
He was thinking about a previous decision.
(*Had made* refers to something that was then in the past.)
He hoped to find a job in the future.
(*Would find* refers to what was then in the future.)

Complex sentences | **Indirect speech**

275 Changes in pronouns

Linda: 'Can I borrow your moped, Susan?'

1 Susan (to her brother):
   Linda asked me yesterday if she could borrow my moped.

2 Linda (to her father):
   I asked Susan yesterday if I could borrow her moped.

As in German, **pronouns** in indirect speech show the **point of view of the person who is reporting**. They depend on the context in which the words are reported. In example 1, it is Susan who is reporting what Linda asked her. So *I* becomes *she*, and *your* becomes *my*.
In example 2, on the other hand, it is Linda herself who is reporting what she asked Susan. So she uses *I* and *her*.

276 Changes in phrases of time and place

a Phrases of time:

Andy (on Sunday): 'I'll give you your CDs back tomorrow, Tracy.'

1 Tracy (two hours later on Sunday):
   When Andy called me two hours ago, he said he'd give me my CDs back tomorrow.

2 Tracy (on Monday):
   When Andy called me yesterday, he said he'd give me my CDs back today.

3 Tracy (on Friday):
   When Andy called me on Sunday, he said he'd give me my CDs back the next day/the following day/on Monday.

Phrases of time sometimes have to be changed in indirect speech. As in German, these **changes** depend on the **point of view of the person who is reporting**. They therefore do **not** happen **automatically**.
That is why in example 1 *tomorrow* stays the same (it is still Sunday when Tracy reports what Andy said), while in examples 2 and 3 it changes (it is a day or several days later when Tracy reports what Andy said).
The following changes are possible in phrases of time in indirect speech:

now	▷ then, at that time
today	▷ (on) that day, yesterday, on/last Monday, …
this week	▷ that week
yesterday	▷ the day before, on/last Monday, …
three days ago	▷ three days before/earlier, on/last Monday, …
last week	▷ the week before/ the previous week
tomorrow	▷ the next/following day, on Monday, today, …
next month	▷ the following month, a month later, in June, …

b Phrases of place:

Dennis (at his hotel in Bristol): 'I've just arrived.'

▷ Susan (in Bristol):
   Dennis phoned to say he had just arrived here.

▷ Frank (in London):
   Dennis phoned from Bristol and said he had just arrived at his hotel.

Changes in **phrases of place** also depend on the **context** in which something is reported.

Complex sentences | **205** | **Indirect speech**

277 Changes in tenses

a Pete: 'I'm in New York for a few days.'
▷ Pete said he was in New York for a few days.
Pete sagte, er sei/wäre für ein paar Tage in New York.

Pete: 'I was very impressed by Washington.'
▷ Pete added that he had been very impressed by Washington.
Pete fügte hinzu, er sei/wäre von Washington beeindruckt gewesen.

When the **reporting verb** is in the **simple past** (e.g. *said, added*, etc.), we usually use a different tense in indirect speech than was used in direct speech.
The **verb forms of direct speech** are '**backshifted**' – moved back a step into the past. This is known as the 'backshift of tenses':
am (present tense) ▷ *was* (past tense)
was (past tense) ▷ *had been* (past perfect)

b **Further examples:**

Pete: 'I write my girlfriend a card every day.'
▷ Pete said he wrote his girlfriend a card every day.

Pete: 'I'm having a really good time.'
▷ Pete said he was having a really good time.

present tense ▷ **past tense**

Pete: 'I saw Bruce Willis in Central Park.'
▷ Pete said he had seen Bruce Willis in Central Park.

Pete: 'They were filming an action scene.'
▷ Pete said they had been filming an action scene.

past tense ▷ **past perfect**

Pete: 'I've met lots of interesting people.'
▷ Pete said he had met lots of interesting people.

Pete: 'I've been doing quite a lot of sightseeing.'
▷ Pete said he had been doing quite a lot of sightseeing.

present perfect ▷ **past perfect**

Pete: 'I didn't take any photos of the Empire State Building because I had forgotten my camera.'
▷ Pete said he hadn't taken any photos of the Empire State Building because he had forgotten his camera.

A verb in the **past perfect stays the same**. (The past perfect cannot be 'backshifted' any further.)

Pete: 'I'll probably go up again.'
▷ Pete said he would probably go up again.

will ▷ **would**

Pete: 'I can't always understand New Yorkers.'
▷ Pete said he couldn't always understand New Yorkers.

can ▷ **could**

Pete: 'I may go to see *Cats* on Friday.'
▷ Pete said he might go to see *Cats* on Friday.

may ▷ **might**

Pete: 'I would like to go to Harlem on Sunday.'
▷ Pete said he would like to go to Harlem on Sunday.

Would, **could** (= *könnte*), **might, should** and **ought to** stay **the same**.

Pete: 'I must fly home on the 4th.'
▷ Pete said he must fly home on the 4th.
▷ Pete said he had to fly home on the 4th.

Must/needn't expressing obligation or lack of obligation can stay the same or change to *had to/didn't have to*.

▶ Tenses of the full verbs: 72, 73
▶ Modal auxiliaries: 22, 23, 25-35, 40, 41

Complex sentences   **206**   **Indirect speech**

> **Notes**
>
> **1**   1   Pete: 'A girl on the phone? Oh, it must be Liz.'
>   ▷ Pete thought it must be Liz on the phone.
>   2   Pete: 'You simply must go to the concert, Liz.'
>   ▷ Pete told Liz that she simply must go to the concert.
>
> **2**   Doctor: 'You mustn't go out just yet.'
>   ▷ The doctor told me I mustn't go out just yet.
>   ▷   … I wasn't to go out …

Must stays the same when it expresses a deduction or certainty (example 1) or when it is used to give advice (example 2).

Mustn't can stay the same, or it can change to *wasn't/weren't to*.

▶ Modal auxiliaries: 42 e, 47

278   Changes or no changes in tenses

a

Alex: 'My sister is at art school.'
▷ Alex said his sister is at art school.
▷ Alex said his sister was at art school.

Claire: 'My visa for Russia has arrived.'
▷ Claire said this morning that her visa for Russia has arrived.
▷ Claire said this morning that her visa for Russia had arrived.

Teacher: 'Sound travels through water five times faster than through air.'
▷ Our teacher told us sound travels through water five times faster than through air.
▷ Our teacher told us sound travelled through water five times faster than through air.

It is never wrong to **change the verb tense** when the reporting verb is in the simple past. But it is **not always necessary** with

- statements which are still true when they are reported

- general truths.

b

Tom: 'I'm 16.'
▷ Did you hear that? Tom said he was 16.
                … sei/wäre …

Head teacher: 'The school will be closed on Monday.'
▷ Somebody said that the school would be closed on Monday.
    … geschlossen sei/wäre.

Mike: 'John is a liar.'
▷ Mike said that John was a liar.
          … sei/wäre.

We **change the verb tense** of the direct speech if we want to make it clear that

- the words that we are reporting are not ours

- we are not sure if the information is true

- we do not agree with what was said.

In German the subjunctive is used.

Complex sentences | **207** | **Indirect speech**

c Vicky: 'I arrived last Sunday.'
   ▷ Vicky told us she arrived last Sunday.
   ▷ (Vicky told us she had arrived last Sunday.)

In informal English, **past tense forms** in direct speech often **stay the same** (i.e. are not changed to the past perfect). This can happen if it is clear from the context, or from the use of a particular phrase, which action took place first. In the example, the phrase *last Sunday* makes it clear that Vicky arrived before the time when her statement was reported.

d Tony: 'There was an accident in the chemistry lab. Some potassium nitrate exploded when two boys set it alight.'
   ▷ Tony said that there had been an accident in the chemistry lab. Some potassium nitrate exploded when two boys set it alight.

When indirect speech continues for **longer than a single sentence** (e.g. on television or in the newspaper), it often happens that only the first simple past form is changed to the past perfect. The other simple past forms stay the same. It is clear from the backshift in the first sentence that the events lie further back in the past.

279 Indirect questions

Reporter: 'What's the title of your new album, Geri?'
▷ The reporter asked Geri what the title of her new album was.

Reporter: 'When will it be released?'
▷ The reporter wanted to know when it would be released.

Reporter: 'Are there any plans for your next concert tour?'
▷ The reporter wondered if/whether there were any plans for her next concert tour.

When the reporting verb is in the simple past (e.g. *asked, wanted to know, wondered*), the **verb tense** of the direct speech is '**back-shifted**' (or not), just as in a statement.

Question words like *how, what, when, where,* etc. are **retained** in an indirect question.

If there is **no question word** in the direct question (i.e. if it is a yes/no question), then we use **if** or **whether** (= *ob*) in the indirect question.

▶ Questions: 4
▶ Question words + *to*-infinitive: 128

		auxiliary	subject	main verb	
Ed:	'What	does	ZIP code	mean?'	
▷ Ed asked what (statement)			ZIP code	meant.	
			ZIP code	means	postcode.
Ed:	'Does		the train	go	north?'
▷ Ed asked if (statement)			the train	went	north.
			The train	goes	north.

The **word order** in an indirect question is **subject – verb**. This is the same word order as in a statement. We do not use *do* before the subject.
As in German, there is **no question mark** after an indirect question.

▶ Word order: 2

Note

What time is it?
▷ Can/Could you tell me what time it is?

When was the Treaty of Maastricht signed?
▷ Do you know when the Treaty of Maastricht was signed?

We also use indirect questions (e.g. *… what time it is*) after certain phrases which signal a question (e.g. *Can you tell me …? Do you know …?*). We do this when we ask politely for information.
In this kind of sentence, too, you need to be careful with the word order.

Complex sentences | 208 | **Indirect speech**

280 Indirect commands, requests, advice and suggestions

a Mother: 'Take your mobile with you, Jenny.'
   ▷ Jenny's mother told her to take her mobile with her.
   or:
   ▷ Jenny's mother told her that she should take her mobile with her.

   Mother: 'Don't pack too many clothes.'
   ▷ Jenny's mother told her not to pack too many clothes.
   or:
   ▷ Jenny's mother told her that she shouldn't pack too many clothes.

Commands and **prohibitions** are usually reported by using **tell sb. + to-infinitive** (negative: *tell sb. not to*). Instead of the infinitive, we can also use a **that-clause with should/shouldn't**.

'One of my Image Consultant* firms advises me to take up the fiddle*; another says I should burn Rome.'

consultant Berater
take up the fiddle anfangen, Geige zu spielen

▶ Verb + object + *to*-infinitive: 123 a/b

Note

Teacher (to class): 'Don't forget the money for the class trip.'
   ▷ The teacher told the class not to forget the money for the class trip.
   or:
   ▷ The class was told not to forget the money for the class trip.

The clause with *tell* can also be passive.

b Jenny: 'Can/Could/Would you lend me your new travel-bag?'
   ▷ Jenny asked her mother to lend her her new travel-bag.
   or:
   ▷ Jenny asked her mother if she could lend her her new travel-bag.

   Mother: 'If I were you, I'd take a rucksack.'
   ▷ Jenny's mother advised her to take a rucksack.

We also normally use a **to-infinitive** to report **requests** and **advice**. We use the reporting verbs *ask* (for requests) and *advise* (for advice).

c Father: 'Let's leave after breakfast.'
   ▷ Jenny's father suggested | leaving after breakfast.
                                | that they should leave …

Suggestions are usually reported with the verb **suggest**. After *suggest* we use the *-ing* form or a *that*-clause with *should*.

▶ Gerund after certain verbs: 139 a

⚠ *Jenny schlug vor, um zehn zu gehen.*
   not: Jenny suggested ~~to leave~~ at ten.
   but: Jenny suggested leaving at ten.

We never use an infinitive after **suggest**.

Appendix

Common mistakes

Many of the mistakes made by German learners of English come from a few relatively limited areas of grammar. The following list of especially common mistakes broadly covers those areas. It is arranged so that you can easily check your knowledge (e.g. before a class test).

1 als (in comparisons)
Mein Handy ist kleiner als deins.

not: My mobile phone's smaller ~~as~~ yours.
but: My mobile phone's smaller **than** yours.

Als after a comparative form translates as *than*.

▶ Sentences with comparisons: 200a, 213a

2 beide
Die beiden Oasis-Alben sind großartig.

not: ~~The both~~ Oasis albums are great.
but: **Both (of) the** Oasis albums are great. / **The two** Oasis albums are great.

Do not use words like *the/these/my*, etc. before *both*.

▶ Position of the article: 187

3 Conditional sentences
Wenn ich Peter auf der Party sehe, gebe ich ihm die CDs.

not: If I see Peter at the party, I ~~give~~ him the CDs.
but: If I see Peter at the party, **I'll give** him the CDs.

Conditional sentences (type I):
if-clause: simple present
main clause: *will*-future

Wenn du mit dem Zug fahren würdest, würdest du Zeit sparen.

not: If you ~~would go~~ by train, you would save time.
but: If you **went** by train, you would save time.

Don't use *would* in the *if*-clause!

▶ Conditional sentences I, II: 252a, 253a

4 Definite article: *the*
Wir sollten die Natur in Ruhe lassen.

not: We should leave ~~the nature~~ alone.
but: We should leave **nature** alone.

Es ist mir egal, was die Leute denken.

not: I don't care what ~~the people~~ think.
but: I don't care what **people** think.

There is no *the* with abstract nouns or nouns in the plural when they are used in a general sense.

▶ Definite article: 183a

5 ..., der/die/das/was ...
(relative pronouns)
Ich kenne viele Leute, die ein Piercing haben.

not: I know a lot of people ~~which~~ have a body piercing.
but: I know a lot of **people who/that** have a body piercing.

When the relative pronoun relates to a person, we use *who* or sometimes *that*. *Which* relates only to things.

Ist das alles, was übrig ist?

not: Is that all ~~what~~ is left?
not: Is that all ~~which~~ is left?
but: Is that **all that** is left?

After *all* the only relative pronoun we can use is *that*.

▶ Relative pronouns: 260 note

Appendix — Common mistakes

6   erklären
Die Lehrerin erklärte uns die Regel.

not: The teacher explained us the rule.
but: The teacher explained the rule to us.

After *explain* we use *to* and an object referring to a person.

▶ Position of the indirect object: 20 d

7   Future forms
Warte auf mich! Ich komme mit.

not: Wait for me! I go with you.
but: Wait for me! I'll go with you.

Use the *will*-future for a spontaneous decision.

Die Carters reisen morgen nach Wales.

not: The Carters travel to Wales tomorrow.
but: The Carters are travelling to Wales tomorrow.

Use the present progressive for definite plans and arrangements.

Pass auf! Die Leiter fällt um!

not: Watch out! The ladder will fall!
but: Watch out! The ladder is going to fall!

Use the *going to*-future if there are already signs that something is going to happen.

▶ *Will*-future: 96 b
▶ Present progressive: 99
▶ *Going to*-future: 98 b

8   gestern
Ich habe Vicky gestern getroffen.

not: I have met Vicky yesterday.
but: I met Vicky yesterday.

With *yesterday* we use the simple past.

▶ Simple past: 86 a

9   es gibt
In unserem Dorf gibt es eine Schule und (es gibt) zwei Diskos.

not: It gives a school in our village, and it gives two discos.
but: There is a school in our village, and there are two discos.

es gibt = *there is*, *there are*

▶ *There + be:* 52

10   gut
Schlaf gut!

not: Sleep good.
but: Sleep well.

To say how someone does something, we use an adverb. The adjective *good* corresponds to the adverb *well*.

▶ Adverbs: 204, 206 b

11   hart/schwer
Du musst hart arbeiten.

not: You must work hardly.
but: You must work hard.

The adverb *hard* has the same form as the adjective.
(The adverb *hardly* means *kaum*.)

▶ *Hard, hardly:* 207, 208

12   Hausaufgaben
Habt ihr viel(e) Hausaufgaben auf?

not: Have you got many homeworks?
but: Have you got much homework?

Homework cannot be plural because it is an uncountable noun.

▶ Uncountable nouns: 177 c

13 Indefinite article: *a/an*

Wir warteten eine Stunde.

not: We waited for ~~a~~ hour.
but: We waited for an hour.

Whether we use *a* or *an* depends on the pronunciation of the following word and not on the spelling.

Tragt ihr eine Uniform?

not: Do you wear ~~an~~ uniform?
but: Do you wear a uniform?

Mandy ist Fernsehmoderatorin.

not: Mandy is ~~TV presenter~~.
but: Mandy is a TV presenter.

We use *a/an* before a word saying what someone's job is.

Ich gehe zweimal in der Woche aus.

not: I go out twice ~~in the~~ week.
but: I go out twice a week.

When we talk about time or frequency, we use *a/an* meaning *per* before a phrase of time.

▶ Indefinite article: 181 b/c, 190, 192

14 *Informationen*

Wir bekamen diese Informationen aus England.

not: We got ~~these informations~~ from England.
but: We got this information from England.

Information cannot be plural because it is an uncountable noun.

▶ Uncountable nouns: 177 c

15 *lassen*

Mrs Flint lässt nicht zu, dass ihre Tochter in die Disko geht.

not: Mrs Flint doesn't let ~~that her daughter goes~~ to the disco.
but: Mrs Flint doesn't let her daughter go to the disco.

let + sb. + infinitive without to = zulassen, dass jemand etwas tut

Die Polizistin ließ mich meine Tasche öffnen.

not: The policewoman made me ~~to open~~ my bag.
but: The policewoman made me ~~opening~~ my bag.
not: The policewoman ~~let me open~~ my bag.
(= *Die Polizistin erlaubte mir, die Tasche zu öffnen.*)
but: The policewoman made me open my bag.

make + sb. + infinitive without to = jemanden dazu veranlassen, etwas zu tun

▶ Let/Make + object + infinitive without *to*: 133

Mrs Croft lässt ihr Auto einmal die Woche waschen.

not: Mrs Croft ~~lets her car wash~~ once a week.
but: Mrs Croft has her car washed once a week.

have + sth. + past participle = etwas (von jemand anderem) tun lassen

▶ Have something done: 156

16 *(der/die/das) meiste*

Die meisten Jungen in meiner Klasse fahren gern Mountainbike.

not: ~~The most~~ boys in my class like mountain-biking.
but: Most (of the) boys in my class like mountain-biking.

Do not use *the* before *most* when it means the same as the German *die meisten*.

▶ Most of + *the*: 187

17 muss nicht/braucht nicht
Du musst/brauchst die Arbeit heute nicht fertig (zu) machen.

not: You ~~mustn't~~ finish the work today.
(= *Du darfst die Arbeit heute nicht fertig machen.*)
but: You needn't finish/ don't have to finish the work today.

The opposite of *must* is *needn't* or *don't/doesn't have to*. (*You mustn't* means the same as the German *du darfst nicht*.)

▶ *Needn't, don't have to, mustn't*: 40, 41

18 Nachrichten
Das sind gute Nachrichten.

not: ~~Those are~~ good news.
but: That's good news.

In spite of the fact that it ends in *-s*, *news* is used as a singular noun.

▶ Uncountable nouns: 177 d

19 The passive
Wir wurden von der Polizei angehalten.

not: We were stopped ~~from~~ the police.
but: We were stopped by the police.

In the passive *by* is the equivalent of the German *von*.

Ihm wurde befohlen anzuhalten.

not: ~~Him~~ was told to stop.
but: He was told to stop.

With *tell* we can form a structure called 'persönliches Passiv' (*he was told*).

▶ Passive: 110, 111 b

20 Polizei
Ist die Polizei schon gekommen?

not: ~~Has~~ the police come yet?
but: Have the police come yet?

Police is used only in the plural.

▶ Collective nouns: 176 b

21 Progressive and simple forms
Schau mal, es schneit.

not: Oh look, it ~~snows~~.
but: Oh look, it's snowing.

We use the present progressive for something happening as we speak.

Gehst du oft aus?

not: ~~Are~~ you ~~going~~ out often?
but: Do you go out often?

We use the simple present for actions or events that happen regularly.

▶ Simple form and progressive form: 68, 78

22 Questions
Was bedeutet dieses Wort?

not: What ~~means~~ this word?
but: What does this word mean?

We form simple present questions with *do/does* and simple past questions with *did*.

Was hast du gestern gemacht?

not: What ~~did~~ you yesterday?
but: What did you do yesterday?

Was passiert in diesem Film?

not: ~~What does happen~~ in this film?
but: What happens in this film?

When we use *what, who* or another question word to ask about the subject, we do not use *do/does/did*.

▶ Word order in questions: 5 b/c, 6 i

Appendix — Common mistakes

23 **Rat(schlag)**
Kannst du mir bitte einen Rat geben?

not: Can you give me ~~an~~ advice, please?
but: Can you give me some advice, please?

We cannot use *an* with *advice* because it is an uncountable noun.

▶ Uncountable nouns: 177c

24 **schlechter/schlimmer**
Ich fühle mich schlechter als gestern.

not: I'm feeling ~~bad(d)er~~ than yesterday.
not: I'm feeling ~~worser~~ than yesterday.
but: I'm feeling worse than yesterday.

The comparative and superlative forms of *bad* are *worse* and *worst*.

▶ Irregular comparison: 198

25 **seit**
Ich bin seit einer Stunde hier.

not: I've been here ~~since~~ an hour.
not: I ~~am~~ here for an hour.
(= *Ich bin für eine Stunde hier.*)
but: I've been here for an hour.

We use *for* with a period of time and *since* with a point of time. If we want to say how long something has lasted, we use the present perfect.

Wir kennen Kate seit letztem Jahr.

not: We ~~know~~ Kate since last year.
but: We've known Kate since last year.

▶ Present perfect: 80b
▶ *Since* and *for*: 84

26 **sich (mich/dich/…)**
Ich habe mich mit meinem Taschenmesser geschnitten.

not: I cut ~~me~~ with my penknife.
but: I cut myself with my penknife.

In the German sentence, *mich* refers back to the subject *ich*. So we have to use the reflexive pronoun *myself* in English.

Können wir uns am Bahnhof treffen?

not: Can we meet ~~ourselves~~ at the station?
but: Can we meet at the station?

We do not use *meet* with *myself*, *ourselves*, etc.

Edward und Sophie lieben sich.

not: Edward and Sophie love ~~themselves~~.
but: Edward and Sophie love each other.

each other = *sich gegenseitig, einander*
(*themselves* = *sich selbst*)

▶ Reflexive pronouns: 233
▶ Each other: 234

27 **sich freuen auf**
Ich freue mich darauf, euch bald zu sehen.

not: I'm looking forward ~~to see~~ you soon.
but: I'm looking forward to seeing you soon.

In *look forward to*, the word *to* is a preposition, and so it must be followed by a gerund (= *-ing* form) rather than an infinitive.

▶ Verb + preposition + gerund: 143

28	***vor*** (in phrases of time) *Ich habe Sue vor drei Tagen getroffen.*	**not:** I ~~have met~~ Sue three days ago. **not:** I met Sue ~~for three days~~. (= *… drei Tage lang*.) **but:** I met Sue three days ago.	In phrases of time, the German word *vor* translates as *ago*. We use the past tense in sentences with *ago*. ▶ Simple past: 86 a
29	***vorschlagen*** *Tracy schlug vor, ins Britische Museum zu gehen.*	**not:** Tracy suggested ~~to go~~ to the British Museum. **but:** Tracy suggested going to the British Museum.	After *suggest* we use a gerund (= *-ing* form) rather than an infinitive. ▶ Gerund after certain verbs: 139 a
30	***wollen, dass …*** *Kevin wollte, dass seine Mutter ihm hilft.* *Ich möchte gern, dass du mitkommst.*	**not:** Kevin wanted ~~that his mother helps~~ him. **but:** Kevin wanted his mother to help him. **not:** I'd like ~~that you come~~ with me. **but:** I'd like you to come with me.	After *want* or *would like* we cannot use a subordinate clause with *that* (= *dass*). ▶ Verb + object + *to*-infinitive: 123 b
31	**Word order** (with adverbs) *Tim öffnete vorsichtig die Tür.*	**not:** Tim opened ~~carefully the door~~. **but:** Tim opened the door carefully.	Do not put an adverb between the main verb and the direct object. ▶ Word order with adverbs: 214 c

Appendix **215** **Word formation**

82-289 Word formation

282-284 Compound words
285 Prefixes
286-288 Suffixes
289 Conversion

When **new words are formed** from existing ones, there are basically four ways in which this happens:
- putting words together to form a compound
- adding a prefix
- adding a suffix
- converting a word to a different part of speech.

282 Compound words

Compound words consist of two or more words. There are not really any fixed rules about whether we write a compound as one word or not. Some are written as one word, some have a hyphen and others are written as separate words. If you are unsure, you should use a dictionary. Usually we stress the first word of a compound noun: e.g. *walking stick* ['– – ,–].

283 Compound nouns

songwriter, ticket office, water power, weather forecast
chewing gum, playing field, swimming pool
air conditioning, taxi-driving, sightseeing
blackboard, madman, high jump

Compound nouns can have the following **structure**:
- noun + noun
- gerund + noun
- noun + gerund
- adjective + noun.

284 Compound adjectives

seasick, fireproof, pollution-free, worldwide
breathtaking, record-breaking, handmade, air-conditioned
Franco-German, dark-brown
English-speaking, well-dressed
a three-hour trip, a ten-mile walk, a five-year-old girl

Compound adjectives can have the following **structure**:
- noun + adjective
- noun + participle

- adjective + adjective
- adjective/adverb + participle
- number + singular noun (+ adjective).

▶ -ing form: 65
▶ Forms of the past participle: 66
▶ Forms of adverbs: 206-208

285 Prefixes

If we **add a prefix** to a noun, adjective, adverb or verb, we can form a new word with a different meaning. But the new word usually belongs to the same part of speech.

a
disadvantage, dissatisfied, disagree, disappear
independence, impossible, illegal, irregular
nonsense, non-smoker, non-stop, non-European
unemployment, unconscious, unfortunately, unload

Prefixes which express an **opposite**:
- dis-
- in-, im-, il-, ir-
- non-
- un-

b

overtime, overcrowded, overload, overburden
sub-standard, subhuman, subnormal
superman, supermarket, superstar, supersonic

Prefixes which express a **lower or higher degree**:
- over- (= zu viel)
- sub- (= nicht ganz, unterhalb)
- super- (= sehr groß, größer als)

c

anti-crime, anti-war, anti-social
pro-government, pro-Indian, pro-integration

Prefixes which express **rejection** or **approval**:
- anti- (= gegen)
- pro- (= für)

d

intercity, inter-school, international
submarine, subway
transport, transatlantic, transfer, transmit

Prefixes which express **place**:
- inter- (= zwischen)
- sub- (= unter)
- trans- (= von einer Stelle zur anderen, jenseits von)

e

ex-president, ex-wife
post-war, postgraduate
precondition, prehistoric, pre-war
reconstruction, rebuild, recycle, redo

Prefixes which express **time**:
- ex- (= früher)
- post- (= nach, auf etwas folgend)
- pre- (= vor)
- re- (= noch einmal)

f

miscalculation, misleading, misunderstand

Prefixes which express the idea that something is done **badly** or **wrong**:
- mis-

Suffixes

With the help of suffixes we can form nouns, adjectives and verbs.

286 Nouns

a

educate – education, organize – organization,
pollute – pollution, decide – decision
move – movement, punish – punishment
perform – performance, exist – existence

Abstract nouns formed from verbs:
- -(a)tion/-sion

- -ment
- -ance/-ence

b

clever – cleverness, polite – politeness
distant – distance, silent – silence
certain – certainty, stupid – stupidity

Abstract nouns formed from adjectives:
- -ness
- -ance/-ence
- -(i)ty

c

teach – teacher, work – worker, act – actor, visit – visitor
assist – assistant, apply – applicant, study – student

Nouns formed from verbs and saying what someone's **job** is or what **group they belong to**:
- -er/-or
- -ant/-ent

d

journal – journalist, type – typist, active – activist
history – historian, republic – republican

Nouns formed from nouns, verbs or adjectives and saying what someone's **job** is or what **group they belong to**:
- -ist
- -(i)an

Appendix | **217** | **Word formation**

287 Adjectives

a
care – care**ful**/care**less**, help – help**ful**/help**less**
artist – artist**ic**, energy – energet**ic**
danger – danger**ous**, fame – fam**ous**
salt – salt**y**, health – health**y**
nation – nation**al**, industry – industri**al**
friend – friend**ly**, month – month**ly**

Adjectives **from nouns**:
- -ful/-less
- -ic
- -ous
- -y
- -al
- -ly

b
drink – drink**able**, eat – eat**able**, read – read**able**

Adjectives **from verbs**:
- -able

c
expense – expens**ive**, act – act**ive**

Adjectives **from nouns** or **verbs**:
- -ive

288 Verbs

legal – legal**ize**, modern – modern**ize**,
popular – popular**ize**
short – short**en**, wide – wid**en**

Verbs **from adjectives**:
- -ize

- -en

289 Conversion

Conversion means that a word can be used as another part of speech without having a prefix or suffix added. So the same word can belong to several different parts of speech.

a Let's go to the new sports shop. — Geschäft — • **noun** and **verb**
  I shop there from time to time. — einkaufen

b What a cold day! — kalt — • **adjective** and **noun**
  My wife has got a bad cold. — Erkältung

c These clothes are dry. — trocken — • **adjective** and **verb**
  The other clothes will soon dry. — trocknen

d I prefer light colours. — hell — • **adjective**, **noun** and **verb**
  You needn't switch on the light yet. — Licht
  Let's light a candle. — anzünden

American English

290-298

290 Present perfect – simple past
291 *Have* and *have got*
292 Irregular verbs
293 Question tags
294 Collective nouns

295 *The*
296 *This* and *that*
297 Adverbs
298 Prepositions

Between **British English (BE)** and **American English (AE)** there are some differences in pronunciation, spelling and vocabulary. But the differences in grammar are very small. The most important of them are described in this chapter.

290 Present perfect – simple past

BE/AE: Peter has just left.
　　　Have you ever eaten 'sushi'?
AE:　 Peter just left.
　　　Did you ever eat 'sushi'?

In AE we can use the **simple past** instead of the **present perfect** with adverbs like *just*, *already*, *yet*, *ever* and *never*.

▶ Present perfect and simple past in contrast: 87

291 Have *and* have got

BE:　 I've got/I have a free ticket.
　　　Has Liz got/Does Liz have any money?
　　　We haven't got/We don't have any time to lose.
AE:　 I have a free ticket.
　　　Does Liz have any money?
　　　We don't have any time to lose.

In BE **have** and **have got** are both possible. *Have got* is preferred in informal BE. In AE *have* is normally used.

▶ *Have* used as full verb: 53-55

292 Irregular verbs

BE:　 dream – dreamed – dreamed
　　　dream – dreamt – dreamt
AE:　 dream – dreamed – dreamed

Some verbs have both regular and irregular forms in BE. In AE the **regular forms** are preferred.

▶ Irregular verbs: 310

293 Question tags

BE/AE: Tom likes fast cars, doesn't he?
AE:　　You'll have to pay the money back, won't you?

AE:　　You'll arrive at 10.30, right?
　　　 We're leaving after breakfast, OK?

Question tags are used less often in AE than in BE. They are used in AE mainly when the speaker expects agreement.
The tags **right?** and **OK?** are often used in AE.

▶ Question tags: 11-12

294 Collective nouns

BE:　 The public was/were not informed early enough.
AE:　 The public was not informed early enough.

In AE a singular verb is preferred after a **collective noun**.

▶ Collective nouns: 176

295 The

BE/AE: Does Greg play the piano?
AE: Does Greg play piano?

BE: My brother is in hospital. (= He is ill.)
AE: My brother is in the hospital. (= He is ill.)
BE: Craig studies at university.
AE: Craig studies at the university.

In AE the **definite article** *the* can be omitted before a musical instrument.

In BE the definite article *the* is omitted before *hospital* and *university* when we are thinking of the purpose of the building. But *the* is normally used in AE.

▶ *The* with *church, school, prison*, etc.: 184

296 *This and* that

BE: (on the phone) Who is that?
AE: (on the phone) Who is this?

If we ask the name of someone speaking on the telephone, in BE the question is **Who is that?**, and in AE it is **Who is this?**

▶ Demonstrative pronouns: 237, 238

297 *Adverbs*

BE/AE: Kathy is a really nice person.
It certainly is hot today.
AE: Kathy is a real nice person.
It sure is hot today.

BE: Sue has probably heard the news by now.
AE: Sue probably has heard the news by now.

In informal AE an **adjective** can sometimes be used **instead of an adverb**.

Adverbs which in BE go in mid-position often come **before the auxiliary** in AE.

▶ Position of adverbs in a sentence: 215

298 *Prepositions*

BE: from Monday till Sunday
AE: from Monday through Sunday

BE: look out of the window
AE: look out the window

BE: round/around the lake
AE: around the lake

BE: in Bond Street
AE: on Fifth Avenue

BE: at the weekend
AE: on the weekend

BE: a player in the team
AE: a player on the team

BE: five past ten
AE: five past/after ten

BE: twenty to four
AE: twenty to/of four

BE: talk to someone
AE: talk to/with someone

BE: meet someone
AE: meet with someone

In **certain phrases** there are some differences in the use of prepositions in BE and AE.

299-301 Emphasis

299 Word stress
300 Special words
301 Special structures

299 Word stress

My father likes football, but *I* don't.
I didn't say I like football. I *don't* like it.
I don't really dislike football, but I don't *like* it either.
I like basketball, but I don't like *football*.

Any word in an English sentence can be emphasized if we give it especially **strong stress** in **speech**. We can often change the meaning of a sentence by changing the stress.

300 Special words

a   Thank you so much. It was such a lovely party.
    I really enjoyed it.
    Vielen, vielen Dank! Es war so eine nette Party. Es hat mir wirklich gut gefallen.
    The blouse was just what I was looking for.
    Die Bluse war genau das, wonach ich gesucht habe.
    That's definitely not true.
    Das ist definitiv nicht wahr.

Certain **individual words** like **so, such, really, just, certainly, definitely** and **absolutely** can be used to add emphasis.

b   Who ever heard of such a story?
    Wer hat denn je …?
    Why on earth didn't you ask for help?
    Warum hast du denn bloß nicht …?
    What the hell is your bike doing in the kitchen?
    Was zum Teufel …?

We can give special emphasis to a question if after a **question word** we add **ever** or phrases like **… in all the world, … in heaven's name, … on earth** or **… the hell** (informal).

c   This is the very book I was talking about.
    Das ist genau das Buch, …
    This is the very best news we've heard for weeks.
    Das ist die allerbeste Nachricht, …
    I hope it'll be the very last time you're late.
    Ich hoffe, dass es das allerletzte Mal ist, …

We can use **very** to emphasize a noun, a superlative or *next, last, first* or *same*.

d   I was very annoyed indeed.
    Ich war wirklich sehr verärgert.
    Thank you very much indeed.
    Vielen herzlichen Dank.

We can use **indeed** to emphasize *very* + adjective or adverb.

301 Special structures

a
I *do* like that jacket.
Ich mag diese Jacke wirklich.
I didn't say eight o'clock. – But you *did* say eight o'clock.
 … – Natürlich hast du acht Uhr gesagt.
Do have another piece of cake.
Nehmen Sie doch bitte noch ein Stück Kuchen!
Do be quiet!
Seid doch endlich leise!

In a statement without an auxiliary we can use **do/does/did** to add emphasis to what we are saying. This kind of emphasis is often used to give greater force to a command or an instruction. *Do/does/did* is always strongly stressed in such sentences. In American English this usage is less frequent.

'I'm sorry, but the doctor no longer sees patients in person. But he does take e-mails from 9:00 until 3:00.'

b
It's Tina who always starts the argument, not Tom.
Es ist Tina, die immer zu streiten anfängt, nicht Tom.
It's her voice (that) I like most.
It was the Clarks who were late.
It was in New York that I first met Sue, not in Boston.

It wasn't us who did the damage.

By using **it is/it was + relative clause** we can emphasize a noun, a pronoun or an adverbial phrase. This kind of emphasis is mainly used to express a contrast.

In this structure, we use the object form of the personal pronoun (i.e. *me, you, us*, etc.).

▶ Relative clauses: 258

c
Never have I felt so embarrassed.
Noch nie habe ich mich so geschämt.
Under no circumstances did she want to see her friend again.
Unter keinen Umständen wollte sie ihren Freund wiedersehen.

Some **adverbials** with a restrictive or negative meaning can go **at the beginning of the sentence** for special emphasis. In this case the word order is:
auxiliary – subject – main verb (inversion).

▶ Inversion: 10 d

d
Judy herself told me the news, so it must be true.
Judy selbst hat mir die Neuigkeit erzählt, …
This time I won't help you. Clean up the mess yourselves.
 … Bringt das Durcheinander selbst in Ordnung.

An **emphasizing pronoun** can emphasize a noun or pronoun which comes earlier in the sentence.

▶ Emphasizing pronoun: 236

e
He's always getting into trouble, that boy down the road.
Er gerät immer in Schwierigkeiten, …
Our neighbours are always quarrelling. We have to turn up the TV.
Unsere Nachbarn streiten sich ständig. …

We can use **always + present progressive** to emphasize the fact that something happens again and again, i.e. very often or too often.

▶ Present progressive: 77 a, note 2

Punctuation

302–304

302 Full stop
303 Exclamation mark
304 Comma

English punctuation is broadly similar to German. This chapter deals only with the most important differences.

302 Full stop (AE: period)

6.5 (six point five) 6,5 (sechs Komma fünf)	In English we use a **decimal point** rather than the comma used in German.
12,000 (twelve thousand) 12.000 (zwölftausend)	With **numbers over 1,000**, English uses a comma (rather than a point) in order to divide the number into thousands.
the year 2001	But when we write the year, we do the same as in German; we do not put any punctuation after the thousand figure.

303 Exclamation mark

Stop that dreadful noise! Hör mit diesem furchtbaren Lärm auf! What a lovely dress! Was für ein hübsches Kleid!	An exclamation mark is used in English only to express **strong feeling**, e.g. anger, enthusiasm or astonishment.
Turn over your papers, please. Dreht bitte die Zettel um! Write at least three sentences. Schreibt mindestens drei Sätze!	After an unemotional instruction, command, request, etc., we use a full stop. Exclamation marks are therefore used much less in English than in German.

304 Comma

a The film was very scary. I could hardly bear to watch it, so I turned it off half way through.
or:
… I could hardly bear to watch it so I turned it off half way through.
Der Film war richtig gruselig. Ich konnte es kaum ertragen, ihn anzusehen, also habe ich ihn mittendrin ausgeschaltet.

In English a comma is often used to indicate a **pause in speech** and to aid understanding. In contrast to German, the comma is not used primarily to divide the sentence into grammatical units.

Appendix — Punctuation

b Alison hasn't got a car, and she hasn't got a motorbike either.
Alison hat kein Auto und sie hat auch kein Motorrad.

Mel didn't really want the beer but she drank it anyway.
Mel wollte das Bier nicht wirklich, aber sie trank es trotzdem.

Main clauses which are connected by the conjunctions **and, but** or **or** may or may not have a comma between them. The longer the sentence, the more likely it is to have a comma.

c Luckily, there was nobody in the lift when it got stuck.
Glücklicherweise war niemand im Aufzug, als er stecken blieb.

Susan, of course, arrived much later than all the others.
Natürlich kam Susan viel später als die anderen.

Under the circumstances, it seemed better not to ask too many questions.
Unter den Umständen erschien es besser, nicht zu viele Fragen zu stellen.

Adverbs or **adverbial phrases** which come **at the beginning** or **in the middle of a sentence** are often separated off by commas.

d If the accident was Tony's fault, he should pay.
Wenn Tony den Unfall wirklich verschuldet hat, sollte er zahlen.

If a **subordinate clause** comes **at the beginning of a sentence**, it is usually separated from the main clause by a comma.

⚠ Is it true that the Robinsons live in Munich?
Stimmt es, dass die Robinsons in München wohnen?

Jenny quickly explained what Lisa had to do.
Jenny erklärte schnell, was Lisa tun musste.

We do not put a comma before a **subordinate clause with *that*, *what*, *where*, *why*,** etc.

e All the people who had known the President were very sad.
Alle Menschen, die den Präsidenten gekannt hatten, waren sehr traurig.

What's the name of the actress who starred in 'Notting Hill' with Hugh Grant?
Wie heißt die Schauspielerin, die mit Hugh Grant in „Notting Hill" gespielt hat?

A **defining relative clause** is not separated off by commas.

Julia Roberts, who has starred in several romantic comedies, is the best-paid actress in Hollywood.
Julia Roberts, die in verschiedenen romantischen Komödien mitgespielt hat, ist die bestbezahlte Schauspielerin in Hollywood.

A **non-defining relative clause** is separated from the main clause by commas.

▶ Relative clauses: 259 b, 265 a

f Sue looked at him and said, 'I can't believe that.'
Sue sah ihn an und sagte: „Ich kann das nicht glauben."

'I can't believe that,' Sue said.
„Ich kann das nicht glauben", sagte Sue.

Before **direct speech** we put a comma in English. In German we use a colon.

Sometimes the clause with the reporting verb comes after the direct speech. In English we put a comma before the second set of quotation marks.

▶ Indirect speech: 273-280

Numbers

305-309

305 Cardinal numbers/Ordinal numbers
306 The number 0
307 Fractions and decimals
308 The date
309 The time of day

305 Cardinal numbers / Ordinal numbers

Cardinal numbers

1	one [wʌn]
2	two
3	three
4	four
5	five
6	six
7	seven
8	eight
9	nine
10	ten
11	eleven
12	twelve
13	thirteen [ˌ– '–]
14	fourteen [ˌ– '–]
15	fifteen [ˌ– '–]
16	sixteen [ˌ– '–]
17	seventeen [ˌ– – '–]
18	eighteen [ˌ– '–]
19	nineteen [ˌ– '–]
20	twenty
21	twenty-one
22	twenty-two
23	twenty-three
30	thirty
40	forty ['– –]
50	fifty
60	sixty
70	seventy
80	eighty
90	ninety
100	one/a hundred
101	one/a hundred and one
200	two hundred
1,000	one/a thousand
1,001	one/a thousand and one
5,169	five thousand one hundred and sixty-nine
100,000	one/a hundred thousand
1,000,000	one/a million
1,000,000,000	one/a billion

Ordinal numbers

1st	(the) first
2nd	(the) second
3rd	(the) third
4th	(the) fourth
5th	(the) fifth
6th	(the) sixth
7th	(the) seventh
8th	(the) eighth
9th	(the) ninth
10th	(the) tenth
11th	(the) eleventh
12th	(the) twelfth
13th	(the) thirteenth [ˌ– '–]
14th	(the) fourteenth [ˌ– '–]
15th	(the) fifteenth [ˌ– '–]
16th	(the) sixteenth [ˌ– '–]
17th	(the) seventeenth [ˌ– – '–]
18th	(the) eighteenth [ˌ– '–]
19th	(the) nineteenth [ˌ– '–]
20th	(the) twentieth ['– tɪəθ]
21st	(the) twenty-first
22nd	(the) twenty-second
23rd	(the) twenty-third
30th	(the) thirtieth
40th	(the) fortieth
50th	(the) fiftieth
60th	(the) sixtieth
70th	(the) seventieth
80th	(the) eightieth
90th	(the) ninetieth
100th	(the) one hundredth
101st	(the) one hundred and first
200th	(the) two hundredth
1,000th	(the) one thousandth
1,001st	(the) one thousand and first
5,169th	(the) five thousand one hundred and sixty-ninth
100,000th	(the) one hundred thousandth
1,000,000th	(the) one millionth
1,000,000,000th	(the) one billionth

Appendix **225** **Numbers**

306 The number 0

The temperature often falls below zero here.
Six minus six is nought (BE)/zero (AE).
My phone number is 4021 (four-oh-two-one).
The final score was 2-0 (two nil/nothing).
Martina Hingis won the final set 6-0 (six love).

We can refer to the number **0** in various ways.
- zero [ˈzɪərəʊ] (on a scale)
- nought [nɔːt] (BE)/zero (AE) (when doing sums)
- „oh" [əʊ] (in telephone and account numbers)
- nil or nothing (in sports results)
- love (in tennis).

307 Fractions and decimals

a ⅝   five eighths

   ⅓ (mile)   one/a third (of a mile)

   ½   one/a half (**but:** ½ mile = half a mile)

   ¾ (hour)   three quarters (of an hour)

   3 ½ (km)   three and a half (kilometres)

   5 ⅔   five and two thirds

Ordinal numbers are also used to form **fractions**.
(exceptions: half and quarter)

b 0.5   (nought) point five (BE)
               zero point five (AE)
   4.25%   four point two five per cent

Decimals have a point in English and not a comma:
four point two five = vier Komma zwei fünf.

308 The date

   May 7(th)   May the seventh
               in AE also: May seventh
   7(th) May   the seventh of May

   1993   nineteen ninety-three
   2003   two thousand and three

There are various ways of saying and writing the **date**.

⚠ 3/7/02   = 3rd July, 2002 (BE)
              = March 7th, 2002 (AE)

When the date is written in figures (e.g. 3/7/02), the order in **BE** is day/month/year, but in **AE** it is month/day/year.

Appendix **Numbers**

309 The time of day

a
| 8.00 | eight o'clock |
| | I'll see you at eight, Jackie. |

| 8.15 | eight fifteen |
| | = (a) quarter past eight |

| 8.20 | eight twenty |
| | = twenty (minutes) past eight |

| 8.30 | eight thirty |
| | = half past eight |

| 8.45 | eight forty-five |
| | = (a) quarter to nine |

| 8.53 | eight fifty-three |
| | = seven (minutes) to nine |

> **Note**
>
> BE: twenty (minutes) to nine
> AE: twenty (minutes) to/of nine
>
> BE: ten (minutes) past six
> AE: ten (minutes) past/after six

We use **o'clock** only on the hour. We can leave it out in informal speech.

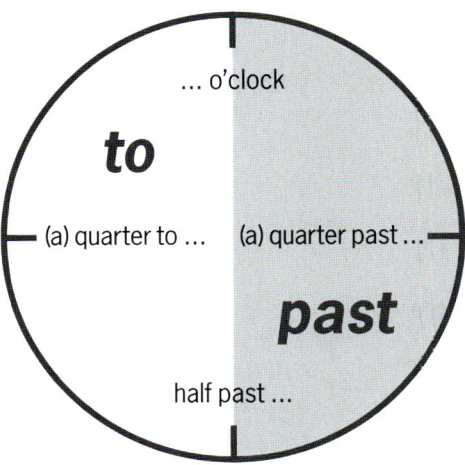

In American English we can use *of* instead of *to* and *after* instead of *past*.

b   8.00 am   eight am [ˌeɪ_'em]
                = eight o'clock in the morning

    8.00 pm   eight pm [ˌpiː_'em]
                = eight o'clock in the evening/at night

c   14.27   fourteen twenty-seven
    20.00   twenty (hundred) hours

If we add **am** (= *before noon*), we can make it clear that we mean the twelve hours **before** midday (= 0.00–12.00).

If we add **pm** (= *after noon*), we can make it clear that we mean the twelve hours **after** midday (= 12.00–24.00).

The 24-hour clock is used mainly in **timetables**.

310 Irregular verbs

infinitive	simple past	past participle	
be	was, were	been	*sein*
bear	bore	borne, born	*(er)tragen*
beat	beat	beaten	*schlagen, besiegen*
become	became	become	*werden*
begin	began	begun	*beginnen, anfangen*
bend	bent	bent	*(sich) biegen; sich beugen*
bet	bet	bet	*wetten*
bind	bound	bound	*binden, verbinden*
bite	bit	bitten	*beißen*
blow	blew	blown	*blasen, wehen*
break	broke	broken	*(zer)brechen; kaputtmachen*
breed	bred	bred	*züchten*
bring	brought [ɔ:]	brought [ɔ:]	*(mit)bringen, (her)bringen*
broadcast	broadcast	broadcast	*senden, übertragen, ausstrahlen*
build	built	built	*bauen*
burn	burnt, burned*	burnt, burned*	*(ver)brennen*
burst	burst	burst	*platzen*
buy	bought [ɔ:]	bought [ɔ:]	*kaufen*
cast	cast	cast	*werfen*
catch	caught [ɔ:]	caught [ɔ:]	*fangen, erwischen*
choose [u:]	chose [əʊ]	chosen [əʊ]	*(aus)wählen, aussuchen*
cling	clung	clung	*sich klammern, festhalten*
come	came	come	*kommen*
cost	cost	cost	*kosten*
creep	crept	crept	*kriechen, schleichen*
cut	cut	cut	*schneiden*
deal [i:]	dealt [e]	dealt [e]	*handeln (von), sich beschäftigen (mit)*
dig	dug	dug	*graben*
do	did	done [ʌ]	*tun, machen*
draw	drew	drawn	*zeichnen; ziehen*
dream [i:]	dreamt [e], dreamed [i:]*	dreamt [e], dreamed [i:]*	*träumen*
drink	drank	drunk	*trinken*
drive	drove	driven	*(Auto) fahren; (an)treiben*
eat	ate [eɪ, BE also: e]	eaten	*essen*
fall	fell	fallen	*(hin)fallen*
feed	fed	fed	*füttern*
feel	felt	felt	*(sich) fühlen*
fight	fought [ɔ:]	fought [ɔ:]	*(be)kämpfen*
find	found	found	*finden*
flee	fled	fled	*fliehen, flüchten*
fling	flung	flung	*schleudern*
fly	flew	flown	*fliegen*
forbid	forbade [æ]	forbidden	*verbieten*
forget	forgot	forgotten	*vergessen*
freeze	froze	frozen	*(ge)frieren; erstarren*

infinitive	simple past	past participle	
get	got	BE: got AE: gotten	*bekommen; (hin)kommen; holen; werden*
give	gave	given	*geben; schenken*
go	went	gone [ɒ]	*gehen; fahren; werden*
grind	ground	ground	*zerkleinern, mahlen*
grow	grew	grown	*wachsen; anbauen, anpflanzen*
hang	hung hanged*	hung hanged*	*hängen; etw. aufhängen* *jd. hängen*
have	had	had	*haben*
hear [ɪə]	heard [ɜː]	heard [ɜː]	*hören*
hide	hid	hidden	*(sich) verstecken*
hit	hit	hit	*schlagen, treffen*
hold	held	held	*(fest)halten*
hurt	hurt	hurt	*verletzen, wehtun*
keep	kept	kept	*(be)halten; aufbewahren; weiter tun*
kneel	knelt, kneeled*	knelt, kneeled*	*knien*
know	knew	known	*kennen; wissen*
lay	laid	laid	*legen*
lead	led	led	*führen, leiten*
leap [iː]	leapt [e], leaped [iː]*	leapt [e], leaped [iː]*	*springen, hüpfen*
learn	learnt, learned*	learnt, learned*	*lernen*
leave	left	left	*weggehen, verlassen; (zurück)lassen*
lend	lent	lent	*(ver)leihen*
let	let	let	*(zu)lassen*
lie	lay	lain	*liegen*
light	lit, lighted*	lit, lighted*	*anzünden; beleuchten*
lose [uː]	lost [ɒ]	lost [ɒ]	*verlieren*
make	made	made	*machen, bauen; (veran)lassen*
mean [iː]	meant [e]	meant [e]	*bedeuten; meinen*
meet	met	met	*(sich) treffen; kennen lernen*
overcome	overcame	overcome	*überwältigen; überwinden*
overtake	overtook	overtaken	*überholen*
pay	paid	paid	*(be)zahlen*
put	put	put	*stellen, legen, setzen*
quit	quit, quitted*	quit, quitted*	*verlassen; aufhören*
read [iː]	read [e]	read [e]	*(vor)lesen*
retell	retold	retold	*nacherzählen*
ride	rode	ridden	*reiten; (Rad) fahren*
ring	rang	rung	*läuten, klingeln; anrufen*
rise [aɪ]	rose	risen [ɪ]	*(an)steigen; sich erheben, aufstehen*
run	ran	run	*laufen, rennen; führen, leiten*
say	said [e]	said [e]	*sagen*
see	saw	seen	*sehen*
seek	sought [ɔː]	sought [ɔː]	*suchen*

infinitive	simple past	past participle	
sell	sold	sold	*verkaufen*
send	sent	sent	*schicken, senden*
set	set	set	*setzen; untergehen (Sonne, Mond)*
sew [əʊ]	sewed [əʊ]	sewn, sewed* [əʊ]	*nähen*
shake	shook	shaken	*schütteln; erschüttern*
shine	shone [BE: ɒ, AE: əʊ]	shone [BE: ɒ, AE: əʊ]	*scheinen (Sonne); leuchten*
shoot	shot	shot	*(er)schießen*
show	showed	shown	*zeigen*
shut	shut	shut	*schließen, zumachen*
sing	sang	sung	*singen*
sink	sank	sunk	*sinken; versenken*
sit	sat	sat	*sitzen*
sleep	slept	slept	*schlafen*
slide	slid	slid	*rutschen*
smell	smelt, smelled*	smelt, smelled*	*riechen*
speak	spoke	spoken	*sprechen*
spell	spelt, spelled*	spelt, spelled*	*buchstabieren*
spend	spent	spent	*(Geld) ausgeben; (Zeit) verbringen*
spit	spat	spat	*spucken*
spoil	spoilt, spoiled*	spoilt, spoiled*	*verderben; verwöhnen*
spread [e]	spread [e]	spread [e]	*(sich) ausbreiten; aufstreichen*
stand	stood	stood	*stehen*
steal	stole	stolen	*stehlen*
stick	stuck	stuck	*kleben*
sting	stung	stung	*stechen*
stink	stank, stunk	stunk	*stinken*
strike	struck	struck	*schlagen; treffen (Blitz, Kugel)*
strive [aɪ]	strove	striven [ɪ]	*sich bemühen, kämpfen*
swear	swore	sworn	*schwören*
sweep	swept	swept	*kehren, fegen*
swim	swam	swum	*schwimmen*
swing	swung	swung	*schwingen*
take	took	taken	*(mit)nehmen; (hin-, weg)bringen*
teach	taught [ɔ:]	taught [ɔ:]	*unterrichten, lehren*
tear [eə]	tore	torn	*(zer)reißen*
tell	told	told	*sagen, nennen; erzählen, berichten*
think	thought [ɔ:]	thought [ɔ:]	*meinen, denken, glauben*
throw	threw	thrown	*werfen*
understand	understood	understood	*verstehen, begreifen*
upset	upset	upset	*erschüttern, verärgern*
wake	woke	woken	*aufwachen; aufwecken*
wear [eə]	wore	worn	*(Kleidung, Brille) tragen, anhaben*
weep	wept	wept	*weinen*
wet	wet	wet	*befeuchten*
win	won [ʌ]	won [ʌ]	*gewinnen*
write	wrote	written	*schreiben*

* Some irregular verbs also have a regular form, which is used more and more frequently.

Grammatical terms

abstract noun	abstraktes Nomen, Begriffswort	*life, love, pollution, …*
active	Aktiv, Tatform	The police *caught* the thief.
activity verb	Tätigkeitsverb, Vorgangsverb	*write, play, rain, grow, …*
adjective	Adjektiv, Eigenschaftswort	*bad, good, big, expensive, …*
adverb	Adverb, Umstandswort	
adverb of degree	Gradadverb	*very* good, *extremely* cold, …
adverb of frequency ['fri:kwənsi]	Adverb der Häufigkeit	*always, never, often, once, …*
adverb of manner	Adverb der Art und Weise	*badly, easily, carefully, well, …*
adverb of place	Adverb des Ortes (oder der Richtung)	*here, there, outside, nowhere, …*
adverb of time	Adverb der Zeit	*now, today, yesterday, …*
adverbial	adverbiale Bestimmung, Umstandsangabe	Come and sit *here/next to me*. I'm leaving *today/on Monday*.
adverbial clause of contrast	Adverbialsatz des Gegensatzes	*Though it was very late*, the dockers went on working.
adverbial clause of place	Adverbialsatz des Ortes	Tell me *where I can leave my stuff*.
adverbial clause of purpose	Adverbialsatz des Zwecks	She hid the letter *so that nobody would read it*.
adverbial clause of reason	Adverbialsatz des Grundes	I fell asleep in the history lesson *because I was bored*.
adverbial clause of time	Adverbialsatz der Zeit	I got a job in a bank *after I left school*.
adverbial phrase	zusammengesetzte adverbiale Bestimmung	*to the shops, in the morning, …*
article	Artikel, Begleiter, Geschlechtswort	*a, an, the*
aspect	Aspekt, *progressive form* vs. *simple form*	
attributive [-'---]	attributiv, vor dem Nomen stehend	a *big* castle
auxiliary [ɔːgˈzɪliəri]	Hilfsverb, Hilfszeitwort	*has* gone, *don't* eat, *can* fly, …
backshift of tenses	Verschiebung der Zeiten (in der indirekten Rede)	Ann: 'I *am* sorry.' ▷ Ann said she *was* sorry.
bare infinitive	Infinitiv ohne *to*	You can *say* that again!
cardinal number ['kɑːdɪnl]	Grundzahl	*one, two, three, ten, …*
clause	Teilsatz (= Haupt- oder Nebensatz)	→ main clause, subordinate clause
clause element	Satzglied (z.B. *subject*, *verb*, *object*)	
collective noun [kəˈlektɪv]	Sammelname, Gruppenbezeichnung	*family, team, people, police, …*
colon	Doppelpunkt	Er sagte*:* "Ich kann das nicht glauben."
comma	Komma	Peter*,* Paul and Mary …
command [kəˈmɑːnd]	Aufforderung(ssatz)	Listen. Let's go to the cinema.
common noun	allgemeines Nomen	*woman, town, month, …*
comparative	Komparativ, erste Steigerungsform	*faster, better, more interesting, …*
comparison	Steigerung; Vergleich	fast – faster – fastest; as fast as …; faster than …
complement ['kɒmplɪmənt]	prädikative Ergänzung (zum Subjekt oder Objekt)	→ subject complement, object complement
complex sentence	Satzgefüge (aus Haupt- und Nebensatz), zusammengesetzter Satz	I can't come *because I'm ill*.
compound adjective	zusammengesetztes Adjektiv	*seasick, well-dressed, …*
compound noun	zusammengesetztes Nomen	*ticket office, sightseeing, blackboard, …*
compound sentence	Satzreihe (aus zwei oder mehr Hauptsätzen)	I like swimming *and* I enjoy dancing.
compound tense	zusammengesetzte Zeit (z.B. *present perfect, past progressive*)	
conditional sentence	Bedingungssatz, Konditionalsatz	*If you help me*, I'll help you.
conjunction	Konjunktion, Bindewort	*and, or, but; after, when, although, …*
consonant ['kɒnsənənt]	Konsonant, Mitlaut	*b, c, d, f, …*; [p], [s], [ʃ], [j], …
contact clause	Relativsatz ohne Relativpronomen	He's the man *I saw yesterday*.
conversion	Konversion, Übergang eines Wortes von einer Wortart in die andere	What a *cold* day! I've got a *cold*.
coordinating conjunction [kəʊˈɔːdɪneɪtɪŋ]	nebenordnende Konjunktion	*and, but, or, …*
countable noun	zählbares Nomen	*house(s), idea(s), child(ren), …*

decimals ['---]	Dezimalzahlen	*1.4, 6.7, ...*
defining relative clause	bestimmender Relativsatz, notwendiger Relativsatz	The boy *who said that* is silly.
definite article	bestimmter Artikel	*the* bag, *the* apples
demonstrative determiner [dɪ'mɒnstrətɪv]	Demonstrativpronomen als Bestimmungswort, Demonstrativbegleiter	*this* man, *these* men, *that* girl, *those* girls
demonstrative pronoun	(nominal gebrauchtes) Demonstrativpronomen, hinweisendes Fürwort	*This* is my sister. Whose shoes are *those*?
determiner [dɪ'tɜːmɪnə]	Bestimmungswort (vor einem Nomen), Begleiter (eines Nomens)	*a* car, *my* bike, *this* house, *some* money, ...
direct object ['daɪrekt]	direktes Objekt (meist Sachobjekt)	I like *pop music*. Carol gave her friend *a tie*.
direct speech	direkte Rede, wörtliche Rede	Ann said, *'I'm sorry.'*
-ed form	*-ed*-Form (der regelmäßigen Verben)	*watched, loved, shouted, ...*
emphasis ['emfəsɪs]	Hervorhebung, Betonung	Thank you *so* much.
emphasizing pronoun ['emfəsaɪzɪŋ]	verstärkendes Pronomen	I saw the accident *myself*.
end-position	Endstellung (des Adverbs)	I opened the door *carefully*.
exclamation [ˌeksklə'meɪʃn]	Ausruf(esatz)	*What a nice cat! How beautiful!*
exclamation mark	Ausrufezeichen	*Don't you dare!*
falling intonation	fallende Intonation	It's too cold in here, *isn't it*?
finite forms	finite, gebeugte Formen (des Verbs)	*does, did, watch, watched, ...*
fixed phrase	feststehende Fügung	*have a party, go by train, ...*
focusing adverb	betonendes Adverb	I *only* got here five minutes ago.
foreign plural	Plural bei Wörtern aus anderen Sprachen	*analyses, stimuli, bacteria, ...*
fractions	Bruchzahlen	*three quarters, one third*
free indirect speech	erlebte Rede	
front-position	Anfangsstellung (des Adverbs)	*Fortunately*, we could all swim.
full stop	Punkt	*The wall's 3.6 m high.*
full verb	Vollverb	*say, sing, laugh, walk, ...*
future	Zeitform der Zukunft, Futur	→ *going to*-future, *will*-future
future perfect	vollendete Zukunft, Futur II	I *will have written*
future progressive	Verlaufsform der Zukunft	I *will be writing*
gender (of nouns) ['dʒendə]	Geschlecht (der Nomen)	*he* (boy), *she* (girl), *it* (table)
gerund ['dʒerənd]	Gerundium, *-ing*-Form	I like *dancing. Dancing* is fun.
gerund construction	Gerundialkonstruktion	Kim *enjoys skating*.
going to-future	Futur mit *going to*	*I'm going to write*
idiomatic expression	idiomatische Wendung	*beat about the bush* = um den heißen Brei herumreden
if-clause	Nebensatz mit *if*, *if*-Satz	*If you help me*, I'll help you.
imperative [ɪm'perətɪv]	Imperativ, Befehlsform, Aufforderung	*Listen. Don't talk.*
indefinite article	unbestimmter Artikel	*a* bag, *an* apple
indirect command ['ɪndərekt]	indirekte Aufforderung	He told me *to leave*.
indirect object	indirektes Objekt (meist Personenobjekt)	Carol gave *her friend* a tie.
indirect question	indirekter Fragesatz	She asked me *where the station was*.
indirect speech	indirekte Rede, nicht wörtliche Rede	Ann said *(that) she was sorry*. Do you know *where Ken is*?
infinitive	Infinitiv, Grundform des Verbs	*(to) go, (to) dance, (to) sit, ...* → passive infinitive, perfect infinitive
infinitive construction	Infinitivkonstruktion	*To know him* is *to love him*.
infinitive without *to*	Infinitiv ohne *to*	You can *say* that again!
-ing form	*-ing*-Form des Verbs	*going, dancing, sitting, ...*
initial sound	Anlaut	bottle: [b]
intransitive verb	intransitives Verb (= kann nicht mit direktem Objekt verbunden werden)	*appear, sleep, laugh, ...*
inversion	Inversion, Umkehr der Stellung von Subjekt und Prädikatskern im Satz	Rarely *does Lee* pay his debts.
irregular verb	unregelmäßiges Verb	*go – went – gone*

linking adverb	satzverbindendes Adverb	Sharon loves parties. After what Ian said to her, *however*, she doesn't feel like going to his party.
linking verb	Verb, das Subjekt und Subjektkomplement miteinander verbindet	*appear, be, become, seem, …*
long form	Langform des Hilfsverbs	She *is* talking. You *need not* go.
main clause	Hauptsatz	*I can't come* because I'm ill.
main verb	Vollverb, wenn es um seine Funktion im Satz geht	She doesn't *like* skating.
material noun	Stoffbezeichnung	*air, bread, milk, sand, …*
mid-position	Mittelstellung (des Adverbs)	You can *always* ask me.
modal auxiliary [ˌməʊdl_ɔːgˈzɪliəri]/ modal/modal verb	modales Hilfsverb	*can, could, may, might, will, would, shall, should, ought to, must, needn't*
name	Eigenname	*July, England, London, …*
nationality word	Nationalitätsbezeichnung	*an Englishwoman, the English*
'natural' adverb	„ursprüngliches", nicht vom Adjektiv abgeleitetes Adverb	*always, perhaps, soon, still, …*
negative infinitive	verneinter Infinitiv	He told me *not to cry*.
negative statement	verneinter Aussagesatz	*I don't like pop music.*
non-defining relative clause [ˈnɒndɪfaɪnɪŋ]	nicht bestimmender Relativsatz, nicht notwendiger Relativsatz	Uncle Bill, *who works there*, should be able to help.
non-finite forms	infinite, nicht gebeugte Formen (des Verbs)	*(to) do, doing, (to) watch, watching*
'notional' subject	Sinnsubjekt	They wanted *him* to be home by ten.
noun	Nomen, Substantiv, Hauptwort	*book, milk, fridge, pain, glasses, …*
number	Zahl(wort)	*one, two, …; first, second, …*
object	Objekt, Satzergänzung	I like *pop music*.
object complement	Objektkomplement, Ergänzung zum Objekt	The waiting made me *nervous*.
object form	Objektform (des Personalpronomens)	*me, you, him, her, it, us, them*
object question	Frage nach dem Objekt	*What did you say? Who did you ask?*
of-phrase	*of*-Fügung	the name *of the street*
open condition	erfüllbare Bedingung	→ real condition
ordinal number [ˈɔːdɪnl]	Ordnungszahl	*first, second, third, tenth, …*
pair noun	Paarwort	*trousers, pyjamas, shorts, …*
part of speech	Wortart (z.B. *adjective, verb*)	
participle [ˈpɑːtɪsɪpl]	Partizip	*helping, going, …; helped, gone, …* → present participle, past participle
participle construction	Partizipialkonstruktion	*Entering the house*, I saw an old man.
passive	Passiv, Leideform	The thief *was caught* (by the police).
passive gerund	Passivform des Gerundiums	I don't like *being called* 'stupid'.
passive infinitive	Passivform des Infinitivs	I want *to be asked*.
passive participle	Passivform des Partizips	Have you ever watched an operation *being performed*?
passive progressive	Verlaufsform des Passivs	The match *is being shown* on TV.
past participle	Partizip Perfekt, Partizip II	Jane has *arrived*. The thief was *caught*. This is the *stolen* car.
past perfect	Plusquamperfekt, Vorvergangenheit	I *had written*
past perfect progressive	Verlaufsform des *past perfect*	I *had been writing*
past progressive	Verlaufsform der Vergangenheit	I *was writing*
past tense	Vergangenheitsform, Präteritum, Imperfekt	I *wrote* – I *was writing*
perfect infinitive	Infinitiv Perfekt	John may *have arrived*.
period of time	Zeitraum	*for three hours*
personal pronoun	Personalpronomen, persönliches Fürwort	*I, you, she, me, them, …*
phrasal verb [ˈfreɪzl]	feste Verb-Adverb-Verbindung	*fill sth. in, put sth. up, go on, …*
phrase of place	Ortsangabe	*near the station, under my bed, there …*
phrase of time	Zeitangabe	*on Monday, next week, yesterday, …*
plural	Plural, Mehrzahl	*chairs, letters, feet; we, yourselves, those, …*
plural noun	Nomen, das nur im Plural steht	*clothes, stairs, glasses, …*
point of time	Zeitpunkt	*at 9:15*
positive statement	bejahter Aussagesatz	*I like pop music.*

possessive adjective [pə'zesɪv]	Possessivpronomen als Bestimmungswort, Possessivbegleiter	→ possessive determiner
possessive determiner	Possessivpronomen als Bestimmungswort, Possessivbegleiter	*my, your, his, her, its, our, their*
possessive form	*s*-Genitiv, besitzanzeigende Form	*Sandra's* bike, *our friends'* car
possessive pronoun	(nominal gebrauchtes) Possessivpronomen, besitzanzeigendes Fürwort	*mine, yours, his, hers, ours, theirs*
predicative [–'–––]	prädikativ, nach dem Verb stehend	The castle is *big*.
prefix ['priːfɪks]	Vorsilbe, Präfix	*dis-, in-, re-, un-, …*
preposition	Präposition, Verhältniswort	*at, in, on, with, by, because of, …*
preposition of place	Präposition des Ortes	*in* the park, *above* the clouds, …
preposition of time	Präposition der Zeit	*at* three o'clock, *on* Sunday, …
prepositional object	Präpositionalobjekt	I'm looking for *my glasses*.
prepositional verb	Verbindung aus Verb + Präposition, präpositionales Verb	*look at* sth., *look for* sth., *listen to* sb., …
present infinitive	Infinitiv Präsens	You may *leave* earlier today.
present participle	Partizip Präsens, Partizip I	I'm *looking* for my bag. I've seen a *flying* saucer.
present perfect	*present perfect* (Perfekt, vollendete Gegenwart)	I *have written*
present perfect progressive	Verlaufsform des *present perfect*	I *have been writing*
present progressive	Verlaufsform der Gegenwart	I *am writing*
present tense	Gegenwartsform, Präsens	I *write* – I *am writing*
primary verb	Verb, das als Hilfs- und Vollverb verwendet werden kann	*be, have, do*
progressive form [prə'gresɪv]	Verlaufsform des Verbs	I *am writing* – I *was writing* – I *have been writing*
progressive infinitive	Verlaufsform des Infinitivs	Mike must *be watching* TV.
pronoun	Pronomen, Fürwort	→ personal/possessive/demonstrative/relative/reflexive/emphasizing pronoun
pronunciation	Aussprache	[prəˌnʌnsi'eɪʃn]
prop-word	Stützwort	a blue car and a red *one*
proper noun	Eigenname	*Belfast, Mr Ferguson, Sunday, …*
punctuation	Zeichensetzung	
quantifier ['kwɒntɪfaɪə]	Mengenbezeichnung	*some, any, much, many, a few, …*
question	Frage(satz)	Is Jill at home? – No, she isn't. Where's Jill? – At school.
question tag	Frageanhängsel, Bestätigungsfrage	It's hot, *isn't it*? You aren't working, *are you*?
question with a question word	Frage mit einem Fragewort, Fragewortfrage	Where's Jill? – At school.
question word	Fragewort	*what, where, who, whose, when, why, which, how*
real condition	erfüllbare Bedingung	*If it rains this afternoon*, the match will be cancelled.
reflexive pronoun [rɪ'fleksɪv]	Reflexivpronomen, rückbezügliches Fürwort	I hurt *myself*.
regular verb	regelmäßiges Verb	*watch – watched – watched*
relative clause	Relativsatz, Bezugssatz	The boy *who said that* is silly.
relative pronoun	Relativpronomen, bezügliches Fürwort	the girl *who/that* you met the car *which/that* was stolen the boy *whose* parents we met
reported speech	indirekte Rede, nicht wörtliche Rede	Ann said *(that) she was sorry*. Do you know *where Ken is*?
reporting verb	einleitendes Verb (der indirekten Rede)	Ann *said/added* she was sorry.
rising intonation	steigende Intonation	The film starts at 8.15, *doesn't it*?
sentence	Satz	*I like music. Do you smoke?* → complex sentence, compound sentence
sentence adverb	Adverb, das sich auf den ganzen Satz bezieht	*Clearly*, there has been a mistake.
-*s*-form	-*s*-Form des Verbs (= 3. Person Singular des *simple present*)	she *knows*, he *likes*, it *tries*
short answer	Kurzantwort	Can you see? – *Yes, I can.* – *No, I can't.*

short form	Kurzform des Hilfsverbs	she's, I've, you needn't, …
sibilant sound	Zischlaut	[ʃ], [s], [ʒ], …
simple form	einfache Form des Verbs	I write – I wrote – I have written – I had written – I will write
simple past	einfache Form der Vergangenheit	I wrote
simple present	einfache Form der Gegenwart	I write
singular ['sɪŋgjələ]	Singular, Einzahl	chair, letter, foot; I, yourself, that, …
sound	Laut	[ə], [ð], [ɲ], …
spelling	Rechtschreibung	
split infinitive	Trennung des to vom Infinitiv durch ein Adverb	It's difficult to really understand him.
statement	Aussagesatz	I (don't) like pop music.
state verb	Zustandsverb	know, hate, want, …
stress	(Wort)Betonung	ˌɪnfəˈmeɪʃn
stressed syllable	betonte Silbe	excla'mation
subject	Subjekt, Satzgegenstand	Sandra likes pop music. The thief was caught.
subject complement	Subjektkomplement, Ergänzung zum Subjekt	He became chairman.
subject form	Subjektform (des Personalpronomens)	I, you, he, she, it, we, they
subject question	Frage nach dem Subjekt	What happened? Who came?
subjunctive	Konjunktiv	Er sagte, er könne das nicht glauben.
subordinate clause [səˈbɔːdɪnət]	Nebensatz, untergeordneter Satz	I can't come because I'm ill. → if-clause, relative clause
subordinating conjunction [səˈbɔːdɪneɪtɪŋ]	unterordnende Konjunktion (zur Einleitung eines Nebensatzes)	because, if, that, when, …
substitute form	Ersatzform	can ▷ be able to; must ▷ have to
suffix ['sʌfɪks]	Nachsilbe, Endsilbe, Suffix	-able, -ful, -ly, …
superlative [suːˈpɜːlətɪv]	Superlativ, höchste Steigerungsform	fastest, best, most terrible, …
syllable	Silbe	fan-ta-stic
tense	(grammatische) Zeitform, Tempus	→ present tense, past tense
time	wirkliche Zeit (im Gegensatz zur grammatischen Zeitform des Verbs)	present, past, future
timetable future	Zukunftsform, die auf fahrplanmäßige Geschehen verweist	The plane to Madrid leaves at 9.55 tomorrow.
to-infinitive	to-Infinitiv	I'd like to leave early.
transitive verb	transitives Verb (= kann mit direktem Objekt verbunden werden)	help sb., love sb., …
uncountable noun	nicht zählbares Nomen	bread, oil, time, information, …
unreal condition	nicht erfüllbare Bedingung	If I were you, I'd take the job.
unstressed syllable	unbetonte Silbe	excla'mation
verb	1. Prädikat(skern), Satzaussage 2. Verb, Zeitwort, Tätigkeitswort	I like pop music. I can play the guitar. be, like, play, sit down, …; can, will, do, …
verb of movement	Verb der Bewegung	come, go
verb of perception	Verb der Wahrnehmung	feel, hear, listen to, notice, see, smell, taste, watch
verb of rest	Verb der Ruhe	lie, remain, sit, stand, stay
verb of speaking and thinking	Verb des Sagens und Denkens	believe, consider, expect, say, think
voiced sound	stimmhafter Laut	[g], [d], [b], …
voiceless sound	stimmloser Laut	[k], [t], [p], …
vowel ['vaʊəl]	Vokal, Selbstlaut	a, e, i, o, u; [ɪ], [ʊ], [ɜː], [eɪ], …
will-future	Futur mit will	I will write
word class	Wortart, Wortklasse (z.B. noun, adjective, preposition)	
word formation	Wortbildung	song + writer = songwriter
word order	Wortstellung, Satzgliedstellung	e.g. subject – verb (S–V)
word stress	Betonung eines Wortes	My father likes tennis, but I don't.
yes/no question	Entscheidungsfrage	Is Jill at home? – No, she isn't.

Index

The numbers refer to the sections of the grammar; *N (1, 2, …)* stands for *note (1, 2, …)*, ⚠ *(1, 2, …)* stands for the warning triangle *(1, 2, …)*. Numbers in **bold** refer to the sections which deal in depth with a word or structure.

A

a/an: 178, **181**, 189-195
   forms and pronunciation 181b/c
   use 170, 177a, **189-195**
   = *per* 192
   after *as, without* 191
   after *half, quite, rather, such,* etc. 194a
   before jobs, nationalities, etc. 190
   or *one* 193
   fixed phrases 195
   + adjective 196d N2
ability: *can, could, be able to* 25, 26, **36, 37**
able → *be able to*
about 247, 250
above 247, 250
abroad: position 215c
absolutely: to emphasize sth. 300a
abstract noun: 286a/b
   use of *the* 183a
according to 247
across 247
active: 72, **107**, 111, 112, 114 N, 120a, 136a, 139a N, 145 ⚠, 153a
activity verb 69, 71, 83 ⚠, **209b**
   do as activity verb 57
   have as activity verb 55
add + indirect speech 274a
adjective: 196-202
   use **196**, 209
   use in AE 297
   used attributively **196b/d**, 199 N
   used predicatively 196b/c
   comparative and superlative 197-200
   in comparisons 200
   used as noun 202
   used as subject complement/object complement 18
   participles used as adjectives 153a N
   after verbs 196b, 209a
   with a suffix 287
   compound adjectives 284
   + gerund 145
   + preposition 246e
   + preposition + gerund 141
   + prop-word *one* **201**, 239
   + *to*-infinitive 124
admit: + gerund 139a
   + indirect speech 274a
advantage of + gerund 142
adverb: 203-216
   form 205-208
   formed from an adjective 206
   with the form of an adjective 207
   with two forms 208
   'natural' adverb 205
   use 203
   comparative and superlative 210-212
   in comparisons 213
   position 2 ⚠1, **214, 215**
   position in AE 297
   of frequency 204, **215b/c**
   of manner 204, **215c/c N**
   of place 204, **215c**
   of time 204, **215b/c**
   adverb of degree 204, **215e**
   focusing adverb 204, **215f**
   linking adverb 204, **215a**
   sentence adverb 204, **215a**
   emphasis 215g
   punctuation 304c
   after verbs 209b
   English verbal expressions for German adverbs 216
   verb + adverb → phrasal verb
adverbial: **17**, 121a
   position 2 ⚠1, 10c/d, 17, 301c
   to emphasize sth. 301c
   punctuation 304c
   with negative or restrictive meaning 10d, 301c
adverbial clause: 267-272
   of time 268
   of place 269
   of reason 270
   of contrast 271
   of purpose 272
   shortened adverbial clause 267d
   infinitive as substitute 267c
   participle as substitute 157-161, 267c
adverbial phrase: 205
   position 2 ⚠1, 10c/d
   punctuation 304c
advice: uncountable noun 177c
advice: *should, ought to, must …* 29, 35, **42**
   in indirect speech 274a, **280b**
advise: passive 111b
   + indirect speech 274a, **280b**
   + object + *to*-infinitive **123a**, 280b
aerobics: singular 177d
a few 178, 217, **219d-f**
afford: not reflexive 233b
afraid: not before a noun 196c

afraid of + gerund 141
afraid/frightened 196c
after: conjunction 268
   preposition 247, 250, 298
   in AE 309 N
   + gerund 144
   + past perfect or simple past 92 N
against 247
ago: position 215c
   in indirect speech 276a
   + past tense 86a, 87
agree: state verb 70
   + indirect speech 274a
   + *to*-infinitive 122
   agree with + gerund 143
ahead of 247
aircraft: singular and plural 172b
a little: 178, 217, **219d/e**
   comparative and superlative 212, 219f
alive: not before a noun 196c
all: 80b, 82a, 87, 178, 217, **221**
   + relative pronoun *that* 260 N
   + *the* 187, **221b**
   all of 221b N1
allow: passive 111b
   + object + *to*-infinitive 123a
   allowed → *be allowed to*
alone: not before a noun 196c
along 247
a lot (of): 178, 217b, **219a/c/f**
   comparative and superlative 219f
already: position 215b
   + present perfect 80a, 87
although: 271
   + shortened adverbial clause 267d
always: position 215b
   + indirect speech 274a
   + present perfect 80b, 87
   + present progressive 77 N2, 301e
   + simple present 75a, 78
am: with time of day 309b
ambulance staff: covering both sexes 169d
American English 186 N, 206 N2, 221 N1, **290-298**, 308 ⚠,309 ⚠
among 247
and: 15
   commas 304b
   between comparatives 200d, 213c
angry about/at + gerund 141
animals: *he/she/it* 228b
   relative pronoun *which* or *who* 260, 261
   possessive form 179b
announce sth. to sb. 20d

Appendix — Index

answer: passive 111b
   + indirect speech 274a
any: with (un)countable nouns 178,
   217b, 218b
   = *jeder beliebige* 218e, 220b/b ⚠
   in questions and negative sentences 218c
   compounds 169 N1, 217d,
   224a/b, 225a
anybody/anyone: 179 N3, **224a/b**, 225a
   + *they/them/their* 169 N2, **225a**
   + *to*-infinitive 126c
anything: 224a/b
   + relative pronoun *that* 260 N
   + *to*-infinitive 126c
anywhere: 224a/b
   + *to*-infinitive 126c
apart from 247
apologize: not reflexive 233b
   apologize for + gerund 143
apostrophe 179a/N1
appear: + adjective 196b
   + subject complement 18
appoint + object complement 18
argue: not reflexive 233b
army + singular or plural 176a
around 247, 298
arrange + *to*-infinitive 122
article → *a/an, the*
as: conjunction 268, 270
   + *a/an* 191
   as … as 200
ask: + indirect question/request 274a, **279,
   280b**
   + object + *to*-infinitive 123a
asleep: not before a noun 196c
as long as 251d
as many/much 219c
aspect 68
assistant: male/female 169b
as soon as 268
at: in phrases of place 247
   in phrases of time **186a, 247, 249a**, 250,
   298
at the moment + present progressive 77a, 78
athletics + singular 177d
attributive use of adjectives 196b/d, 199 N
audience + singular or plural 176a
author: male/female 169b
auxiliaries: *be, have* and *do* 49
   modal auxiliaries 22-48
   short forms 58-60
   to form negatives **3b**, 11, 13b,
     41c, **49**, 50b, 56 ⚠, **74, 85**
   to form questions **5b**, 41c, 49, 56 ⚠,
     74, 85
   to form question tags 11
   in short answers 7b, 8b
   + infinitive without *to* 23a, 95, **131**
avoid + gerund 139a

B

backshift of tenses 274d, 277, 278
bad: comparative and superlative 198
   bad at + gerund 141
   badly: comparative and superlative 212
band + singular or plural 176a
BBC + singular or plural 176a
be: auxiliary 49, 76, 81, 88, 93, 97, 101,
   108
   full verb 10 N1, **50-52**
   state verb 70
   linking verb 18, **51**, 196b
   short forms 58a, **59**, 60
   it is/was … + relative clause 301b
   + adjective 71 N1, 196b
   + gerund 137a
   + passive infinitive 120a N
   + subject complement 18
be able to **36, 37**, 122
be about to + infinitive 106c
be allowed to **38, 39**, 122
be bound to + infinitive 106d
because 270
because of 247, 270 ⚠
be certain to + infinitive 106d
become: + adjective 196b
   + subject complement 18
before: adverb + present perfect 80a, 87
   conjunction 268
   preposition 247
   + gerund 144
begin: + gerund or *to*-infinitive 139b
   + indirect speech 274a
behind 247, 250
believe: state verb 70
   + indirect speech 274a
   + object + *to be* 123c
   + object complement 18
   + *will*-future 96a
   believe in + gerund 143a
be likely to + infinitive 106d
belong to: state verb 70
belongings: plural 175b
below 247
be on the point of + gerund 106c
beside 247, 250
besides 247
be supposed to 42d
be sure: + indirect speech 274a
   be sure to + infinitive 106d
be to 42c, 106b
better, best 198, 212
between 247
be unlikely to + infinitive 106d
be used to + gerund 86d/d ⚠, 141
beyond 247
billiards: singular 177d
binoculars: pair noun 175a
bit: *a bit of* 177b/c
black: noun 202c

C

both: 222a/a ⚠/b N
   + *the* 187
bring + two objects 20
busy + gerund 145
but: 15
   commas 304b
buy + two objects 20
by: 247
   with the passive 110
   + gerund 144
   + phrase of time with the future perfect 104
by the time 268

call + object complement 18
can: **25**, 36-39, 43-45, 47
   substitute forms 36, 38
   in indirect speech 277b
can't/cannot **36, 38**, 45
   and *be not allowed to* 39
cardinal numbers 217a, **305**
carry on + gerund 139a
catch + present participle 155b
Catholic: noun 202c
cattle: plural noun 176b
cause + object + *to*-infinitive 123b
certainly: to emphasize sth. 300a
chairperson: covering both sexes 169d
chance of + gerund 142
change: not reflexive 233b
chief: before noun 196d
child/children 172a
choice between + gerund 142
choose + *to*-infinitive 122
church: use of *the* 184
class: use of *the* 184a
   + singular or plural 176a
clause element 17-20
clear: comparative and superlative 197
clever: comparative and superlative 197c
   clever at + gerund 141
close: adjective/adverb 207
   close to 247
clothes: plural 175b
club + singular or plural 176a
coach: male/female 169b
colleague: male/female 169b
collective nouns: 176
   in AE 176, 294
college: use of *the* 184a
come + present participle 155a
comma 16b, 119 ⚠, 251c, 259b, 265a,
   267b, 274b, **304**
command: 13
   in indirect speech 274a, 280a
   with question tags 12 N1
   emphasis with *do* 301a
committee + singular or plural 176a
common: comparative and superlative 197c

common mistakes 281
common noun 168a
comparative and superlative:
   of the adjective 197-200
   of the adverb 210-212
   of quantifiers 219f
comparison: with adjective 200
   with adverb 213
complain: not reflexive 233b
   + indirect speech 274a
   complain about + gerund 143
complement 17, 18
complementation of the verb 17-20, 51
   → subject complement, object complement
complex sentence 16, 251-280
   commas 267b, **304**
compound adjective 284
compound noun: 283
   plural 172 N
compound sentence: 15
   commas 304
compounds: of words 282-284
   with *some, any, every, no* 169 N1, 217d, **224, 225**
concentrate on: not reflexive 233b
conditional sentences: 251-257
   conditional sentence I 251b, **252**, 253b
   conditional sentence II 251b, **253**
   conditional sentence III 251b, **254**
   mixed types 252c, **255**
   omission *if* + inversion 256
   shortened clauses 257
congratulations: plural 175b
conjunctions: coordinating conjunctions 15
   subordinating conjunctions 16, **267a**, 268-272
   with a participle 159 N, **161**
Conservative: noun 202c
consider: + gerund 139a
   + object (+ *to be*) 123c
   + object complement 18
consist of: state verb 70
consonant 64b, 65b, 66b, 171b, 181a/b, 197a, 206b
contact clause 264
continue: + gerund/*to*-infinitive 139b
   + indirect speech 274 a
continuous form → progressive form
conversion 289
cook + two objects 20
coordinating conjunctions 15
cost: state verb 70
could/couldn't: **26**, 36, 37, 43-45, 47
   substitute forms 36, 38
   in conditional sentence II 253a/c
   in conditional sentence III 254a
   in indirect speech 277b
countable noun 168b, **170-174**, 178, 217
couple + singular or plural 176a
court: use of *the* 184a
cousin: male/female 169b

crazy about + gerund 141
crew + singular or plural 176a
crossroads: singular and plural 172b
crowd + singular or plural 176a
cup: *a cup of* 177b

D

daily: adjective/adverb 207
   position of the adverb 215c
damage: uncountable 177c
danger of + gerund 142
date 308
death: use of *the* 183a
   possessive determiner and plural 231c
decide + *to*-infinitive 122
   decide against + gerund 143
decimals 302, **307**
declare + object + *to be* 123c
deep: adjective/adverb 207
defining relative clauses: 259-264
   use 259
   contact clauses 264
   participle as substitute **153c**, 258b
   to-infinitive as substitute **126b/c**, 258b
   commas 259b, **304e**
   → relative pronoun, non-defining relative clauses
definite article → *the*
definitely: to emphasize sth. 300a
delay + gerund 139a
deliver sth. to sb. 20d
demonstrative determiner 237, 238
demonstrative pronoun: 237, 238
   in AE 296
deny + gerund 139a
depend on: state verb 70
   + gerund 143
describe sth./sb. to sb. 20d
despite 247
determiner: with (un)countable nouns 178
   quantifier as determiner 217b
   my, your, etc. 230
   this, these, that, those 238
   what, which, whose 241-244
   after *all* 221b
   + gerund 148
   + *the* 187
die/dying 65 ⚠
difficulty (in) + gerund 142
direct object: 19, 20
   as subject of a passive sentence 111, 112
direct speech: punctuation 273, 304f
   → indirect speech
disappointed about/at + gerund 141
dislike: state verb 70
   + gerund 139a
do: auxiliary **3c**, 5b, **49**, 59a
   full verb 3 ⚠, 5 ⚠, **56, 57**
   activity verb 57

   to emphasize sth. 13 N1, 301a
   to form negatives **3c**, 11, 13b, 41c, **49**, 50b, 56 ⚠, **74, 85**
   to form questions **5b**, 41c, 49, 56⚠, **74, 85**
   to form question tags 11
   with inversion 10a
   negative short forms 13b, 22, **59a**
   + infinitive without *to* 3c, 5b, **131**
doctor: male/female 169b
double + *the* 187
doubt: state verb 70
doubt about + gerund 142
down: preposition 247
dream of/about + gerund 143
driver: male/female 169b
drop: *some drops of* 177b
due/duly 206b
due to 247
dull/dully 206b
during 186a, 247

E

each: 217, **220a/a** ⚠
   + *they/them/their* 169 N2, **225b**
each other 234
early: adjective/adverb 207
   comparative and superlative 211a
earnings: plural 175b
economics: singular 177d
-ed **form** 66
either 217, **222b/b N**
elder/eldest: 199 N
   before noun 196d
elect + object complement 18
emphasis: 77 N2, 299-301
   with adverbs 204, **215f**
   with emphasizing pronouns 236
   with special structures 301
   with special words 300
   of adverbs 215g
   of individual words 299
   of *the, a/an* 181 N
emphasizing pronoun 235, 236, 301d
encourage + object + *to*-infinitive 123a
end-position of the adverb 214c, **215c/d**
enemy + singular or plural 176a
enjoy + gerund 139a
   enjoy doing = gern tun 216
   enjoy yourself 233a
equipment: uncountable 177c
even if/even though 271
ever: position 215b
   to emphasize sth. 300b
   + present perfect 80a, 87
every: 217, **220a/b** ⚠, 225b
   compounds 196 N1, **224c**
   + phrase of time 75, 78

Appendix 238 Index

everybody/-one: 179 N3, 221b ⚠, **224c**
  + *they/them/their* 169 N2, **225a**
everything: 221b ⚠, **224c**
  + relative pronoun *that* 260 N
everywhere: **224c**, 269
  position 215c
evidence: uncountable 177c
except (for) 247
excited about + gerund 141
exclamation 14
exclamation mark 13 ⚠, 303
expect: expressing future time 96a, **106a**
  + object + *to*-infinitive 123b
  + *to*-infinitive 122
explain sth. to sb. 20d

F

fair adjective/adverb 207
  fairly/fair 208
family + singular or plural 176a
famous for + gerund 141
far: adjective/adverb 207
  comparative and superlative **198, 199,** 212
  farther/farthest **198, 199,** 212
  farther/further **198, 199,** 212
fast: adjective/adverb 207
feel: state verb 209b
  activity verb 209b
  verb of perception 71
  not reflexive 233b
  + adjective/adverb 196b, **209b**
  + object + infinitive without *to* 134
  + object + present participle 154a
  + subject complement 18
  feel like + gerund 143
female/male (model) 169c
fetch + two objects 20
few 178, **219e/f**
find: + object complement 18
  + present participle 155b
fine: not before a noun 196c
finish + gerund 139a
finite forms of the verb 118
fire fighter: covering both sexes 169d
first: ordinal number 305
  emphasis 300c
  the first + *to*-infinitive 125
fish: singular and plural 172a/N
flight attendant: covering both sexes 169d
fixed phrases 113, 132, 163, 188, 195, 245, 250
follow: passive 111b
foot/feet 172a
for: 80b, **84,** 87, 247
  fixed phrases 250
  and *since* with the present perfect 84

  + gerund 144
  + indirect object 20b
  + present perfect 80b, **84,** 87
  + present perfect progressive 82a
force + object + *to*-infinitive 123a
foreigner: male/female 169b
forget + gerund or *to*-infinitive 139c
formal English 5b, 8a, 10d, 149 N, 166d, 167c, 219e, 229a, 242b, 253b ⚠, 256, 257a, 259a, 262 N, 263 N, **p. 6**
former: before noun 196d
  the former 199 N
fractions 307
free: adjective/adverb 207, 208
  comparative and superlative 197c
  freely/free 208
free indirect speech 273 N
friend: male/female 169b
friendly/in a friendly way 206b
frightened/afraid 196c/c ⚠
from 247
front-position of the adverb 214a, **215a**
  to emphasize sth. 301c
full/fully 206b
full stop 302
full verb 21, 50-57, **61-71**
  definition 61
  forms 62-66
  be, have and *do* 21, **50-57**
  negatives 3
  tenses of the full verbs 67, **72-94**
fun + gerund 146
furniture: uncountable 177c
further: *further/furthest* **198, 199,** 212
  further/farther **198, 199,** 212
future perfect 73, **103-104**
future progressive 73, **101-102**
  and *will*-future 102a
future time: 73, 95-106
  ways of expressing future time **73,** 75e/f, 77c, **95-106**
  in adverbial clauses of time 268 ⚠
  in subordinate clauses of time and *if*-clauses 75f
  expressed with modal auxiliaries 23f
  → *going to*-future, *will*-future

G

gender of nouns 169, 228
gerund: 136-150
  spelling 65
  forms 136
  followed by various elements 137b
  used as object after certain verbs 19 N, 137a, **139,** 280c
  used as subject 137a, **138**
  after adjective + preposition 141
  after adjectives 145
  after *be* 137a

  after determiners 148
  after fixed phrases 147
  after nouns 146
  after noun + preposition 142
  after prepositions 137a, **144,** 267
  after verb + preposition 143
  or *to*-infinitive after certain verbs 139c
  other structures instead of a gerund 150
  passive 116
  subject in gerund constructions 118c, **149**
get: passive 108 N3/N4
  + adjective 196b
  + object + past participle 156 N
  + present participle 155b
  + subject complement 18
  + two objects 20
give: passive 112
  + two objects 20
give up + gerund 139a
glad: not before a noun 196c
  glad about + gerund 141
glasses: pair noun 175a
go + present participle 155a
goggles: pair noun 175a
***going to*-future**: 73, **97-98,** 102b
  and *will*-future 98 ⚠
good: comparative and superlative 198
  good/well 206b
  good at + gerund 141
go on: + gerund 139a
  + gerund or *to*-infinitive 139c
  go on doing = weitermachen 216
government + singular or plural 176a
grammatical terms 311
group + singular or plural 176a
group words: 286c
  with *a/an* 190
grow + adjective 196b
  + subject complement 18

H

had → *have*
  had better + infinitive without *to* **42b,** 132
hair: countable/uncountable 177 N1
half 307
  half/halves 112b
  with time of day 309
  + *a/an* 194a
  + *the* 187
happen to do = *zufällig tun* 216
hard: adjective/adverb 207, 208
  + gerund 145
  hardly/hard 208
  hardly: position 215e
  + *any* 218 N2
  hard time + gerund 146
hate: state verb 70
  + gerund or *to*-infinitive 139b
  hate doing = sehr ungern tun 216

hätte 253a ⚠, 254 ⚠2, 274c
have: auxiliary **49**, 79, 81, 91, 93, 103
  full verb 53-55
  activity verb 55, 71 N2
  state verb 54, 70, 71 N2
  short forms 58b, **59**, 60
  + object + past participle 156
  + present participle 155b
  have and *have got* in AE 291
  have got 53, 54, 283
  have got to 41 ⚠1
  have to: substitute form of *must* **40, 41**, 122
    in indirect speech 277b
  having + past participle 158, 159
he 169a, **227**, 228b/c
headphones: pair noun 175a
headteacher: covering both sexes 169d
hear: state verb 70
  verb of perception 71
  + object + infinitive without *to* 134
  + object + present participle 154a
help: passive 111b
  + object + *to*-infinitive 123a
  help yourself 233
her: personal pronoun 169a, **227**
  possessive pronoun 169a, 178, **230**, 231
here: position 215c
hero/heroes 171b
hers **230**, 231
herself 232, 233
hide: not reflexive 233b
high: adjective/adverb 207, 208
  highly/high 208
him 169a, **227**
himself 232, 233
his 169a, 178, **230**, 231
history: use of *the* 183a
homework: uncountable 177c
hope: expressing future time 96a, **106a**
  + *to*-infinitive 122
  I hope (to) = *hoffentlich* 216
hopeless + gerund 145
hope of + gerund 142
hospital: use of *the* 184, 295
house/houses: pronunciation 171c ⚠
housework: uncountable 177c
hovercraft: singular and plural 172b
how: **241a**, 245
  in exclamations 14b
  in indirect questions 279
  + *to*-infinitive 128
however: position 215a
how long: + present perfect 80b
  + present perfect progressive 82a
how many/much 219c
hurry (up): not reflexive 233b

I

I 227
idea of + gerund 142
if: in indirect questions 279
  in *if*-clauses 251c/d/d ⚠
  conditional sentence without *if* 256
  if I were you 253b ⚠
if-clause → conditional sentence
if only 257c
ihr/Ihr: English equivalents 230 ⚠1
ill: not before a noun 196c
imagine: state verb 70
  not reflexive 233b
  + gerund 139a
  + object + *to be* 123c
imperative: 13
  negative imperative **13b**, 49, 50b
  in indirect speech 274a, 280a
  with question tags 12 N1
  emphasis with *do* 301a
in: in phrases of place 247, 298
  in phrases of time 86a, 87, 186a, **215c, 247, 249b**
  fixed phrases 250
in case 251d
include + gerund 139a
indeed: to emphasize sth. 300d
indefinite article → *a/an*
indirect object: 19, 20
  as subject of a passive sentence 112
indirect speech: 273-280
  and direct speech 273
  characteristics 274
  commands, prohibition 274a, **280a**
  questions 274a, **279**
  requests, advice 274a, **280b**
  suggestions 274a, **280c**
  reporting verb **274a/d**, 277a, 278a, **279**, 280
  changes in phrases of time and place 276
  changes in pronouns 275
  changes in tenses 274d, 277, **278**
  punctuation 274b, 279 ⚠
in favour of 247
infinitive: 63, **119-134**
  functions 121
  forms 120
  passive infinitive 115, **120a**
  perfect infinitive 23g, 37h, 41b, 42b, 47, **120a**
  present infinitive **120a**
  negative infinitive 120c
  split infinitive 130b
  progressive form 120b
  to form the *going to*-future 97
  to form the *will*-future 95
  used as subject 121a
  subject in infinitive constructions 118c, **127**
  infinitive without *to* 119, **131-134**
    after auxiliaries 23a, 95, 131
    after fixed phrases 132
    after *let/make* + object 133
    after verbs of perception 134, 154b
  to-infinitive 119, **122-130**
    special features 130
    after adjectives 124
    after certain verbs 122, 139b
    after certain verbs + object 123
    after nouns 126
    after question words 128
    after *the first, the last*, etc. 125
    or gerund after certain verbs 139c
    used as object **19 N**, 121a
    instead of a relative clause 126b/c, 258b
    instead of an adverbial clause 267c
    in indirect commands/requests 280a/b
    to indicate a purpose 129
informal English 41a, 52b, 54, 60, 108 N3, 123c, 139 N, 149 N, 166d, 167c, 196 N2, 206 N1/2, 211b N, 219a/d N1/N2/e, 222c N, 225b, 259a, 260, 263a, 272, 278c, 291, **p. 6**
information: uncountable 177c
in front of 247
-ing form: **65**, 76, 81, 88, 93, 101, **135**
  → gerund, present participle
in order (not) to + infinitive 129
inquire + indirect question 274a
inside (of) 247
insist on + gerund 143
in spite of: 247
  + gerund 144
instead of: 247
  + gerund 144
instructions: *should, ought to, must …* 42
  emphasis with *do* 301a
  punctuation 303
interest in + gerund 142
interested in + gerund 141
into 247, 250
intonation: of questions 4
  of question tags 12a
introduce sth./sb. to sb. 20d
inversion **10**, 256, 301c
  in questions 5a
invitations: *can, could, will, won't …* 25, 27, 28, **44**
invite + object + *to*-infinitive 123a
involve + gerund 139a
irregular verbs 66a, 151a, **310**
  in AE 292
it 169a, **227**, 228b/c, 230 ⚠, 238 ⚠
item: *several items of* 177b
its 169a, 178, **230**, 231
itself 232, 233

J

jeans: pair noun 175a
jeder: English equivalents 220a/b

jobs 286c/d
  male/female 169d
  with *a/an* 190
join: passive 111b
just: position 215b/e
  to emphasize sth. 300a
  + present perfect 80a, 87
  + present progressive 77a, 78
justify + gerund 139a
jury + singular or plural 176a

K

keen: comparative and superlative 197c
  keen on + gerund 141
keep: + gerund 139a
  + present participle 155b
  keep (on) doing = weitermachen 216
kind of 204 N
know: state verb 70
  + indirect speech 274a
  + object + *to be* 123c
knowledge: uncountable 177c

L

lassen 133, 156, 218 Nr. 15
last: emphasis 300c
  in indirect speech 276a
  + past tense 86a, 87, 89a
  the last + *to*-infinitive 125
  last/latest 199
late: adjective/adverb 199, **207**, 208
  lately/late 208
  latest/last 199
latter: *the latter* 199 N
learn + *to*-infinitive 122
least 212
leave: + passive infinitive 120a N
  + present participle 155b
  + two objects 20
leggings: pair noun 175a
lend + two objects 20
less 200, **212**, 219d N2
let + object + infinitive without *to* 133
  let's: in imperatives 13c
  + infinitive without *to* 132
lie: not reflexive 233b
  + present participle 155a
  lie/lying 65 ⚠
life: use of *the* 183a
  possessive determiner and plural 231c
  life/lives 171b
like: preposition 247
like: state verb 70
  + gerund or *to*-infinitive 139b
  like doing = gern tun 216
likely: comparative and superlative 197c
linking adverb 204, **215a**

linking verb 18, **51, 196b**
listen to: + object + infinitive without *to* 134
  + object + present participle 154a
little: 178, 217b, **219d/e**
  comparative and superlative 198 N, 219f
lively/in a lively way 206b
living/alive 196c ⚠
long: adjective/adverb 207
long forms 5d, 7b, **22**
look: activity verb 209b
  state verb 70, 209b
  + adjective/adverb 196b, **209b**
  + subject complement 18
  look forward to + gerund 143
looks: plural 175b
lots (of) 217, **219a/c**
love: state verb 70
  + gerund or *to*-infinitive 139b
love = 0 306
lovely/in a lovely way 206b
low: adjective/adverb 207
luck + gerund 146

M

main: before noun 196d
main clause: 15, 16
  → complex sentence
main verb **3**, 5, 9, 10, 214b/c
majority + singular or plural 176a
make: + object + infinitive without *to* 133
  + object complement 18
  + two objects 20
male/female (*model*) 169c
man: English equivalents 108 N2, 229
man/men 172a
management + singular or plural 176a
manner: *in a … manner* 206b
manners: plural 175b
many 178, 217, **219b/c/f**
  comparative and superlative 219f
material nouns: use of *the* 183a
mathematics/maths: singular 177d
may/may not: **32, 38, 39**, 44, 47
  and *be (not) allowed to* 39
  in indirect speech 277b
me 8c, 227
mean: state verb 70
  + gerund or *to*-infinitive 139c
means: singular and plural 172b
measles: singular 177d
meet: not reflexive 233b
mention: *mention sth. to sb.* 20d
  + gerund 139a
  + indirect speech 274a
mid-position of the adverb 214b, 215b
might: 33, 47
  in conditional sentence II 253a
  in conditional sentence III 254a
  in indirect speech 277b

mind: state verb 70
  + gerund 139a
mine **230**, 231
minority + singular or plural 176a
miss + gerund 139a
modal auxiliaries: 22-48
  forms 22
  functions 24
  characteristics 23
  substitute forms **23d**, 36-41
  use 25-48
  expressing future time 23f
  in conditional sentences 252a
  in imperatives **13 N3**
  in indirect speech 277b
  passive 108c
  + infinitive without *to* 131
  + perfect infinitive 23g
more: comparative 212
  to form the comparative and superlative
    of adjectives 197b/c
  to form the comparative and superlative
    of adverbs 211b
most: superlative 212
  to form the comparative and superlative
    of adjectives 197b/c
  to form the comparative and superlative
    of adverbs 211b
  most (of) + *the* 187
  mostly/most 208
mouse/mice 172a
mouth/mouths: pronunciation 171c ⚠
move: not reflexive 233b
much: 178, 217, **219b/c/f**
  comparative and superlative 212, **219f**
must: **29, 40-42**, 47
  and *have to* 40, 41a/c/d
  in indirect speech 277b/b N
mustn't: 30, **38, 39**
  and *be not allowed to* 38, 39
  and *needn't* 41 ⚠3
  in indirect speech 277b/b N
my 178, **230**, 231
myself 232, 233
  instead of *I* 233 N2

N

name + object complement 18
names: use of *the* 185
nationality words: **173**, 190 ⚠
  with *a/an* 190
native: noun 202c
'natural' adverb 205
nature: use of *the* 183a
near: 247
  nearest/next 199
  nearly/near 208
  nearly: position 215e

necessity: *must, need not, have to* 29, **40**, **41**
need: state verb 70
    as full verb/modal auxiliary 41 N
    + gerund 139a N
needn't: **31**, 40, 41
    and *mustn't* 41 ⚠3
    and *not have to* 40
    in indirect speech 277b
    + perfect infinitive 41b
negatives: form/word order **3**, 49, 50, 56 ⚠, **74**, **85**, 88, 91, 93, 95, 97,101
    gerund 136b
    imperative **13b**, 49, 50b
    infinitive 120c
    modal auxiliaries **22**, 23c, 36, 37d, 38, 40, 41c
    questions 4, **5d**
    question tags 11
    short answers 7b
    short forms 59
    statements **3**, 11
neighbour: male/female 169b
neither: *neither (of)* 217, **222c/c N**
    neither … nor 10b
never: position 10d, **215b**
    + *any* 218c N2
    + present perfect 80a, 87
    + simple present 75a
news: singular 177d
next: in indirect speech 276a
    emphasis 300c
    the next + *to*-infinitive 125
    next/nearest 199
    next to 247
nicht wahr? 12a
nil 306
no: quantifier 178, 217b/⚠, **223a/b**
    compounds 196 N1, **224d**
    + gerund 148
nobody/no one: 179 N3, **224d**
    + *they/them/their* 169 N2, **225a**
    + *to*-infinitive 126c
non-defining relative clauses: 265
    which relating to a clause 266
    commas 265a, **304e**
    → defining relative clauses
none (of) 217c ⚠, **223c**
non-finite forms of the verb 118
not: **3**, 22, 59, 120c/c N, 136b
nothing: 224d
    + *to*-infinitive 126c
    = *0* 306
notice: verb of perception 71
    + object + infinitive without *to* 134
    + object + present participle 154a
'notional' subject 127, 149, 162
nought 306
noun: 168-180
    with suffixes 286
    compound nouns 283
    gender 169, 228
    nouns covering both sexes 169d
    plural 171-174
    plural nouns 175a
    pair words 175
    collective nouns 176
        in AE 294
    determiners before noun **178**, 183a, **217b**
    with *(a) few* 219d
    in the plural with *many/a lot of /lots of* 219a/b
    in the plural with *some/any* 218b
    of-phrase 180
    possessive form 179
    as subject complement/object complement 18
    adjective used as noun 202
    emphasis 300c, 301b/d
    + gerund 146
    + preposition 246e
    + preposition + gerund 142
    + *to*-infinitive 126
    → (un)countable nouns
nouns referring to people: male/female 169b
now: position 215b
    in indirect speech 276a
    + present progressive 77a, 78
nowhere 224d
null: English equivalents 306
numbers 302, **305-309**

O

object 19, 20
    position 2, **20**, 214c/c⚠
    position with phrasal verbs 166a-c
    position with prepositional verbs 167a/b
    in a passive sentence 111, 112
    gerund used as object 137a, **139**
    infinitive used as object 19 N, 121a
    relative pronoun used as object **261**, 264a/b, 265c
    subordinate clause used as object 19 N
    + infinitive without *to* 133, 134
    + past participle 156
    + present participle 154
    + *to*-infinitive 123
    → direct/indirect object
object complement 18
object form → personal pronoun
object question 6 ⚠, 242a/b
obligation: *should, ought to, must …* 35, **42**
    in indirect speech 277b
o'clock 309a
of: preposition 247, 298
    of which 262 N
    → *of*-phrase

off 247
offer: passive 112
    + *to*-infinitive 122
    + two objects 20
offers: *can, could, will, won't …* 25, 27, 28, 32, **44**
***of*-phrase 180**, 183b, 185b, 186b, 217c, 220a ⚠, 223c, 231b ⚠/d, 243b, 244c ⚠
    in expressions of quantity 180c, 217c
often: position 215b
    + present perfect 80a, 87
    + simple present 75a, 78
oh = *0* 306
OK? 293
on: in phrases of place 247, 298
    in phrases of time 75a, 78, 99, **215c, 247, 249c**, 298
    fixed phrases 250
    + gerund 144
once: conjunction 268
    + shortened adverbial clauses 267d
one: prop-word 201, **239**
    number **178**, 181 N, 193, **305**
    = *man* 229a
one another 234
oneself 232, 233
only: *only a little/a few* 219e
    the only + *to*-infinitive 124
onto: 247, 250
on top of 247
open: not reflexive 233b
open conditions 251b, 252 N1, 253b
opportunity of + gerund 142
opposite: preposition 247
opposition + singular or plural 176a
or: 15
    commas 304b
order: + indirect command 274a
    + two objects 20
ordinal numbers: 305
    + *one* 239b
ought to: **35, 42, 47**, 122, 131
    in indirect speech 277b
our 178, **230**, 231
ours **230**, 231
ourselves 232, 233
out (of) 247, 298
outside 247
over: preposition 247
    over and above 250
overalls: pair noun 175a
owing to 247
own: state verb 70
own: to emphasize sth. 231b/b ⚠

P

packet: *a packet of* 177b
pair: *a pair of* 175a

pair words 175a
pants: pair noun 175a
paper: countable/uncountable 177 N1
participle: 151-163
  forms 65b, 66b, **151**
  compound participles 151b
  and adjective 153a N
  and participle with an object or noun 153c
  use 152
  with a noun 153
  after conjunctions 159 N, **161**
  after verbs 154
  instead of an adverbial clause **157-161**, 267c
  instead of a relative clause **153c**, 258b
  instead of a subordinate clause 16a
  passive 117
  subject in participle constructions 118c, 157, **162**
  fixed phrases 163
party + singular or plural 176a
pass + two objects 20
passive: 72, **107-117**, 120a, 136a, 139a N, 145⚠, 152a
  form 108
  passive progressive 108b
  with *get* 108 N3/N4
  with a modal auxiliary 108c
  with *by* 110
  'persönliches Passiv' **111b**, 112, 114
  'unpersönliches Passiv' 114
  use 109
  with verbs of saying and thinking 114
  with verbs with one object 111
  with verbs with two objects 112
  with prepositional verbs and with fixed phrases 113
  with phrasal and prepositional verbs 164c
  passive infinitive **115**, 120a
  gerund 116
  participle 117
  past participle with passive meaning 108, 153a/⚠2
  instead of *man* 229c
past: preposition 247, 290
  with time of day 309a
past participle: form **66**, 151a
  passive meaning 108, **153 a/⚠2**
  to form certain forms of the verb 23g, 79, 91, 103, 108a, 120a, **152a**
  have + object + past participle 156
past perfect: 72, **91**, **92**
  and simple past 92b
  in conditional sentence III 254a, 256
  in indirect speech 277
past perfect progressive: 72, **93**, **94**
past progressive: 72, **88-90**
  and simple past 90
  in conditional sentence II 253a
  in indirect speech 277
  passive 108b

past tense → simple past, past progressive
penny/pence 172a
people: plural noun 176b
  use of *the* 183
  = *man* 229b
  = *Volk* 176b N
per 247
permission: *can, may, could, be allowed to* 25, 26, 32, **38**, **39**
personal pronoun: **227-229**, 233 ⚠
  subject form 227a
    in short answers 7b
  object form 227a
    after *than/as* 200b, 213b
    after verbs and prepositions 227b
    in short answers, comparisons and after *be* 7b, 8c, 227c
    before *to*-infinitive 123b
  and reflexive pronoun 233 N1/ ⚠
  in question tags 11
  changes in indirect speech 275
'persönliches Passiv': **111b**, 112, 114
phrasal verbs: 164-166
  meaning 165
  stress 164b
  use 166
  position of the object 166a-c
  passive 164c
phrases of place: 248
  adverbs of place 204, **215c**
  position 215c
  in indirect speech 276b
  in the possessive form 179c
phrases of time: adverbs of time **204**, 215b/c, **249**
  position 215b/c
  with *since/for* 84
  with *a/an* = *per* 192
  use of *the* 186
  in indirect speech 276a
  in the possessive form 179e
physics: singular 177d
piece: *a piece of* 177b/c
plan + *to*-infinitive 122
pleasant: comparative and superlative 197c
pleased: not before a noun 196c
pliers: pair noun 175a
plural nouns: 175
plural of nouns: 171-176
  form 171-174
  possessive form in the plural 179a
  foreign plurals 174
pm: with time of day 309b
point sth. out to sb. 20d
police: plural noun 176b
police officer: covering both sexes 169d
polite: comparative and superlative 197c
politics: singular 177d
position → word order
possessive determiner: 230, 231
  with parts of the body/items of clothing 231c

possessive form: 179
  in phrases of place 179c
  in phrases of time 179e
possessive pronoun: 230, 231
  of mine/yours, etc. 231d
  changes in indirect speech 275
possibility: *may, might, can, could, needn't, should, must* … 25, 32, 33, **47**
possibility of + gerund 142
potato/potatoes 171b
practise + gerund 139a
predicative use of adjectives 71 N1, **196b/c**
prefer: state verb 70
  + gerund or *to*-infinitive 139b
  prefer doing = *lieber tun* 216
prefixes 285
prepositional verbs: 164, 167
  meaning 167a
  stress 164b
  position of the object 167a/c N
  passive 113, 164c
  + gerund 143
prepositions: 246-250
  form and function 246
  position 5e, 113, **246c-e**, 263a
    in indirect questions 246d
    in infinitive constructions 126b, **246d**
    in passive sentences 113, **246d**
    in questions 5e, **246d**
    in relative clauses **246d**, 263a
  meaning 247
  of place and direction 248
  with phrases of time 249
  in AE 298
  fixed phrases 250
  with *who/whom* 242c
  in combination with other words 246e
  + gerund 137a, **140-144**, 267c
  verb + prepostion → prepositional verb
present participle: form **65**, 151a
  spelling 65
  active meaning 153a
  to form certain forms of the verb 81, 88, 108b, 120b, **152a**
  after verbs of rest and movement 155
  after verbs of perception 154
present perfect: 72, **79**, **80**
  simple and progressive 83
  for a state 80b
  with *since/for* 84
  and simple past 80c, 86a ⚠, 87
  and simple past in AE 290
  in indirect speech 274d, **277b**
present perfect progressive 72, **81-83**
present progressive: 72, **76-78**
  expressing future time 73, 77c, **99**, 102b
  and simple present 78
  in indirect speech 277
  passive 108b

present tense 72
→ simple present, present progressive
press + singular or plural 176a
prettily/pretty 208
prison: use of the 184
probability: *may, might, can, could, should, must …* 26-29, 35, **47**
problem of + gerund 142
progress: uncountable 177c
progressive form: **68-71**, 76-78, 81-83, 88-90, 93, 94, 99, 101
  formed with the present participle 152a
  with *be* + adjective 71 N1
  not with certain verbs 70
  of the infinitive 120b
  in the passive 108b
  → present progressive, past progressive, past perfect progressive, present perfect progressive, future progressive
prohibition: *cannot, may not, must not, be not allowed to* 25, 26, 30, 32, **38**, **39**
  in indirect speech 280a
promise: in indirect speech 274a
promise: passive 112
  + indirect speech 274a
  + *to*-infinitive 122
  + two objects 20
pronouns: 226-239
  with collective nouns 176a
  with uncountable nouns 177c
  used as object 20c
  in indirect speech 275
  emphasis 301b/d
  emphasizing pronoun **235, 236**, 301d
proper names: 168a
  use of *the* 185
propose + indirect speech 274a
prop-word *one* 201, **239**
Protestant: noun 202c
proud of + gerund 141
public + singular or plural 176a
public/publicly 206b
punctuation: 302-304
  comma 16b, 119 ⚠, 251c, 259b, 265a, 267b, 274b, **304**
  exclamation mark 13 ⚠, **303**
  full stop 302
  question mark 279
  quotation marks 273, 274b, **304f**
  in direct speech 273, **304f**
  in indirect speech 274b, 279 ⚠
pupil: male/female 169b
pyjamas: pair noun 175a

Q

quantifiers: 217-225
  as determiners 217b
  comparative and superlative 219f
  with an *of*-phrase 217c

  with and without a noun 217c
  + *that* 260 N
quarter: 307
  with time of day 309a
question: 4-9
  form/word order **5, 6, 9**, 49, 50b, 56 ⚠, 74, 85
  question with a question word **4**, 8, **240, 241**
  yes/no question **4**, 7
  negative question 4, 5d
  object question **6** ⚠, 242a/b
  subject question **6**, 8b, 242a
  emphasis 300b
  intonation 4
  answering questions **7, 8**, 238d ⚠
  in indirect speech 274a, **279**
question mark 279
question tag **11, 12**
  intonation 12a
  in AE 293
question word: 240-245
  as subject 6
  in a complex sentence 16a
  in indirect speech 279
  fixed phrases 245
  + *to*-infinitive 128
quit + gerund 139a
quite: position 215e
  + *a/an* 194a
quotation marks 273, 274b, **304f**

R

rarely: position 10d, **215b**
rather: position 204, **215e**
  + *a/an* 194a
  rather than + infinitive without *to* 132
  would rather 132
read + two objects 20
reader: male/female 169b
real conditions 251b, 252 N1, 253b
realize: state verb 70
really: position 206 N2, **215e**
  to emphasize sth. 300a
reason for + gerund 142
recognize: state verb 70
refer to: not reflexive 233b
reflexive pronoun: 232-234
  stress 232
  and personal pronoun 233 N1/⚠
  changes in indirect speech 275
reflexive verb in German, not reflexive verb in English 233b
refusals: *won't, wouldn't* 27, 28, **46**
refuse: + *to*-infinitive 122
  + two objects 20
rejections: *won't, wouldn't* 27, 28, **46**
relative clauses: 258-266
  → defining relative clauses,

  non-defining relative clauses
relative pronoun: 258a, **260-263**, 265, 266
  whose 262, 265e
  which relating to a clause 266
  used as object **261**, 264a/b, 265c
  used as subject **260**, 264b ⚠, 265b
  in a complex sentence 16
  contact clauses 264
  + prepositions 263, 265d
relax: not reflexive 233b
rely on: + gerund 143
  not reflexive 233b
remain: + adjective 196b
  + passive infinitive 120a N
  + present participle 155a
  + subject complement 18
remains: plural 175b
remember: state verb 70
  not reflexive 233b
  passive 111b
  + gerund or *to*-infinitive 139c
remind + object + *to*-infinitive 123a
report: *report sth. to sb.* 20d
  + indirect speech 274a
reported speech → indirect speech
reporting verb 274a/a N/d
requests: *can, could, will, would* 25-28, 39b, **43**
  in indirect speech 274a, **280b**
  with question tags 12 N1
  punctuation 303
require + gerund 139 N
rest: not reflexive 233b
right: adjective/adverb 207, 208
  rightly/right 208
  right? 293
risk + gerund 139a
  risk of + gerund 142
roof/roofs 171b
round: preposition 247, 298

S

safe: comparative and superlative 197c
same: emphasis 300c
say: *say sth. to sb.* 20d
  + indirect speech 274a/b
  say/tell 274a ⚠
school: use of *the* 184
scissors: pair noun 175a
see: activity verb 71
  state verb 70, 71
  verb of perception 71
  + object + infinitive 134
  + object + present participle 154a
seem: state verb 70
  + adjective 196b
  + subject complement 18
  + *to*-infinitive 122
  seem to do = anscheinend tun 216

-self/-selves 232-236, 301d
sell + two objects 20
send: + two objects 20
   + present participle 155b
sentence: 1-20
   exclamations 14
   imperatives **13**, 43
   questions 4-9
   statements 2, 3, 9
   main clause and subordinate clause 15, 16
sentence adverb 204, **215a**
series: singular and plural 172b
-s form of the verb 64, 74
shall: **34, 35**, 45
   expressing future time 95
shan't: expressing future time 95
she 169a, **227**, 228b/c
sheep: singular and plural 172b
shopping: uncountable 177c
short answers 7b, 8b
short forms 13b, 22, **58-60**
shortened adverbial clause 267d
shortened relative clause 257
shorts: pair noun 175a
should: **35**, 42, 47
   in conditional sentences 256
   in indirect speech 277b, **280a**
show: passive 112
   + two objects 20
shy/shyly 206b
sibilant sound 64b/c, 171 a/c
sick of + gerund 141
sie/Sie: English equivalents 227b ⚠
silly/in a silly way 206b
simple: comparative and superlative 197c
simple form of the verb 68-74, 79, 85
simple past: 72, **85-86**
   form **66**, 85
   and past perfect 92b
   and past progressive 90
   and present perfect 80c, 86a ⚠, 87
   and present perfect in AE 290
   in conditional sentence I 252 N1
   in conditional sentence II 253a
   in indirect speech 274c, 277, **278c/d**
simple present: **72-75**
   form 64
   and present progressive 78
   expressing future time 73, 75e, **100**
   in a subordinate clause of time referring to the future 75f
   in conditional sentence I 75f, **252a/b**
   in indirect speech 274d, **277**
   with reporting verbs 274d
since: conjunction 84 N1, 268, 270
   preposition 247
   and *for* with the present perfect 84
   + present perfect 80b, **84**, 87
   + present perfect progressive 82a
singer: male/female 169b
singular: of the nouns 170, 176

use of uncountable nouns 177
of verb/pronoun with collective nouns 176a
sit + present participle 155a
sit down: not reflexive 233b
slice: *a slice of* 177b
sleeping/asleep 196c ⚠
smell: state verb 209b
   activity verb 71, 209b
   verb of perception 71
   + adjective/adverb 209b
   + object + infinitive without *to* 134
   + object + present participle 154a
so: 219c
   to emphasize sth. 300a
so as (not) to + infinitive 129
society: use of *the* 183a
so far + present perfect 80a, 87
sole: before noun 196d
so many/much 219c
some: with (un)countable nouns 178, **217b, 218**
   pronunciation 218a N
   in offers and requests 218d
   in positive statements 218c
   compounds 196 N1, **224a**
   with numbers 218d N2
somebody/-one: 179 N3, **224a, 225a**
   + *they/them/their* 169 N2, **225a**
   + *to*-infinitive 126c
something: 224a
   + *to*-infinitive 125c
sometimes: position 215b
   + simple present 75a, 78
somewhere: 224a
   + *to*-infinitive 126c
soon: position 215b
sorry: not before a noun 195c
   sorry about/for + gerund 141
sort of 204 N
so that 272
sound: state verb 70, **209b**
   activity verb 209b
   + adjective/adverb 196b, 209b
   + subject complement 18
spacecraft: singular and plural 172b
specialize in + gerund 143
species: singular and plural 172b
split infinitive 13Cb
spoken language 153c, 157
spokesperson: covering both sexes 169d
sport: countable/uncountable 177 N1
staff + singular or plural 176a
stairs: plural 175b
stand + present participle 155a
start + gerund or *to*-infinitive 139b
statement: 2, 3
   word order **2, 3, 9**, 10
   negative statement **3**, 11
   emphasis with *do* 301a
   in indirect speech 274a

state verb: 70, 71, 83 ⚠, 159, **209**
   have (got) used as state verb 54
stay: + present participle 155a
   + adjective 196b
still: position 215b
   + present progressive 77a, 78
stop: + gerund 139a
   + gerund or *to*-infinitive 139c
stress: in phrasal/prepositional verbs 164b
   in reflexive pronouns 232
strong obligation: *must, need not, have to* 29, **40, 41**
student: male/female 169b
stupid: comparative and superlative 197c
subject: 17
   position **2**, 5, 6, **9**, 10, 279
   question word used as subject 6
   gerund used as subject 137a, 138
   infinitive used as subject 121a
   relative pronoun used as subject 260, 264b, 265b
   in the passive 111, 112
   in infinitive constructions 118c, **127**
   in gerund constructions 118c, **149**
   in participle constructions 118c, 157, **162**
subject complement 18, 121a
subject form → personal pronoun
subject question 6, 8b, 242a
subjunctive in indirect speech 274c
subordinate clause: 16
   word order 16 ⚠2, 258 ⚠
   adverbial clause 267-272
   if-clause 251-257
   relative clause 258-266
   used as object 19 N
   with comparisons 200c
   commas 16b, 251c, 259b, 265a, 267b, 274b, **304d**
   → complex sentences
subordinating conjunctions 16, **267a**, 268-271
substitute forms of the modal auxiliaries 23d, 36-41
subtle: comparative and superlative 197c
succeed in + gerund 143
such: to emphasize sth. 300a
   + *a/an* 194a
suffixes 286-288
suggest: + gerund 139a, 280c ⚠
   + indirect speech 274a, 280c/c ⚠
   suggest sth. to sb. 20d
suggestions: *Shall I/we …?, can, could* 25, 26, 34, **45**
   in indirect speech 274a, 280c
superlative: 197-199, 210-212
   emphasis 300c
   + *one* 239b
suppose: state verb 70
   + object + *to be* 123c

Appendix — Index

+ *will*-future 96a
I suppose = *vermutlich* 216
suppose/supposing 251b
supposed → *be supposed to*
sure: comparative and superlative 197c
    → *be sure*
surroundings: plural 175b
swimming trunks: pair noun 175a

T

take + two objects 20
talk about/of + gerund 143
taste: state verb 209b
    activity verb 71, **209b**
    verb of perception 71
    + adjective/adverb 196b, 209b
teach: + object + *to*-infinitive 123a
    + two objects 20
teacher: male/female 169b
team + singular or plural 176a
tell: passive 112
    + indirect speech 274a/b, **280a**
    + object + *to*-infinitive 123b
    + two objects 20
    tell/say 274a ⚠
tense: tense/time 67
tenses of the full verb 72-94
than 200, 213
thank: passive 111b
thanks: plural 175b
that: demonstrative determiner 178, **238a-d**
    conjunction 280a/c
    relative pronoun 260, 261
    commas 304d ⚠
    in AE 296
the: 181-188
    form and pronunciation 181a/c
    use 182-188
    with abstract nouns 183a
    with *all, both, most,* etc. 187, 221b, 222a ⚠
    with *church, school, prison,* etc. 184
    with material nouns 183a
    with phrases of time 186
    with plural nouns 183
    with proper nouns 185
    with (un)countable nouns 178
    fixed phrases with and without *the* 188
    in AE 184 N, 295
    after determiners 187
    + adjective used as noun 202
    + gerund 148
    + prop-word *one* 239 ⚠
    the ... the = *je ... desto* 200e, 213d
their: 178, **230**, 231
    after *nobody,* etc. 169 N, **225a**
theirs **230**, 231
them: 227
    after *nobody,* etc. 169 N, **225a**

themselves 232-234
then: position 215a
there: position 215c
    + *be* 52
these: 178, **238a/b**
    in indirect speech 276a
they: **227**, 238 ⚠
    = *man* 229b
    after *nobody,* etc. 169 N, **225a**
thief/thieves 171b
think: state verb 70
    used as reporting verb 274a/b
    + object complement 18
    + *will*-future 96a
    think of + gerund 143
this: 178, **238a-d**
    in indirect speech 276a
    in AE 296
    + gerund 148
    + phrases of time 99
those 178, **238a/b**
though: 271
    + shortened adverbial clause 267d
threaten + indirect speech 274a
through 247, 298
throughout 247
throw + two objects 20
tie/tying 65 ⚠
tights: pair noun 175a
till: conjunction 268
    preposition 247, 298
time: and tense 67
time of day 309
timetable future 100
tired of + gerund 141
to: 247, 250, 298
    to indicate the purpose of an action 129
    before infinitive 119, **122-130**
    instead of a *to*-infinitive 130a
    with time of day 309
    + indirect object 20b
today: in indirect speech 276a
    possessive form 179e
    + present progressive 78
to-infinitive → infinitive
tomato/tomatoes 171b
tomorrow: in indirect speech 276a
    possessive form 179e
too: position 215e
    too many/much 219c
tooth/teeth 172a
tourist: male/female 169b
towards 247
trouble (in) + gerund 142
trousers: pair noun 175a
true: comparative and superlative 197c
    true /truly 206b
try: + gerund or *to*-infinitive 139c
    + *to*-infinitive 122
turn + subject complement 18
    turn round: not reflexive 233b

twice + *the* 187
typical behaviour: *will, would* 27, 28, **48**

U

ugly/in an ugly way 206b
uncountable noun: 168b, **177**, 178, 194 ⚠, 217b
    with *(a) little* 178, **219d**
    with *a lot of, much* 178, **219a/b**
    with determiners 178
    with *some/any* 178, 217b, **218b**
    with *what* in exclamations 14 ⚠
under 247
understand: state verb 70
United States: singular 177d
university: use of *the* 184, 295
unless 251d
unlike 247
'unpersönliches Passiv' 114
unreal conditions 251b, 253a/b, 254a
until: conjunction 268
    preposition 247
    + shortened adverbial clause 267d
up: preposition 247
upset: not before a noun 196c
up to 247
up to now + present perfect 80a, 87
us 227
USA: singular 177d
used to + gerund 86, 141, 141 N
    + infinitive 86d, 141 N
    used to = *früher* 216
usually: position 215b
    + simple present 75a, 78
utter: before noun 196d

V

verb: 21-167
    types of verbs 21
    full verbs 50-57, 61-71
    tenses of the full verbs (summary) 72, 73
    modal auxiliaries 22-48
    be, have and *do* used as auxiliaries 49
    activity verb **69**, 71, 83 ⚠, **209b**
    state verb **70**, 71 , 83 ⚠, 159, **209b**
    of liking, disliking and wishing 70b
    of perception 37e, **71**
    of perception + object + infinitive without *to* 134, 154b
    of perception + object + present participle 154
    of rest/movement + present participle 155
    of saying and thinking **114**, 123c
    of thinking, inferring and knowing 70b
    reporting verb **274a/d**, 277a, 278a, **279**, 280

irregular verbs 66a, 151a, **310**
   in AE 292
   not in the progressive form 70
   passive with different kinds of verbs
      111-114, 164c
   reflexive verb in German, not reflexive verb
      in English 233b
   English verbal expressions for German
      adverbs 216
   phrasal verbs 164-166
   prepositional verbs 164, 167
   with suffixes 288
   position and form **2**, 3, **5,
      6**, 9, 16b ⚠1/2, 17, 18, 279 ⚠
   + adverb 164, 167, 209b
      → phrasal verbs
   + direct object **19, 20**, 111
   + gerund 19 N, 137a, **139**, 280c
   + infinitive without *to* **131**, 133, 134
   + object + *to*-infinitive 123
   + participle 154
   + preposition 164-166
      → prepositional verbs
   + preposition + gerund 143
   + *to*-infinitive **122**, 139b
   + two objects **20**, 112
very: position 204, **215e**
   to emphasize sth. 300c/d
very many/much 219c
via 247
visitor: male/female 169b
voiced sound at the end of the word 64c,
   66c, 171c
voiceless sound at the end of the word
   64c, 66c, 171c
vowel 64b, 65b, 66b, 171b, 181a/b, 197a

W

wages: plural 175b
want: state verb 70
   expressing future time 106a
   + gerund 139 N
   + object + *to*-infinitive 123b
   + *to*-infinitive 122
   want to know + indirect question 274a
   want sb. to do sth. + indirect command
      274a
wäre 253a ⚠, 254 ⚠2, 274c
warn + object + *to*-infinitive 123a
was/were in conditional sentence II 253b ⚠
watch: + object + infinitive without *to* 134
   + object + present participle 154a
way: *in a … way* 206b
   way of + gerund 142
we 227
weigh: state verb 71 N3
   activity verb 71 N3
well: adjective/adverb 206b/b ⚠
   not before a noun 196c

comparative and superlative 212
   position 215c
werden (with the passive) 108a
were/was in conditional sentence II 253b ⚠
what: 5, 6, **241a**/N/b, 244a/c, 245
   in exclamations 14b
   in indirect questions 279
   commas 304d ⚠
   + *a/an* 194b
   + *to*-infinitive 128
   what if 257d
when: question word 5, **241a**
   in indirect questions 279
   conjunction 251d ⚠, 252b, 267d, **268**
   used as relative pronoun 263b
   + past tense 87, 89
   + shortened adverbial clause 267d
   + *to*-infinitive 128
whenever 252b, 268
where: question word 5, **241a**
   in indirect questions 279
   conjunction 267d, **269**
   commas 304d ⚠
   used as relative pronoun 263b
   + shortened adverbial clause 267d
   + *to*-infinitive 128
whereas 271
wherever 269
whether: in indirect questions 279
   + *to*-infinitive 128
which: question word 5, 6, **241a**/b, 243b,
   244b/c
   relative pronoun 260, 261, 265b/c, 266
   relating to a clause 266
   + *one* 239b
   + *to*-infinitive 128
while: 268, 271
   + shortened adverbial clause 267d
white: noun 202c
who: question word 5, 6, 41a/b, **242**,
   243a
   relative pronoun 260, 261, 265b
   + *to*-infinitive 128
whole/wholly 82a, 206b
whom: question word 242b/c
   relative pronoun 261 N, 265c
whose: question word 5, 6, **241a**/a ⚠/b
   relative pronoun 262, 265e
why: 5, **241a**, 245
   commas 304d ⚠
   why (not) + infinitive without *to* 132
wide: adjective/adverb 207
will: **27**, 43, 44, 47, 48
   short form 58c, **59**, 60
   in an *if*-clause 252 N2
   in indirect speech 277b
will-future: 73, **95-96**
   for predictions 96a
   for spontaneous decisions 96b
   to form the future progressive 101
   and future progressive 102a

and *going to*-future 98 ⚠
   in conditional sentence I 252a
   in indirect speech 277b
wise: comparative and superlative 197c
wish: state verb 70
with 247, 290
within 247
without: 247
   + *a/an* 191
   + gerund 144
woman/women 172a
wonder: state verb 70
   not reflexive 233b
   + indirect question 247a, **279**
won't: in the *if*-clause 252 N2
   expressing future time 95, 101, 103
   used as modal auxiliary **27**, 44, 46
word formation: 282-289
   conversion 289
   suffixes 286-288
   prefixes 285
   compounds 282-284
word order: statement **2, 3, 9**,
   question **5, 6, 9**
   indirect question 279 ⚠
   subordinate clause **16** ⚠2, 258 ⚠
   relative clause 258 ⚠
   negative sentence 3, **74, 85**
   adverbs/adverbials 2 ⚠1,
      10c/d, 17, **214-215**
   a/an after *half, quite, such* 194a
   the after *all, both*, etc. 187
   direct/indirect object 20
   object with phrasal verbs 166a-c
   object with prepositional verbs
      167a/c N
   participle with a noun 153c
   prepositions 5e, 113, **246c-e**, 263a
   emphasizing pronoun 236
   inversion **10**, 256, 301c
worried about + gerund 141
worry: not reflexive 233b
   worry about + gerund 143
worse, worst 198, 212
worth + gerund 145, 145 ⚠
would/wouldn't: **28**, 43, 44, 46-48
   short form 58c, **59**, 60
   in conditional sentence II 253a/a ⚠
   in conditional sentence III 254a/⚠1
   in an *if*-clause 253a ⚠/c N
   in indirect speech 274c ⚠, **277b**
   + infinitive without *to* 48, 86 N1
would hate + *to*-infinitive 139 ⚠
would like: expressing future time 106a
   + object + *to*-infinitive 123b ⚠, 139b ⚠
   + *to*-infinitive 122
would love: + object + *to*-infinitive 123b ⚠,
   139b ⚠
   + *to*-infinitive 122
would prefer + *to*-infinitive 139 ⚠
would rather + infinitive without *to* 132

would sooner + infinitive without *to* 132
write: + indirect speech 274a
  + two objects 20
writer: male/female 169b
written language 153c, 157, 166d, 169b N, 267c
wrong: adjective/adverb 207, 208
  wrongly/wrong 208
würde 274c ⚠

Y

yes/no question: **4**, 7
  in indirect speech 279
yesterday: in indirect speech 276a
  possessive form 179e
  + past tense 86a, 87
yet + present perfect 80a, 87
you: 227
  referring to several people 227 N
  = *man* 229b
your 178, **230**, 231
yours 230, 231
yourself/-selves 232, 233

Z

zero 306

Bildquellen

Atlantic Syndication Partners, Sarasota, FL: S. 75 (© 2001 Atlantic Syndication Partners, Reprinted by Permission, and Distributed by Copley News Service); Bulls Press, Frankfurt a. M.: S. 39 oben (© 2001 KFS/Distr. Bulls), S. 88 (© Mirror/Distr. Bulls); The Cartoon Bank, Dobbs Ferry, NY: S. 30 (Drawing by Mankoff; © 1993 The New Yorker Magazine, Inc.); CartoonStock, London (www.CartoonStock.com): S. 8, 12, 22, 27, 35, 37, 39 unten, 42, 48, 59, 61, 64, 71, 83, 95, 96, 101, 104, 105, 108, 116, 118, 122, 123, 135, 150, 162, 168, 170, 171, 172, 194, 202, 218; Creators Syndicate International, Los Angeles: S. 7, 141, 142 (© 1998 by Far Works, Inc.); Exley Publications, Watford: S. 131; Randy Glasbergen, New York (www.glasbergen.com): S. 14, 55, 94, 147, 156, 165, 184, 188; Sidney Harris: S. 86, 221; Kipkakomiks, München: S. 93 (© 2000 United Feature Syndicate, Inc.); Private Eye, London: S. 52; Punch Ltd, London: S. 10, 13, 21, 36, 38, 44, 92, 145, 180, 190, 192, 208; The Spectator, London: S. 18, 26, 67, 72, 98, 113, 133, 138, 158.

Textquellen

Oxford University Press, Oxford: S. 100 (Reproduced by Permission of Oxford University Press from the Oxford Advanced Learner's Dictionary Sixth Edition, Copyright © Oxford University Press 2000)

Nicht alle Copyright-Inhaber konnten ermittelt werden. Deren Urheberrechte werden hiermit vorsorglich und ausdrücklich anerkannt.